雅舍小品

FROM A COTTAGER'S SKETCHBOOK
vol. 1

陳達遵

二〇〇毛年十月

中國現代文學中英對照系列
Bilingual Series on Modern Chinese Literature

編輯委員會 Advisory Committee

中國現代文學中英對照系列

Bilingual Series on Modern Chinese Literature

雅舍小品選集(卷一)

From A Cottager's Sketchbook vol. 1

中英對照版

Chinese-English Bilingual Edition

梁實秋 著

陳達遵 英譯

Original Chinese Text by
LIANG SHIH-CHIU
Translated by Ta-tsun Chen

The Chinese University Press

《雅舍小品選集》(卷一)（中英對照版）
梁實秋 著
陳達遵 英譯

© **香港中文大學** 2005（中英對照版）

初集及續集中文版1988年由台灣正中書局印行

國際統一書號 (ISBN) 962–996–218–7

出版：中文大學出版社
　　　香港中文大學 • 香港 新界 沙田
　　　圖文傳真：+852 2603 6692
　　　　　　　　+852 2603 7355
　　　電子郵遞：cup@cuhk.edu.hk
　　　網　　址：www.chineseupress.com

鳴謝：梁文薔女士惠贈梁實秋先生相片
　　　劉永寧女士提供雅舍重建後的相片，及其畫作為插圖

From A Cottager's Sketchbook, Volume 1
(Chinese-English Bilingual Edition)
　Chinese text by Liang Shih-chiu
　Translated by Ta-tsun Chen

© **The Chinese University of Hong Kong**, 2005
(Chinese-English Bilingual Edition)

Chinese edition of *From A Cottager's Sketchbook*, Parts 1 and 2,
　published in 1988 by Cheng Chung Book Company, Taiwan

ISBN 962–996–218–7

Published by The Chinese University Press,
　The Chinese University of Hong Kong,
　Sha Tin, N.T., Hong Kong.
　Fax: +852 2603 6692
　　　+852 2603 7355
　E-mail: cup@cuhk.edu.hk
　Web-site: www.chineseupress.com

Photographs of Mr. Liang Shih-chiu courtesy of Ms. Liang Wenchiang
Illustration and photograph of the rebuilt Cottage courtesy of Ms. Liu Yongning

Printed in Hong Kong

出版人的話

近二十年，中國與外界接觸日趨頻繁，影響所及，華文作家在世界文學圈中益受注目。二〇〇〇年諾貝爾文學獎由高行健先生獲得，或非偶然。

中文大學出版社一向秉承促進中西方文化交流的使命，故於年前開始籌劃「中國現代文學中英對照系列」，邀得鄭樹森教授出任編輯委員會主席，及幾位國際著名學者出任成員，挑選中國著名作家之重要作品及現有之最佳英譯本，以中英文雙語對照排列出版，計劃每年出書五至六種。個別名作亦會另邀翻譯界高手操刀。各書均邀學界專家特撰新序，以為導讀。

本社謹對編輯委員會及各界友人之鼎力協助，致以熱切謝忱。

Publisher's Note

It is a recent phenomenon that authors of Chinese origin have been attracting more international attention in the literary world, probably as a result of China's increasing cultural interactions with the outside world in the past two decades. As such, it was not coincidental that the 2000 Nobel Prize was awarded to Gao Xingjian, an author of Chinese origin.

With the mission to bridge the gap between Chinese and Western cultures, The Chinese University Press is uniquely situated to play an active role in this area. Thus, this *Bilingual Series on Modern Chinese Literature* has come into existence. Under the able guidance of Professor William Tay and other members of the Advisory Committee, it is planned that five to six titles will be added to the list annually. They will be important works by major authors and will be presented in a bilingual format for cross-cultural appreciation. This means the Committee has either to identify the best existing translations, or to commission experts who can do the job equally well. Each author in the series will also be introduced by a noted scholar in the field to put the work in a critical perspective.

The publisher appreciates the invaluable advice of the Advisory Committee, and sincerely thanks all those who have helped to make this series a reality.

Contents

目錄

Introduction

Ta-tsun Chen

The present volume is a labor of love, prompted by a fervent wish to introduce English readers to the works of one of the foremost Chinese essayists of modern times. In its original, this collection of essays would need no introduction, as it has long enjoyed among the Chinese a popularity comparable to that of the *Essays of Elia* in the United Kingdom and *The Sketch Book of Geoffrey Crayon* in the United States. For foreign readers, however, a short biographical note on the author would seem in order.

Liang Shih-chiu, a renowned educator, writer, translator, literary critic and lexicographer, was born on 6 January 1903 (not 8 December 1902, as given in the *New Encyclopaedia Britannica*, 15th edition) into a well-to-do family in Beijing, the fourth among eleven children. In 1915, he was admitted to Tsing Hwa College in Beijing, a school with an eight-year program designed to prepare students for further study in the United States. While at Tsing Hwa, especially in his final years there, he began to manifest his literary interest and talent by joining literary clubs, dabbling in modern poetry and short story writing, and editing and frequently contributing to the school journal, *Tsing Hwa Weekly*. Before he was twenty, his critical reviews of works of contemporary poets and writers began to appear in literary journals.

導　論

陳達遵

　　本書中譯英是我多年的夙願，希望把這位現代中國散文大家的作品介紹給英語讀者：這項工作雖然艱辛，我卻甘之如飴。這本散文集的原作在華人世界，與查理·蘭姆 (Charles Lamb) 的《伊利亞隨筆》在英國及華盛頓·歐文 (Washington lrving) 的《見聞雜記》在美國，享有同等的盛譽，本來無需在卷首冠以序言，但對國外讀者來說，似有必要在此略述作者的生平。

　　梁實秋先生是著名的教育家、作家、翻譯家、文學批評家和辭典編輯，1903年1月6日 (《大英百科全書》第十五版中小傳誤作1902年12月8日) 生於北京，家境殷實，兄弟姊妹十一人中，先生行四。1915年，他考入北京清華學校，該校八年制課程，專為學生作留美準備。在清華時期，尤其是最後幾年，他開始展露文學的志趣與才華，參加文學社團，嘗試新詩和短篇小說的創作，擔任校刊《清華週刊》的編輯工作，並經常為其撰稿。未滿二十歲，他已在幾份文學雜

After his graduation from Tsing Hwa in 1923, he went to study in the United States on a government scholarship. After graduating from Colorado College (Colorado Springs) in 1924, he proceeded to Harvard where he studied Shakespeare under George Lyman Kittredge and literary criticism under Irving Babbitt. The influence of Babbitt's new humanism and conservative criticism, which was to remain undiminished to the end of his life, helped to shape his literary tenets and led him to rebel against what he saw as the romantic excesses of modern Chinese literature. A number of treatises he wrote during this period (such as "The Romantic Trends in Contemporary Chinese Literature" and "Lord Byron and Romanticism") constituted his literary manifesto. In the fall of 1925, he transferred to Columbia University to continue his graduate study in English literature.

In July 1926, he gave up the last two years of his scholarship and returned to China to marry his fiancée, as he had promised. In this same year, at the age of twenty-four, he was appointed professor of English by the Southeastern University in Nanjing and began a teaching career that spanned forty years (interrupted only briefly during World War II) and included important teaching and administrative positions at several top-notch universities in the country. In the next twenty years, he also served as editor for a succession of magazines and literary supplements, including the famous *Crescent Moon Monthly*, of which he was a co-founder. These were also his prolific years as a writer, translator and literary critic. The series of short satires he wrote for a newspaper in Shanghai was reissued in one volume, entitled *The Art of Reviling* (1927). His literary treatises, which covered a wide range of topics (Aristotle, Cicero, Horace, Carlyle, Oscar Wilde, literary discipline, dramatic art, etc.) were later collected and published under the title *The Romantic and the Classical* (1927). Two dozen other discourses he contributed to the *Crescent Moon Monthly* (on such topics as "Literature and Revolution", "The Seriousness of Literature", "The

誌陸續發表對當時詩人和作家作品的多篇評論。1923年，他從清華
學校畢業，公費赴美留學。1924年畢業於科泉的科羅拉多學院，轉
入哈佛大學，從喬治·吉特列治教授攻讀莎士比亞，又從歐文·白璧
德教授研習文學批評。白璧德的新人文主義和穩健的批評對他的影
響尤深，終生不減，極有助於他的文學理論的形成，亦使他對當時
目睹的現代中國文學的極端浪漫趨勢產生反感。在這個時期，他所
撰寫的幾篇論文(如〈現代中國文學之浪漫的趨勢〉和〈拜倫與浪漫主
義〉)即是他的文學宣言。1925年秋，他轉入哥倫比亞大學，修習英
國文學研究所課程。

　　1926年7月，他放棄最後兩年的公費，依約回國與未婚妻程季
淑完婚。同年他二十四歲，獲南京東南大學聘為英語系教授，開始
長達四十年的教學生涯(只在抗戰時期略告中斷)，歷任國內多所著
名高等學府的重要教職和行政工作。其後二十年，先後兼任若干雜
誌和文學副刊的編輯，其中包括著名的《新月月刊》，並為月刊創辦
人之一。這個時期，他在寫作、翻譯和文學批評等方面的成果也很
豐碩。他在上海某報發表的多篇諷刺小品結集出版，書名為《罵人的
藝術》(1927年)；多篇文學評論(分別討論亞里斯多德、西塞羅、何
瑞斯、喀賴爾、王爾德、文學的紀律、戲劇藝術等)嗣後也結集出
版，書名為《浪漫的與古典的》(1927)；在《新月月刊》發表的二十

Permanence of Literature", "The Future of Poetry" and "Literary Heritage") were collected and reissued as *A Collection of Prejudices* (1934). His translations in this period included *The Love Letters of Abelard and Héloïse* (1928), James Barrie's *Peter Pan* (1929), *Selected Writings of Cicero* (1931) and George Eliot's *Silas Marner* (1932). In December 1930, the idea of translating the complete works of Shakespeare was first proposed to him and a group of his associates, but eventually he was left to take up this enormous challenge single-handedly. His translations of *Hamlet, Macbeth, King Lear, Othello, The Merchant of Venice, As You Like It, The Tempest* and *Twelfth Night* were published in 1936.

Meanwhile, his condemnation of the romantic, naturalist and decadent trends in literature placed him at odds with the literary establishment. He upheld the classical belief that human life and human nature are the only appropriate subjects for literature and cited Pope's famous saying ("The proper study of mankind is Man.") as his authority. He treated literature as a serious profession and frowned upon literary dilettantism. His theories about literature, though they might lack originality, had a definite impact on his own and subsequent generations. His advocacy of the intrinsic value of literary works as something that transcends social classes and his opposition to the use of literature for propagandist purposes quickly drew him concerted attacks from leftist writers, including false accusations and attempts at character assassination. This defamation campaign followed him wherever he went and culminated in 1942, when he was singled out and publicly branded by Mao Zedong as a champion of bourgeois literature and art.

Liang's teaching career was put on hold by the outbreak of the Sino-Japanese War (known to the Chinese as the "War of Resistance") in July 1937. Fleeing Japanese occupation, he left Beijing and took a circuitous route, by sea and land, to reach the wartime capital Chongqing (formerly

多篇論文(其中包括〈文學與革命〉、〈文學的嚴重性〉、〈文學的永久性〉、〈詩的將來〉和〈文學遺產〉)結集出版為《偏見集》(1934)。這個時期他的譯作包括《阿伯拉與哀綠綺思的情書》(1928)、詹姆斯·巴利的《潘彼得》(1929)、《西塞羅文錄》(1931)和喬治·哀利奧特的《織工馬南傳》(1932)。1930年12月,胡適向他及同儕數人提出翻譯莎士比亞全集的計劃,但此一艱鉅事業後來卻靠先生獨力完成;其所譯莎劇《哈姆雷特》、《馬克白》、《李爾王》、《奧塞羅》、《威尼斯商人》、《如願》、《暴風雨》和《第十二夜》於1936年問世。

與此同時,他譴責文學的浪漫主義、自然主義和頹廢趨勢,與當時的文壇意見相左。他秉持古典的信念,認為人生與人性是文學唯一適當的主題,並援引波普的名言(「人類之正當研究的對象是人」)為證。他將文學看作一種嚴肅的事業,因而不贊成淺薄涉獵文學。他的文學理論或許缺乏獨特見解,但對時人與後代有確實的影響。他主張文學作品本身的價值超越社會階級,反對利用文學作為宣傳工具,因而立即遭受左翼作家群起攻訐,包括誣告和誹謗人格。這種醜化宣傳到處跟隨,於1942年達到高潮,是年毛澤東點名批判他主張資產階級的文藝。

1937年7月中日戰爭(中國人稱為「抗戰」)爆發,他的教學生涯頓告中斷。他為了逃難,倉皇離開北平,水陸輾轉入蜀,抵達陪都重

Chungking) in Sichuan province. In the spring of the following year, he was elected to the National Council and was soon placed in charge of a project whose mission was to produce a new series of textbooks for primary and secondary schools. To escape the frequent and massive air raids conducted by the Japanese against the city, the project was soon relocated to a rural area called Beipei where, for seven years, he shared a small cottage with another family. For the greater part of this period, he lived alone, until his wife and children arrived from Beijing to join him in the summer of 1944. However, these difficult circumstances did not seem to affect his literary activities. He completed his translation of Emily Brontë's *Wuthering Heights* in 1942 and *Mr. Gilfil's Love Story* by George Eliot in 1944.

In the summer of 1946, nearly one year after V-J Day, Liang returned with his family to Beijing and quickly resumed his teaching career. In 1948, however, he was uprooted once again by the outbreak of civil war. He and his family took separate routes to reach Guangzhou but, for some reason, only his wife and their youngest daughter accompanied him when he resettled in Taipei in 1949. From then on and until his retirement in 1966, he taught at Taiwan Normal University, serving first as chairman of the English Department and later as dean of the College of Arts. During this period, to satisfy an urgent educational need, he devoted most of his spare time to the compilation of a set of English textbooks for secondary schools and a series of English-Chinese and Chinese-English dictionaries, of which the latter remain very popular in and outside of Taiwan. Collections of his essays, both old and new and on various subjects, appeared as *Selected Works* (1961) and *Miscellanies* (1963). After his retirement, he was able to concentrate his energy on the three tasks he had set for himself: his unfinished translation of Shakespeare's canon; a history of English literature (in Chinese); and a history of Chinese literature (in English). The first task, after thirty-eight years of intermittent work, was completed in 1967, but the work was

慶。翌年春膺選為國民參政會參政員，旋兼任中小學教科書編輯組
主任。不久，編輯組為逃避日軍經常大規模空襲，遷往鄉下地區北
碚辦公，先生與朋友一家分住一幢小平房，歷經七年；其中大部分
時間，他孑然一身，直至1942年夏夫人攜子女三人逃離北京抵達四
川，全家始告團聚。但是這種艱苦情況似未影響他的文學活動，他
在1942年譯完愛美萊·白蘭台的《咆哮山莊》，又在1944年譯完喬治·
哀利奧特的《吉爾菲先生的情史》。

　1946年夏，日本投降後將近一年，先生攜眷返北平，迅速重執
教鞭。但是1948年內戰爆發，他又開始流離，全家分道抵達廣州，
卻因某種緣故，1949年先生赴台北定居時，只有夫人與小女偕行。
此後即在台灣師範大學執教，歷任英語系主任及文學院院長，直至
1966年退休。在此期間，為適應教育方面的迫切需要，他把課餘時
間大部分用於編撰一套中學英語教科書和一系列英漢及漢英辭典，
這些辭典在台灣和外地至今仍然十分暢銷。他討論各種問題的新舊
文章結集出版為《梁實秋選集》(1961) 和《秋室雜文》(1963)。退休
後，他把精力集中於自訂的三項任務：莎士比亞全集尚未完成的翻
譯工作、撰寫一本英國文學史 (中文) 和一本中國文學史 (英文)。第
一項任務，斷斷續續前後歷經三十八年，終於1967年完成，至1983

not printed until 1983. In the previous year, he had edited a commemorative volume on the occasion of Shakespeare's 400th birthday, to which he contributed three monographs. His *Random Notes Written in Seattle* (1972) was a travelogue describing the tour he made with his wife in the United States in 1970, which he humorously referred to as their belated honeymoon. The next year, he published *The Cloud Watcher*, a collection of elegiac pieces in memory of his old friends. He started his second major task towards the end of 1973 and completed the final draft in December 1983, when he was nearly eighty-one years old. This monumental work, which was published two years later, consisted of a history and a companion anthology of works of major British authors which he had translated into Chinese, each occupying three large volumes. The tragic death of his wife of forty-seven years, which occurred in April 1974 during a visit to their youngest daughter in Seattle, nearly crushed him. This prompted him to write his *Reminiscences at the Acacia Memorial Park* in four months. In 1975, he returned to Taipei to marry his second wife. His second marriage did much to revive his interest in life as well as to sustain him in his monumental project. His writings continued to be eagerly sought after by publishers and editors. During his final years, he continued to write with the same elegance and refined taste but seemed to confine himself to trivial subjects, such as plants, pets and gourmet cooking. He died suddenly of a heart attack on 3 November 1987 before he could embark on his third major project.

Liang will go down in history as the first person to have translated the complete works of Shakespeare into Chinese. Literary historians will remember him as a literary critic and theorist with a conservative leaning—perhaps chiefly for his "war of words" with Lu Xun, the acknowledged leader of leftist writers in the 1930s. The general public will always associate his name with the textbooks and dictionaries he edited. But his claim to lasting fame will be based, first and foremost, on the hundreds of short essays he produced, especially those he wrote

年方始刊行。在前一年 (1966)，他主編《莎士比亞誕辰四百週年紀念集》，內載他的三篇專文。他的《西雅圖雜記》(1972) 是他1970年偕夫人到美國旅行的見聞錄，他戲稱此行是補度蜜月。翌年他出版《看雲集》，載有悼念故友的多篇文章。1973年底，他著手進行第二項艱鉅任務，至1983年12月完成定稿，此時他將屆八秩晉一的高齡；這部曠代鉅著於兩年後問世，包括一套《英國文學史》和一套《英國文學選》(其中將英國歷代主要作家的著作選譯成中文)，每套各三巨冊。1974年4月，在西雅圖探視幼女期間，與他結褵四十七載的夫人突遭意外去世，使他悲痛欲絕，終於在四個月內寫完《槐園夢憶》。1975年，他回台北再婚。第二次婚姻大有助於重新激發他對生命的志趣，並支持他完成這部曠代鉅著。出版家和編輯繼續向他索稿。他晚年的文章始終保持原來的雋永和韻味，但似乎以書寫花草、寵物、美食等瑣事自限。他在1987年11月3日心臟病突發逝世，尚未著手進行第三項任務。

先生將因獨力迻譯莎士比亞全集的第一人而名留青史。文學史家會追念他，視其為傾向保守的文學批評家和理論家——也許主要因為他曾在1930年代與左翼作家公認的領袖魯迅「筆戰」；一般人看到他的名字，總會聯想到他所編撰的教科書和辭典；但是，將來使

under the general title of *Yashe Xiaopin* (*A Cottager's Sketchbook*). As predicted by one of his friends long ago, the *Sketchbook* is now considered by many as an even greater contribution to literature than his *Shakespeare*.

The *Sketchbook* had an almost accidental origin. In 1940, at the invitation of its editor, who was a friend, Liang started to write short and delightful articles for *Weekly Review* in Chongqing. These essays, which deal with familiar and timeless topics and in which social satire is tempered with light humor, met with instant and wide acclaim. Those articles on barbers, *nouveaux-riches* and foreign tourists are reminiscent of Sir Thomas Overbury's *Characters*, which satirize human types rather than individuals. He was as ready to ridicule old traditions and personal failings as to poke fun at himself. His weaknesses (such as craving for certain foods) and idiosyncrasies (such as his morbid fear of dogs) made him delightfully human. These are things that endear him to his readers. The success of these essays was also attributable, in no small measure, to the elegant and highly polished language he employed. At a time when the common cry was "to write as one would speak" and a battle line was drawn between two linguistic camps: the vernacular against the classical, Liang was able to create a rich and effective medium by skillfully blending the two. He made free and extensive use of classical expressions and frequently quoted classical poets and writers (as well as foreign authors)—both to good purposes. In this respect, he obviously took a leaf out of the books of such writers as Samuel Johnson, Lamb and Irving. This distinctive style, marked by brevity and conciseness, has had an enormous influence on and is much imitated by a subsequent generation of essayists. The first ten essays were contributed to *Weekly Review*. An additional ten appeared elsewhere, after the *Review* had ceased publication. These, together with the fourteen articles that were written in Beijing after the war, formed the original *Sketchbook*, which was published after he had resettled in Taiwan in 1949. For the next four decades, he continued to produce

他的盛譽永垂不朽的必定是他留下的數百篇短文,尤其是收入《雅舍小品》的幾十篇短文。誠如很久以前他的朋友朱光潛所預料,現在有許多人認為《雅舍小品》對文學的貢獻甚至在他的莎士比亞之上。

說到《雅舍小品》的起源,幾乎事出偶然。1940年,先生應友人的邀約,為友人在重慶主編的《星期評論》撰寫專欄。這些小品文均以尋常普通、永不過時的事物為題,諷刺社會百態而文字略帶幽默,立即廣受讀者推崇。關於理髮、暴發戶和外國遊客的幾篇令人聯想起湯馬斯·歐佛伯萊爵士的《人物描寫》,諷刺的是各類人物,而非個人。他隨時可以譏諷古老傳統和個人缺點,也隨時可以取笑自己。他的各種弱點(如對某些食物的饞吻)和怪癖(如對狗的過度恐懼)使他的人性越發顯得率真可喜,這一切都使讀者對他感到親切。他的文筆幽雅洗練,也是這些文章成功的一大原因。當時大眾的口號是「我手寫我口」,主張白話與文言的兩個陣營壁壘分明,他卻能將兩種文體巧妙融合,成為一種既典雅又實用的文字工具。他把古文的辭藻字句,信手拈來,大量運用,又時常引用古代詩人和作家(乃至外國文豪)的話——無不恰到好處。在這方面,他顯然也師法約翰孫、蘭姆、歐文等外國作家。這種與眾不同的風格,以簡潔精煉為特色,對後一輩的散文作家影響至鉅,引起他們競相模仿。最早十篇在《星期評論》上發表,另外十篇,在《星期評論》停刊後,散見於當地其他報刊。抗戰結束後,在北京又發表十四篇。這三十四篇構成《雅舍小品》初集,於1949年先生定居台北之後出版。其後四

such literary gems, which appeared first in newspapers and periodicals and were subsequently collected and reissued under the same general title: 32 essays in Volume II (1973), 37 in Volume III (1982) and 40 in Volume IV (1986). Although the craftsmanship remains unchanged, a careful observer may discern in the later volumes a steady increase in depth and a subtle shift from poignant sarcasm to benign humor as he mellowed. His nostalgia for his hometown only increased with age. The seventy essays contained in the present book are random selections from the total of 143, but follow their order in the original volumes. The footnotes have been added for clarification of certain points in the texts. I have adopted the officially promulgated *pinyin* system for transliterating geographical names (e.g., Chongqing instead of Chungking) and have taken the liberty of substituting Beijing for the older name Peiping for easier recognition.

Throughout the years, the popularity of the *Sketchbook* has not been affected appreciably by changing tastes. By 1986, one year before his death, it had gone through more than forty reprints in Taiwan, without counting the many pirated editions that were produced elsewhere. In 2000, it was chosen by a group of eminent judges from Taiwan to top the list of the greatest prose works produced by Chinese writers in the twentieth century. For nearly half a century, his works were banned in Mainland China, while they attracted an increasing interest in Europe and America. In recent years, however, there has been a growing demand within the Chinese academia for a more objective re-evaluation of his achievements, and many of his writings, including his polemic treatises and informal essays, have been reissued in various collections, which have become bestsellers. A project is now underway to have the hillside cottage—the birthplace of this *Sketchbook*—restored at public expense and preserved as a national historic site. Perhaps the day will not be far away when his contributions to Chinese literature will be fully recognized.

October 2002

十年間，先生繼續撰寫此類文學珍品，先在報刊發表，然後結集出版，每集沿用《雅舍小品》總名：二集計三十二篇 (1973)、三集計三十七篇 (1982)、四集計四十篇 (1986)。雖然他的寫作技巧始終不變，但如細心觀察，卻不難看出作者的態度日趨穩健，後來的幾集逐漸增加深度，又從尖刻的諷刺微妙地轉向謔而不虐的幽默。他的鄉愁卻與歲月俱增。本書所載七十篇文章是從合訂本總共一百四十三篇中隨便挑選出來，但按照在原來各集中的先後次序排列。為了解釋原文中的某些字句，加添了腳註。地名的翻譯採用漢語拼音，並擅自把原文的舊地名北平改為北京，使外國讀者容易辨認。

多年來，《雅舍小品》受歡迎的程度不因大眾品味的逐漸改變而受到顯著的影響。截至1986年，即作者去世前一年，在台灣就發行了四十多版，外地許多盜印版尚未計算在內。2000年，台灣一批有名的學者評選出二十世紀中國作家最偉大的散文作品，《雅舍小品》高居榜首。將近半個世紀，先生的作品在中國大陸列為禁書，在歐美卻日益引人矚目。近年來，中國學術界人士日益主張更客觀地重新評估先生的成就。在當地，他的許多作品，包括辯論文章和隨筆，已經彙編成各種不同的版本重新發行，成為暢銷書。目前正計劃由公家撥款修建山坡上那幢小平房——《雅舍小品》的誕生地——作為國家歷史古蹟。先生對中國文學的貢獻充分得到世人公認之日，可能為期不遠。

2002年10月

梁實秋先生攝於1960年代後
期。
Photographs of Mr. Liang
Shih-chiu taken in the late
1960s.

重建後的雅舍新貌，現址中國重慶。

The rebuilt *Yashe* [Mr. Liang's cottage] in Chongqing, China.

本書譯者陳達遵先生 (右) 於1974年專程赴美國西雅圖謁見梁實秋先生 (左)
時留影；背景為本書〈窗外〉一文 (頁290–299) 提到的「白屋」。

The picture was taken in 1974 during a visit pad to Mr. Liang Shih-qiu
(left) by Mr. Ta-tsun Chen (right), translator of this volume, in Seattle,
Washington, U.S.A. The backdrop was the "White House" described in
the article "View from a Window" (pp. 290–299).

雅舍小品初集

From A Cottager's Sketchbook, Part 1

My Cottage

Since coming to Sichuan, I have found that the local people have a most economical way of building their houses. Kiln-fired bricks are commonly used for columns. A set of four such columns, standing far apart and supporting a wooden truss, looks gangly and skeletal and pitiably frail. But, after tiles have been laid on the roof and bamboo slats installed on all sides as walls and plaster spread over them, no one can deny that the thing does look like a house when seen from a distance. The cottage I presently call home is precisely one of this type of dwellings. Needless to say, it has those brick columns, those bamboo slats for walls and all the other architectural features of such houses. Speaking of housing, my experience cannot be called limited, as I have at different times taken up residence in what is known as a "pigeon hole", an arcaded mansion, a two-family house, a "three-up-three-down", a garret, a thatched hut, a baronial palace, a skyscraper and other types of dwellings. After living in a place for some time, whatever its type, I tend to develop an attachment to it and a reluctance to move unless absolutely necessary. When I moved into this cottage, I did not expect it to do much except to shelter me from the elements. Now that I have lived in it for more than two months, it begins to grow on me, although I have gradually come to realize that it cannot shelter me from the weather. Since it has windows but no glass panes, it is as open as a pavilion to the winds. Since the tile roof has quite a

雅　舍

　　到四川來，覺得此地人建造房屋最是經濟。火燒過的磚，常常用來做柱子，孤另另的砌起四根磚柱，上面蓋上一個木頭架子，看上去瘦骨嶙嶙，單薄得可憐；但是頂上鋪了瓦，四面編了竹箆牆，牆上敷了泥灰，遠遠的看過去，沒有人能說不像是座房子。我現在的「雅舍」正是這樣一座典型的房子。不消說，這房子有磚柱，有竹箆牆，一切特點都應有盡有。講到住房，我的經驗不算少，什麼「上支下摘」，「前廊後廈」，「一樓一底」，「三上三下」，「亭子間」，「茆草棚」，「瓊樓玉宇」和「摩天大廈」，各式各樣，我都嘗試過。我不論住在那裏，只要住得稍久，對那房子便發生感情，非不得已我還捨不得搬。這「雅舍」，我初來時僅求其能蔽風雨，並不敢存奢望，現在住了兩個多月，我的好感油然而生。雖然我已漸漸感覺它是並不能蔽風雨，因為有窗而無玻璃，風來則洞若涼亭，有瓦而空隙不

few leaks, the cottage transforms itself into a sort of clepsydra on a rainy day, with water dripping continuously. Though unable to protect me from the weather, my cottage has a character that is entirely its own. And I love anything that has character.

My cottage sits halfway up a hill and is connected to the road below by some seventy or eighty earthen steps. Across the road lie whorls of paddy fields and, beyond them in the distance, stretches of verdant mountains. The cottage itself is flanked on both sides by sorghum farms, bamboo groves, ponds and open pits of night soil. Behind it is an untamed hillside overgrown with thickets. Even though my cottage is located in an isolated area, I often have visitors on moonlit nights and even on stormy days, as it is true in most cases that friendship bridges distance and distance tests friendship. A visitor must mount the several dozen steps before reaching my door. He must continue to climb even after he has been admitted, because the floor of my cottage has been laid in such a way as to conform to the natural incline of the hillside, with the result that one end of the floor is significantly higher than the other. All my visitors, without exception, have found this surprising, but I have grown used to it after a while. Going from my study to the dining room is uphill; after each meal, with my stomach full, I go downhill. I have been making these trips every day without feeling any great inconvenience.

The cottage has six rooms, but I take up only two. Since the bamboo slat walls are not impervious, nor are the windows airtight, my neighbors and I can hear clearly all the sounds and noises that originate from each other's quarters. All the time, the sounds of my neighbors, whether holding a drinking party, chanting poetry, whispering, snoring, sneezing, slurping soup, ripping up paper, or taking off shoes, keep rippling through the cracks and crevices in the windows and the walls to break the peace and quiet in my home. At night, as soon as I

少，雨來則滲如滴漏。縱然不能蔽風雨，「雅舍」還是自有它的個性。有個性就可愛。

「雅舍」的位置在半山腰，下距馬路約有七八十層的土階。前面是阡陌螺旋的稻田。再遠望過去是幾抹蔥翠的遠山，旁邊有高粱地，有竹林，有水池，有糞坑，後面是荒僻的榛莽未除的土山坡。若說地點荒涼，則月明之夕，或風雨之日，亦常有客到，大抵好友不嫌路遠，路遠乃見情誼。客來則先爬幾十級的土階，進得屋來仍須上坡，因為屋內地板乃依山勢而鋪，一面高，一面低，坡度甚大，客來無不驚嘆，我則久而安之，每日由書房走到飯廳是上坡，飯後鼓腹而出是下坡，亦不覺有大不便處。

「雅舍」共是六間，我居其二。篦牆不固，門窗不嚴，故我與鄰人彼此均可互通聲息。鄰人轟飲作樂，咿唔詩章，喁喁細語，以及鼾聲，噴嚏聲，吮湯聲，撕紙聲，脫皮鞋聲，均隨時由門窗戶壁的隙處蕩漾而來，破我岑寂。入夜則鼠子瞰燈，纔一合眼，鼠子便自

close my eyes, the rats will go on a rampage, either rolling walnuts downhill on the floor, or knocking down a candlestick while sipping the vegetable oil in a lamp, or scampering up to the top of my mosquito net, or grinding their teeth on the door jamb or a table leg—all these make it impossible for me to enjoy a peaceful sleep. But, regarding the rats, I must admit with shame that I "can do nothing" about them. "Can do nothing" is often cited by foreigners as the pet phrase that best reflects the typical Chinese attitude toward life marked by indolence and resignation. In fact, I have not been indolent in dealing with the rats. I have pasted the windows with paper, but a rat can puncture it with a single poke of its claw. I have kept every door tightly closed, but a rat has sharp teeth and can gnaw a hole through it in no time. I would like to ask, "What, then, can I do?" Let a foreigner move into my cottage; he will prove just as helpless. Mosquitoes are an even greater nuisance. My cottage is infested with an incredibly large population of mosquitoes that far exceeds anything I have seen before. Here, the common saying that "a swarm of mosquitoes hums like thunder" is literally true. Every day, from dusk to dawn, the rooms are so full of mosquitoes that I keep bumping up against them. These creatures are black and unusually large and seem to have frames of steel. They are particularly active in and around my cottage, even when their season has already ended in other parts of the region. My visitors are likely to leave with legs covered in bumps from mosquito bites that resemble corn on the cob, if they drop their guard even for a moment. But I am taking all this in my stride. The mosquitoes will vanish when winter sets in. And who knows if I will still be a tenant of this cottage next summer?

It takes a moonlit night to bring out the best in my cottage—as it occupies an elevated position and is the first house around here to catch the moonlight. The sight of the moon emerging from behind a mountain top like a bright red disk bursting forth and instantly

由行動，或搬核桃在地板上順坡而下，或吸燈油而推翻燭臺，或攀援而上帳頂，或在門框棹腳上磨牙，使得人不得安枕。但是對於鼠子，我很慚愧的承認，我「沒有法子」。「沒有法子」一語是被外國人常常引用著的，以為這話最足代表中國人的懶惰隱忍的態度。其實我的對付鼠子並不懶惰。窗上糊紙，紙一戳就破；門戶關緊，而相鼠有牙，一陣咬便是一個洞洞。試問還有什麼法子？洋鬼子住到「雅舍」裏，不也是「沒有法子」？比鼠子更騷擾的是蚊子。「雅舍」的蚊風之盛，是我前所未見的。「聚蚊成雷」真有其事！每當黃昏時候，滿屋裏磕頭碰腦的全是蚊子，又黑又大，骨骼都像是硬的。在別處蚊子早已肅清的時候，在「雅舍」則格外猖獗，來客偶不留心，則兩腿傷處累累隆起如玉蜀黍，但是我仍安之。冬天一到，蚊子自然絕跡，明年夏天──誰知道我還是住在「雅舍」！

「雅舍」最宜月夜──地勢較高，得月較先。看山頭吐月，紅盤乍湧，一霎間，清光四射，天空皎潔，四野無聲，微聞犬吠，坐客

spreading its pure light in all directions, making the firmament clear and spotless, when the surrounding areas have settled into a profound stillness broken only by the barely audible bark of a distant dog, will hush all my visitors into a state of self-imposed silence. When the moon is high in the sky, its light will filter through the foliage of the two pear trees in front of my cottage, creating bizarre patterns on the ground, and the whole place will acquire a kind of serene beauty that is nonpareil. After the party has broken up and the visitors have left, I will retire to my room and turn in, while the moonlight continues to stream in through the window as if to console me during the hours of solitude. When rain comes in a drizzle, my cottage will present an equally inspiring view. I will push open a window and the panoramic view before my eyes will greatly resemble a landscape painting by Mi Fei,[1] in which the scenery is typically blurred either by clouds or mist. However, I will grow fidgety if the drizzle turns into a downpour. Wet spots will appear here and there on the ceiling, first as big as rice bowls, but soon developing to the size of cooking pots. Then they will start to drip continually until the plastered seams of the roof finally crack, causing the wet spots to burst open like the sudden blooming of flowers and release torrents of muddy water. This will instantly put my home in great disorder and render useless my attempts at rescue and salvage. This experience has already repeated itself quite a few times.

The furnishings in my cottage can only be described as simple and spare, but they are kept spotless through constant dusting and polishing. Since I am not a public figure, no photographs of political leaders or government dignitaries have found their way into my home. Since I am not a dentist, no diplomas are displayed on my walls. Since

---

1　Mi Fei (1051–1107), also pronounced Mi Fu, alias Mi Yuanzhang, a prominent scholar, poet, painter and calligrapher of the Song dynasty.

無不悄然！舍前有兩株梨樹，等到月升中天，清光從樹間篩灑而下，地上陰影斑斕，此時尤為幽絕。直到興闌人散，歸房就寢，月光仍然逼進窗來，助我淒涼。細雨濛濛之際，「雅舍」亦復有趣。推窗展望，儼然米氏章法，若雲若霧，一片瀰漫。但若大雨滂沱，我就又惶悚不安了，屋頂濕印到處都有，起初如碗大，俄而擴大如盆，繼則滴水乃不絕，終乃屋頂灰泥突然崩裂，如奇葩初綻，砉然一聲而泥水下注，此刻滿室狼藉，搶救無及。此種經驗，已數見不鮮。

「雅舍」之陳設，只當得簡樸二字，但灑掃拂拭，不使有纖塵。我非顯要，故名公巨卿之照片不得入我室；我非牙醫，故無博士文

I am not a barber, my rooms are not decorated with silk tapestries representing the scenic views of the West Lake, or photographs of movie stars. I have one desk, one chair and one bed, which are enough to satisfy my needs to read, to write and to sleep, and I will not ask for more. Although my furniture is spare, I like to rearrange it from time to time. People in the West often ridicule the fondness of women for constantly changing the arrangements of their furniture and regard it as a proof that women are fickle by nature. Whether this allegation is true or false, I myself like changes. The arrangement of furniture in old-fashioned Chinese homes follows a set pattern. There is always a long, narrow counter placed against the center wall of the living room. In front of it is a square table with a high-backed chair on each of the four sides. On either side of the room stands a tea table flanked by two high-backed chairs. I believe that interior decoration must, first and foremost, avoid symmetry and that efforts should be made to achieve a natural elegance marked by an uneven configuration. My home does not contain anything novel, but each piece of furniture has been arranged to suit my own unconventional taste. The moment a visitor steps into my apartment, he or she can tell that it is my home. I fully agree with the comments made by Li Liweng[2] in his *Random Thoughts at a Leisure Hour* on this subject.

I am not the owner of my cottage, only one of its tenants. Yet, when I consider that "the universe is but a temporary abode for all living creatures", and that human beings are transients at the universal inn, for each day that I occupy a part of the cottage, I may regard that part of the cottage as mine. Even if I cannot regard it as mine, at least all the experiences it has given me—some good, some bad, some bitter and some sweet—are mine and mine alone. "The inn," says

---

2   Literary name of Li Yu (1611–1679?), a famous writer and music composer of the Qing dynasty.

憑張掛壁間；我不業理髮，故絲織西湖十景以及電影明星之照片亦均不能張我四壁。我有一几一椅一榻，醋睡寫讀，均已有著，我亦不復他求。但是陳設雖簡，我卻喜歡翻新佈置。西人常常譏笑婦人喜歡變更棹椅位置，以為這是婦人天性喜變之一徵。誣否且不論，我是喜歡改變的。中國舊式家庭，陳設千篇一律，正廳上是一條案，前面一張八仙棹，一邊一把靠椅，兩傍是兩把靠椅夾一隻茶几。我以為陳設宜求疏落參差之致，最忌排偶。「雅舍」所有，毫無新奇，但一物一事之安排佈置俱不從俗。人入我室，即知此是我室。笠翁《閒情偶寄》之所論，正合我意。

「雅舍」非我所有，我僅是房客之一。但思「天地者萬物之逆旅」，人生本來如寄，我住「雅舍」一日，「雅舍」即一日為我所有。即使此一日亦不能算是我有，至少此一日「雅舍」所能給予之苦辣酸

Liu Kezhuang,[3] "is like a home to me, while my home is like an inn." Right now and as long as I am a tenant, the cottage is my home away from home. Even I cannot say for sure if it is more like a home or an inn.

These days, as time hangs heavy on my hands, I have begun to jot down whatever thoughts happen to cross my mind, for my own amusement and without paying attention to either form or design. I have given these random notes the general title of *A Cottager's Sketchbook*, merely to indicate where and under what circumstances they have been written.

---

3   Liu Kezhuang (1187–1269), a poet of the Southern Song dynasty.

甜，我實躬受親嘗。劉克莊詞：「客裏似家家似寄。」我此時此刻卜居「雅舍」，「雅舍」即似我家。其實似家似寄，我亦分辨不清。

長日無俚，寫作自遣，隨想隨寫，不拘篇章，冠以《雅舍小品》四字，以示寫作所在，且誌因緣。

Children

Charles Lamb lived and died a bachelor. Being childless, he asserted in his article entitled "A Bachelor's Complaint", which has been collected into his *Essays of Elia*, that children were not rarities; rather, they were as common as the rats in underground gutters. For that reason, parents should not air their pride in front of him.[4] Lamb's remark, justifiable though it might be, carries with it a slight acerbic taste—like sour grapes.

All my life I have never shared the common belief that the children of today are the masters of tomorrow, for I have seen with my own eyes that, everywhere, children are acting like the masters of today. Children's activities take place primarily in the confines of their homes and nowadays there are few homes in which children are not the center of attention. A man and his wife alone do not make a home. A childless house is like a fruitless tree. Something is lacking. Only after a baby is born does the family begin to settle on a solid foundation, the husband and wife begin to assume their respective roles of father and mother, and all at last have found their proper niches. Once I

---

4   Lamb's own words are: "When I consider how little of a rarity children are—that every street and blind alley swarms with them... I cannot for my life tell what cause for pride there can possibly be in having them."

孩　子

蘭姆是終身未娶的，他沒有孩子，所以他有一篇〈未婚者的怨言〉收在他的《伊利亞隨筆》裏。他說孩子沒有什麼希奇，等於陰溝裏的老鼠一樣，到處都有，所以有孩子的人不必在他面前炫耀。他的話無論是怎樣中肯，但在骨子裏有一點酸——葡萄酸。

我一向不信孩子是未來世界的主人翁，因為我親見孩子到處在做現在的主人翁。孩子活動的主要範圍是家庭，而現代家庭很少不是以孩子為中心的。一夫一妻不能成為家，沒有孩子的家像是一株不結果實的樹，總缺點什麼；必定等到小寶貝呱呱墜地，家庭的柱石纔算放穩，男人開始做父親；女人開始做母親，大家纔算找到各

asked a child who was by no means a prodigy, "What does your mom do?" "She sews my clothes," the child replied. "And your dad?" The child rolled his eyes and said, "He reads newspapers." But he hastened to correct himself and said, "He makes money for us." The child's answers are perfectly correct. Parents are there merely to provide service to their children. If the mother eats a rice porridge for breakfast, she serves the child eggs. If the father has eggs for breakfast, he supplements the child's diet with cod liver oil. Unless the child is presented with the best of things, the parents will have a guilty conscience as if they had committed some terrible crime or mortal sin. The child's health and comfort becomes a priority concern to be taken into consideration in each and every family decision. This tradition has existed since ancient times but has now become more widespread. With the emergence of the nuclear family as an institution, the position of the child has risen sharply. The term "filial piety", once referring to the respect shown by a child to his or her parents' wishes, has now come to mean the respect shown by parents to the wishes of their children. The child is the boss in the family; the parents must respect his or her wishes.

This new definition of "filial piety" is by no means an exaggeration. I have seen many children who are capable of raising a hubbub at home like a battalion of troops in battle. They fight each other with the ferocity of gang war and attack their food like tigers on the hunt. They behave like savages towards their elders and family guests. They fly into a tantrum and roll on the floor, as if in an epileptic seizure, when they are cross. They overturn furniture and mess up everything in their excited romping, turning their house into a burglary scene. But their doting parents remain unruffled and turn a blind eye to all such licentious behavior. In extreme cases, the parents may frown, but the frown will last only a few seconds and quickly change into a smile. Only when such behavior has gone so far as to jeopardize their

自的崗位。我問過一個並非「神童」的孩子：「你媽媽是做什麼的？」他說：「給我縫衣的。」「你爸爸呢？」小寶貝翻翻白眼：「爸爸是看報的！」但是他隨即更正說：「是給我們掙錢的。」孩子的回答全對。爹媽全是在為孩子服務。母親早晨喝稀飯，買雞蛋給孩子吃；父親早晨吃雞蛋，買魚肝油精給孩子吃。最好的東西都要獻呈給孩子。否則，做父母的心裏便起惶恐，像是做了什麼大逆不道的事一般。孩子的健康及其舒適，成為家庭一切設施的一個主要先決問題。這種風氣，自古已然，於今為烈。自有小家庭制以來，孩子的地位頓形提高。以前的「孝子」是孝順其父母之子，今之所謂「孝子」乃是孝順其孩子之父母。孩子是一家之主，父母都要孝他！

「孝子」之說，並不偏激。我看見過不少的孩子，鼓噪起來能像一營兵；動起武來能像械鬥；吃起東西來能像餓虎撲食；對於尊長賓客有如生番；不如意時撒潑打滾有如羊癇，玩得高興時能把傢俱什物狼藉滿室，有如慘遭洗劫……但是「孝子」式的父母則處之泰然，視若無睹，頂多皺起眉頭，但皺不過三四秒鐘仍復堆下笑容，危及父母的生存和體面的時候，也許要狠心咒罵幾聲，但那咒罵大

lives or dignity will the parents harden their hearts and utter a few words of censure, but such verbal censure will by and large take the form of a grumble or an entreaty. It might include a hint of threat, but that kind of threat can only make the children snicker, because it is never carried out. When Meng Yizi[5] inquired about the quintessence of filial piety, Confucius said, "Non-contradiction of wishes." The doting parents of today follow this advice scrupulously. They believe that parents should try all possible means to accommodate every wish of their children so that the children will not have the slightest feeling of being thwarted. The advice about "non-contradiction of wishes" and the theory concerning "character development" being championed by modern experts in children's educational psychology are as like as two peas.

Corporal punishment has long been rejected as harmful to the psychological health of children. This brings to mind a story from a foreign source:

Once a mother took her little son to a department store. As they walked past the toys department, the boy discovered a hobby-horse and immediately hopped into the saddle. He kept rocking it back and forth with unreserved pride and would not get down. The hobby-horse, being part of the store's furnishings, was not for sale. When the employees of the store took turns to ask the child to get down, he refused. When his mother told him to get down, he only grew more obstinate. She promised to take him to buy ice cream, but he remained unmoved. She offered to buy him chocolate candy, but he appeared more obdurate. All the promises she made were rejected out of hand. The negotiations became deadlocked and quickly turned into an impasse. At last, a clever employee came up with a suggestion: "Why not ask our resident child psychologist for help?" All agreed. Thereupon the child psychologist, who had been born with the dignified looks of

---

5   Like Confucius, he was a senior official in the state of Lu.

部分是哀怨乞憐的性質，其中也許帶一點威嚇，但那威嚇只能得到
孩子的訕笑，因為那威嚇是向來沒有兌現過的。「孟懿子問孝，子
曰：『無違。』」今之「孝子」深韙是說。凡是孩子的意志，為父母者宜
多方體貼，勿使稍受挫阻。近代兒童教育心理學者又有「發展個性」
之說，與「無違」之說正相符合。

體罰之制早已被人唾棄，以其不合兒童心理健康之故。我想起
一個外國的故事：

一個母親帶孩子到百貨商店。經過玩具部，看見一匹木馬，孩
子一躍而上，前搖後擺，躊躇滿志，再也不肯下來。那木馬不是為
出售的，是商店的陳設。店員們叫孩子下來，孩子不聽；母親叫他
下來，加倍不聽；母親說帶他吃冰淇淋去，依然不聽；買朱古律糖
去，格外不聽。任憑許下什麼願，總是還你一個不聽；當時演成僵
局，頓時膠著狀態。最後一位聰明的店員建議說：「我們何妨把百貨
商店特聘的兒童心理學專家請來解圍呢？」眾謀僉同，於是把一位天
生成有教授面孔的專家從八層樓請了下來。專家問明原委，輕輕走

a college professor, was brought down from the eighth floor. Having been informed of the situation, the expert stepped quietly over to the child and whispered something into his ear. Instantly the child slid down from his mount, as if he had been hit by an electric shock, grabbed his mother's skirt and left with her in great haste. When asked what exactly he had said to the child, the expert replied, "I said to him, 'If you don't get off the horse, I'm going to smash your skull!'"

This expert was not called an expert for nothing, but one would rather suspect that he was not a doting father. If the child had become used to empty threats of punishment, the psychologist's trick would not have worked as it had. Dr. Samuel Johnson argued against the abolition of corporal punishment, believing that such punishment had the advantage of producing instant results. But Johnson lived in the eighteenth century and his ideas are out of tune with contemporary thinking.

A short poem by Thomas Hardy[6] tells the following story. A newborn child is treated as a precious pearl. When he gets a little older, everybody admires him for his good looks and comely figure. After he has grown up, he falls into evil ways and ends up on the gallows. The old poet was perhaps a bit over-pessimistic. But to show prodigious promise as a child, cherish high ambitions as a youth, fade into obscurity as an adult, and be finally left to rot in the company of the common criminals—this is, indeed, a formula of

---

6   Hardy's poem contains the following two stanzas:

> They see as a palace their cottage-place,
> Containing a pearl of the human race,
> A hero, may be, hereafter styled,
> Do John and Jane with a baby-child.

> They rate the world as a gruesome place,
> Where fair looks fade to a skull's grimace,
> As a pilgrimage they would fain get done—
> Do John and Jane with their worthless son.

到孩子身邊，附耳低聲說了一句話，那孩子便像觸電一般，滾鞍落馬，牽著母親的衣裙，倉皇遁去。事後有人問那專家到底對孩子說的是什麼話，那專家說：「我說的是：『你若不下馬，我打碎你的腦殼！』」

這專家真不媿為專家，但是頗有不孝之嫌。這孩子假如平常受慣了不兌現的體罰，威嚇，則這專家亦將無所施其技了。約翰孫博士主張不廢體罰，他以為體罰的妙處在於直截了當，然而約翰博士是十八世紀的人，不合時代潮流！

哈代有一首小詩，寫孩子初生，大家譽為珍珠寶貝，稍長都誇做玉樹臨風，長成則為非做歹，終至於陳屍絞架。這老頭子未免過於悲觀。但是，「幼有神童之譽，少懷大志，長而無聞，終乃與草木同朽」──這確是個可以普遍應用的公式。「小時聰明，

life with universal applicability. After all, there is a famous saying: "A bright child may turn out to be a dull man." Most parents are optimists, however. When a child has managed to get on a rocking horse by himself, his parents begin to have visions of him riding a steed as the commander of an army one hundred thousand strong. When a child is barely able to hum a wartime ditty, her parents begin to dream of big concerts at which she will enthrall the audience with her angelic voice and receive thunderous applause. When a child is seen accidentally toying with the beads on an abacus, his parents begin to predict in secret that he will one day hold the powerful position of the minister of finance, while at the same time trading in speculative markets as an avocation. Such optimism often reveals itself in conversation among parents until it becomes downright showoff, making it impossible for the people around them to volunteer any comment. I have seen a caricature, which shows a child kneeling on his father's lap and using a toy to hit his father on the head. The father, with eyes narrowed into a smile, seems to exclaim: "Look, this is my son. How active! How cute!" A guest, who sits close by, keeps his mouth wide open as if laughing heartily, in an attempt to show that he is watching the act intently and with profound interest. The picture has a one-word caption: "Histrionics". Indeed, one has to be a well-trained actor to watch the antics of someone else's child and be able to dissemble an interest. Obviously, Lamb did not like to take up this kind of acting.

Parents tend to reserve the greatest share of their love for the dullest, the laziest, the wiliest, the rudest, the ugliest, the weakest or the least-liked among their children. This may seem quite a puzzle. Actually, we have only to recall that, in *Record of a Journey to the West*,[7] the favorite disciple of the holy monk is Pigsy.

7　Chinese title *Xi You Ji,* a popular Chinese comic novel written by Wu Cheng'en (1500–1582) and based on an actual pilgrimage made by the famous Buddhist

大時未必了了。」究竟是知言，然而為父母者多屬樂觀。孩子纔能騎木馬，父母便幻想他將來指揮十萬貔貅時之馬上雄姿；孩子纔把一曲抗戰小歌哼得上口，父母便幻想著他將來喉聲一囀彩聲雷動時的光景，孩子偶然撥動算盤，父母便暗中揣想他將來或能掌握財政大權，同時兼營投機買賣……這種樂觀往往形諸言語，成為炫耀，使旁觀者有說不出的感想。曾見一幅漫畫：一個孩子跪在他父親的膝頭用他的玩具敲打他父親的頭，父親瞇著眼在笑，那表情像是在宣告：「看看！我的孩子！多麼活潑，多麼可愛！」旁邊坐著一位客人裂著大嘴做傻笑狀，表示他在看著，而且感覺興趣。這幅畫的標題是：「演劇術」。一個客人看著別人家的孩子而能表示感覺興趣，這真確實需要良好的「演劇術」。蘭姆顯然是不歡喜演這樣的戲。

孩子中之比較最蠢，最懶，最刁，最潑，最醜，最弱，最不討人歡喜的，往往最得父母的鍾愛。此事似頗費解，其實我們應該記得《西遊記》中唐僧為什麼偏偏喜歡豬八戒。

There is a proverb: "A growing tree straightens itself." It means that children may be a little wild and unruly, but they will mature and outgrow their youthful faults without any disciplinary measures taken against them. But can a crooked sapling grow into a straight tree by itself? I will not bet on it.

---

monk Xuanzang (alias Sanzang) (Tripitaka) to India in the seventh century. In this novel, the holy monk is accompanied on his long journey by three disciples, namely, the smart and resourceful Monkey, who was born of a stone and endowed with magical power, the clumsy and philandering Pigsy and the loyal and reliable Sandy, a fish spirit. This novel is available in English translation under the title of *Monkey* (1942).

　　諺云：「樹大自直」，意思是說孩子不需管教，小時恣肆些，大了自然會好。可是彎曲的小樹，長大是否會直呢？我不敢說。

Music

A friend said in a letter he wrote to me: "...I have never experienced as great an annoyance as now. My next-door neighbors are a group of young women who work for XXX. The moment they get home, they start singing loudly. They sing nothing but the XX type of songs, but the way they sing clearly indicates that they never take into consideration what effects the composers expect these songs to produce. I cannot tell them to shut up, nor can I shout out a vulgarity. I can only plug my ears with two wads of cotton, the way my barber does before shampooing my hair... "

I can sympathize with this friend, but he cannot claim this annoying experience as exclusively his. It has recently occurred to me that the thing we call music is the most aggressive among all the arts. All the other arts, such as sculpture, are static. If you do not like them, you can shut them out of your sight and need not be bothered with them. But the same cannot be said of music. Once a note is struck, the sound will follow the rippling effect of air and invade your ears straight away. And our ears, which are normally unprotected, are left entirely at the mercy of the vibrations and irritations created by the sound in a completely defenseless manner. It is true that sometimes a self-styled painter or calligrapher can be just as annoying. There is a joke about someone who knelt before a calligrapher-cum-painter while holding

音　樂

　　一個朋友來信說：「……我從來沒有像現在這樣煩惱過。住在我的隔壁的是一群在××服務的女孩子，一回到家便大聲歌唱，所唱的無非是些××歌曲，但是她們唱的腔調證明她們從來沒有考慮過原製曲者所要產生的效果。我不能請她們閉嘴，也不能喊『通』！只得像在理髮館洗頭時無可奈何的用棉花塞起耳朵來……」

　　我同情於這位朋友。但是他的煩惱不是他一個人有的。我嘗想，音樂這樣東西，在所有的藝術裏，是最富於侵略性的。別種藝術，如圖畫雕刻，都是固定的，你不高興欣賞便可以不必寓目，各不相擾；惟獨音樂，聲音一響，隨著空氣波盪而來，照直侵入你的耳朵，而耳朵平常都是不設防的，只得毫無抵禦的任它震盪刺激。自以為能書善畫的人，誠然也有令人不舒服的時候；據說有人拿著

a blank Chinese fan in his hands. He was not asking the artist to produce a piece of art; on the contrary, he was begging the artist to show mercy and refrain from ruining the fan with his brush. After all, this was an exceptional case, since calligraphers and painters do not compel other people to look at their works. On the other hand, the thing that we call music enforces its reception by every person within the reach of its sounds without regard to whether it has the effect of stirring one's heart or turning one's stomach.

My friend has expressed an aversion to the singing of his neighbors, but this cannot be considered a grave situation. Once I had the misfortune to attend the performance of a singing quartet. That experience has since caused me to shy away from concerts and similar gatherings. When the group appeared on stage amid loud applause, the pianist started to play and the four vocalists simultaneously opened their lips to sing. Instantly I felt that my eardrums were being violently assaulted by five different tunes that varied widely in pitch and tempo—four from the mouths of the vocalists and a fifth from the piano! The five strands of sounds were thrown together to form one tangled and totally disharmonious mixture. At that moment I felt myself trembling with fear and becoming lightheaded as if I were losing my balance. The next moment I felt as if I had come to a forked road, unable to make a decision. I turned my head to look at other people in the audience and found them staring at each other in bewilderment, as if preparing to run for their lives, while an air of disunity and discord permeated every corner of the hall. Music like this is extremely harmful to human health.

Not everyone has a "musical ear" —I grant you that. Perhaps I was simply not born with such an ear. Or perhaps I grew up under unfavorable circumstances, which prohibited the proper development of such an ear. I recall the time when I was a student living in a

素扇跪在一位書畫家面前，並非敬求墨寶，而是求他高抬貴手，別
糟塌他的扇子。這究竟是例外情形。書家畫家並不強迫人家瞻仰他
的作品，而所謂音樂也者，則對於凡是在音波所及的範圍以內的
人，一律強迫接受，也不管其效果是沁人肺腑，抑是令人作嘔。

我的朋友對於隔壁音樂表示不滿，那情形還不算嚴重；我曾經
領略過一次四人合唱，使我以後對於音樂會一類的集會輕易不敢問
津。一陣彩聲把四位歌者送上演臺，鋼琴聲響動，四位歌者同時張
口，我登時感覺到有五種高低疾徐全然不同的調子亂攪我的耳鼓，
四位歌者唱出四個調子，第五個聲音是從鋼琴裏發出來的！五縷聲
音攪做一團，全不和諧。當時我就覺得心旌戰動，飄飄然如失卻重
心，又覺得身臨歧路，徬徨無主的樣子。我迴顧四座，大家都面面
相覷，好像都各自準備逃生，一種分崩離析的空氣瀰漫於全室。像
這樣的音樂是極傷人的。

「音樂的耳朵」不是人人有的，這一點我承認，也許我就是缺乏
這種耳朵。也許是我的環境不好，使我的這種耳朵，沒有適當的發
育。我記得在學校宿舍裏住的時候，對面樓上住著一位音樂家，還

residence hall. In another hall across the lawn lived a musician—and a Chinese classical musician at that—who had the habit of sitting by a window at dusk and singing an aria ("I may be compared to...") at the top of his lungs, while providing his own accompaniment with a *huqin*.[8] At such a moment I could hardly control myself. I had a strong urge to walk over to my window and tell him loudly what he might be compared to. I have a morbid fear of the sound of the *huqin*. Many times in the past I have heard Mr. XX, the most celebrated huqinist, play his instrument. For all his consummate skill, I could not help thinking that the screechy notes produced by his instrument resembled the sound made by scratching glass with fingernails. I have no particular dislike for any other musical instrument. I have heard "The Wutong Trees in the Rain" played on the *guqin* [9] and "Ambush All Round" on the *pipa*,[10] both of which appealed to me as music. But the *huqin* and I are just not meant for each other. In *The Merchant of Venice*, Shakespeare mentions people who, "when the bagpipe sings in the nose, cannot contain their urine," but that is only a personal oddity. My abhorrence for the *huqin* is perhaps also nothing but an oddity. The young female characters in Peking opera singing in high-pitched falsetto, either in a theater or in a public square, can make one's hair stand on end—even more disconcerting when they give recitals. A sudden squeal released from the throat of such a female character is enough to make me instinctively raise my feet, thinking that I might have stepped on somebody's neck. Recently I went to hear a Hubei opera, in which even the black-faced fellow and the painted-faced fellow[11] screeched and screamed, making the audience nervous and uneasy. Shaanxi opera is sung in an even more passionate and agitated fashion, which often

---

8   A two-stringed bowed instrument commonly used in Peking opera.

9   A seven-stringed plucked instrument sometimes called the Chinese Zither.

10 A four-stringed plucked instrument resembling the lute.

11 Both are stock male characters in Chinese opera.

是「國樂」，每當夕陽下山，他就臨窗獻技，引吭高歌，配合著胡琴
他唱「我好比……」，在這時節我便按捺不住，頗想走到窗前去大聲
的告訴他，他好比是什麼。我頂怕聽胡琴，北平最好的名手××我
也聽過多少次數，無論他技巧怎樣純熟，總覺得唧唧的聲音像是指
甲在玻璃上抓。別種樂器，我都不討厭，曾聽古琴彈奏一段〈梧桐
雨〉，琵琶亂彈一段〈十面埋伏〉，都覺得那確是音樂，惟獨胡琴與我
無緣。莎士比亞的《威尼斯商人》裏曾說起有人一聽見蘇格蘭人的風
笛便要小便；那只是個人的怪癖。我對胡琴的反感亦只是一種怪癖
罷？皮黃戲裏的青衣花旦之類，在戲院廣場裏令人毛髮倒豎，若是
清唱則尤不可當，嘤然一叫，我本能的要抬起我的腳來，生怕是腳
底下踩了誰的脖子！近聽漢戲，黑頭花臉亦唧唧銳叫，令人坐立不
安；秦腔尤為激昂，常令聽者隨之手忙腳亂，不能自己。我可以聽

causes the audience to panic in spite of itself. I can enjoy music. But in the case of music produced through the human larynx, I have to turn my eyes away from the swollen neck and reddened face of the singer. There I see danger and I am worried.

A real aficionado of Peking opera will come to the theater with two packets of choice tea and take a seat in a side box. As he listens to the beautiful singing on the stage, he will nod his head and beat time with his hand and, with closed eyes, quietly savor the intoxicating effects of an aria. Such an emotional experience is something with which I can empathize. But this has been achieved at an enormous cost. He must endure many unpleasant sounds as the price he must pay in order to win a moment's delight in music. Nowadays, listeners are in the minority at an opera house; spectators form the majority. And the singers vie with one another in popularizing a style that prizes "strong lungs and long wind" above other things, and they no longer pay attention to tonal quality and charm. Most people can still appreciate simple rhythms. The noise and clangor of the drums and the gongs and the glissando of the winds and the strings constitute the simplest kind of music. For that reason, it is extremely popular among such people as pot-bellied business executives, politicians, college professors, debutantes, socialites and persons of power, who lack an artistic taste but pride themselves on being music lovers.

As a result of the East-West cultural exchange, our music (with the exception of Chinese opera) is also undergoing a process of metamorphosis. Everything we have, from "Drizzling Rain" to popular songs in the hit parade category, represents a cross between the Chinese ditty and some sort of Western music. Sometimes it is like Chinese food served at a European restaurant; sometimes it is the other way around. I have no way of knowing what form it will finally assume. Since I am not capable of making the slightest contribution to

音樂，但若聲音發自人類的喉嚨，我便看不得粗了脖子紅了臉的樣子。我看著危險！我著急。

真正聽京戲的內行人懷裏揣著兩包茶葉，踱到邊廂一坐，聽到妙處，搖頭擺尾，隨聲擊節，閉著眼睛體味聲調的妙處，這心情我能了解，但是他付了多大的代價！他聽了多少不願意聽的聲音纔能換取這一點音樂的陶醉！到如今，聽戲的少，看戲的多。唱戲的亦競以肺壯氣長取勝，而不復重韻味，惟簡單節奏尚是多數人所能體會，鏗鏘的鑼鼓，油滑的管絃，都是最簡單不過的，所以缺乏藝術教養的人，如一般大腹賈，大人先生，大學教授，大家閨秀，大名士，大豪紳，都趨之若鶩，自以為是在欣賞音樂！

在中西文化的交流中，我們的音樂(戲劇除外)也在蛻變，從〈毛毛雨〉起以至於現在流行的×××之類，都是中國小調與西洋某一級音樂的混合，時而中菜西吃，時而西菜中吃，將來成為怎樣的定

music, I have relinquished my right to enjoy it—and this I have done willingly and without regret. I will shun any musical event unless my presence is absolutely required by the occasion. As to the kind of nuisance created by neighbors, about which my friend complains, I consider it as unavoidable as a natural phenomenon, just as people living in the vicinity of a slaughterhouse cannot avoid hearing the death squeals of pigs. Heard for the first time, the sound can be heartrending, but one will get used to it after a while. Occasionally, a person may be heard singing loudly a snatch from an opera ("I'm a lone rider crossing the border of Xiliang...") when he walks down a deserted street at the dead of night on his way home. I can forgive him because he is afraid of ghosts and tries to steel himself with singing. His action may be reprehensible, but his situation deserves sympathy. But I cannot understand the reason why anyone should pick an early hour at dawn to practice on the bugle. Toot—ta—ta—tee—each note rising higher than the last until the sound cracked. The bugler was obviously going through an ordeal, but he was also robbing many people of their sleep. Why couldn't he practice at another hour?

In principle, as far as man-made music is concerned, one should rather go without than settle for something shoddy. For, without man-made music, the worst scenario for us might be a world of quiet solitude. But as a matter of fact, human beings will never find themselves in quiet solitude. There will always be the wails and laughter of children, the cries of street peddlers, the shouts of quarreling neighbors, the clamor of the marketplace, and the ubiquitous question "Have you eaten?" This question was originally a polite greeting but has now become an exchange of solicitude concerning a matter of life and death.[12]

---

12 In practice, this question is equivalent to the English greeting "How are you?" But, as a result of food shortages during the war years, it was thought to have taken on a new meaning.

型，我不知道。我對音樂既不能作絲毫貢獻，所以也很坦然的甘心放棄欣賞音樂的權利，除非為了某種機緣必須「共襄盛舉」不得不到場備員。至於像我的朋友所抱怨的那種隔壁歌聲，在我則認為是一種不可避免的自然現象，恰如我們住在屠宰場的附近便不能不聽見豬叫一樣，初聽非常淒絕，久後亦就安之。夜深人靜，荒涼的路上往往有人高唱「一馬離了西涼界……」我原諒他，他怕鬼，用歌聲來壯膽，其行可惡，其情可憫。但是在天微明時練習吹喇叭，則是我所不解。「打——搭——大——滴——」一聲比一聲高，高到聲嘶力竭，吹喇叭的人顯然是很吃苦，可是把多少人的睡眠給毀了，為什麼不在另一個時候練習呢？

在原則上，凡是人為的音樂，都應該寧缺毋濫。因為沒有人為的音樂，頂多是落個寂寞。而按其實，人是不會寂寞的。小孩的哭聲，笑聲，小販的吆喝聲，鄰人的打架聲，市裏的喧豗聲，到處「吃飯了麼？」「吃飯了麼？」的原是應酬而現在變成性命交關的問答聲——

Even in the most solitary village, there will be the barks of dogs and the clucks of chickens. But the most unforgettable are what we called the sounds of nature. When the autumn winds rise, the rustling leaves create wave after wave of sound, resembling the onrush of tides, the taps of pelting rain, the hoofbeats of galloping horses, or the quick march of cavalry. Even after the winds have stopped, if you listen carefully, you can still hear the sound of falling leaves hitting the ground one by one. When autumnal rain arrives, it begins with a low rustling like the sound of silkworms nibbling on mulberry leaves. Then it turns into a loud and clear drip-drop when it hits the leaves of some banana tree. The sounds of wind and rain, as well as the chirping of insects and the warbling of birds, make up the music of nature, each capable of appealing to me and dispelling my feeling of solitude. Why do people prefer listening to such singing as "I may be compared to..."? But the secret delight I find in nature's music cannot be easily explained to the uninitiated.

實在寂寞極了還有村裏的雞犬聲！最令人難忘的還有所謂天籟。秋風起時，樹葉颯颯的聲音，一陣陣襲來，如潮湧，如急雨，如萬馬奔騰，如銜枚疾走；風定之後，細聽還有枯乾的樹葉一聲聲的打在階上。秋雨落時，起初如蠶食桑葉，悉悉喙喙，繼而淅淅瀝瀝，打在蕉葉上清脆可聽。風聲雨聲，再加上蟲聲鳥聲，都是自然的音樂，都能使我發生好感，都能驅除我的寂寞，何貴乎聽那「我好比⋯⋯我好比⋯⋯」之類的歌聲？然而此中情趣，不足為外人道也。

Anonymous Letters

The mailman has just brought me an anonymous letter. For two reasons I can tell—even before opening it—that it is anonymous. First, I know in my heart that it is about time I received such a letter (if no such letter turns up, it will mean that I am wrong in taking too dim a view of human nature). Second, the envelope looks a little awkward, with my name and address written in two lines of teetering characters, but not scrawled, in a style that is known as "crude", an imitation of the distinctive style of the calligrapher Zheng Banqiao[13] or merely the clumsy brushwork of an elementary schoolboy. The falling strokes are either too long or too short and all the characters reveal a deliberate effort to disguise for fear of revealing the writer's identity. In the lower left corner appear the words: "See Inside". [14] Nowadays, people no longer write "See Inside" on the front of an envelope, just as they no longer write the words: "Like A Bottle"[15] across the flap on its back. Under normal circumstances, the sender would have given his name and return address. Now that he must conceal his identity, he has subconsciously put down the words "See Inside" to fill the space.

---

13 Literary name of Zheng Xie (1693–1765), a famous poet, painter and calligrapher.
14 Short for "see inside for sender's name and return address".
15 Short for "sealed like a bottle". It has the same purpose as the sealing wax in olden times—to prevent unauthorized opening.

匿名信

　　郵局遞來一封匿名信，沒啟封就知道是匿名信，因為一來我自己心裏明白，現在快要到我接匿名信的時候了（如果竟無匿名信到來，那是我把人性估計太低了），二來那隻信封的神情就有幾分尷尬，信封上的兩行字，傾斜而不潦草，正是書法上所謂「生拙」，像是鄭板橋體，又像是小學生的塗鴉，不是撇太長，就是捺太短，總之是很矜持，唯恐露出本來面目。下款署「內詳」二字。現代的人很少有寫「內詳」的習慣，猶之乎很少有在信封背面寫「如晤」的習慣，其所以寫「內詳」者，乃是平常寫慣了下款，如今又不能寫真姓名，於是於不自覺間寫上了「內詳」云云。

My heart bleeds for writers of anonymous letters, because they must be under extreme compulsion to do such a sneaky thing, just as people will not turn themselves into thieves or prostitutes unless they are driven by the need to survive. One can imagine that the senders must be livid with rage when they conceive the idea and lay the plot. "When anger rises in the heart, evil intent is bound to start." They have simply lost control of themselves. They repeatedly ask themselves: "Must I?" and invariably come to the same conclusion: "I must!" Then they lock their doors, shutter their windows and begin to compose the kind of letters that are unfit to be included in their collected works. Anger and hatred can be most valuable emotions if they are expressed in a proper form and at a proper time, as everybody is familiar with the story that, in a fit of anger, King Wen set out to found the Zhou dynasty. But anonymous letters, in addition to their function as a safety valve for anger and hatred, also expose another facet of human nature—cowardice. Nor is cowardice something uncommon. It is said that certain pirates in the West, cold-blooded murderers though they were, had jitters about signing the ultimatum to the captain of their ship when they plotted to mutiny. That ultimatum created a serious problem, because the first one to sign it would expose himself to greater risk. So they invented the round-robin, in which all the signatures were arranged in a circle, without a beginning or an end, so as to leave no clue as to the order of signing. This method, though also a mark of cowardice, shows far greater courage than sending an anonymous letter. Hiding behind the shield of anonymity, one may say anything that he (or she) may not say to another person face to face, or that would make the speaker blush, or that should never come out of a person's mouth—and say it as freely as water out of a sluice.

　　我同情寫匿名信的人，因為他或她肯幹這種勾當，必定是極不得已，等於一個人若不為生活所逼便絕不至於會男盜女娼一樣。當其蓄謀動念之時，一定有一副血脈僨張的面孔，「怒從心上起，惡向膽邊生。」硬是按捺不住，幾度心理猶豫，「何必？」又幾度心理堅決，「必！」於是關門閉戶獨自去寫那將來不便收入文集的尺牘。憤怒怨恨，如果用得其當，是很可寶貴的一種情感，所謂「文王一怒」那是無人不知的了，但是匿名信則除了發洩憤怒怨恨之外還表現了人性的另一面——怯懦。怯懦也不希奇。聽說外國的殺人不眨眼的海盜，如果蓄謀叛變開始向船長要挾的時候，那封哀的美敦書的署名是很成問題的，領銜的要冒較大的危險，所以他們發明了round-robin法以姓名連串的寫成一圓圈，無始無末，渾然無跡。這種辦法也是怯懦，較之匿名信還是大膽的多。凡是當著人不好說出口的話，或是說出口來要臉紅的事，或是根本不能從口裏說出來的東西，在匿名的掩護之下可以一洩如注。

When someone takes out a sheet and bites his pen as an overture to writing an anonymous letter, he has one more thing to reckon with— his handwriting is an obstacle. More than the handwriting in any other language, Chinese calligraphy tends to reveal the writer's personality. People who write a neat hand like print tend to be meek and docile. Those who refuse to stay within the assigned printed spaces, regardless of the number of strokes in a character, are usually aggressive and uninhibited. There is even a perceived link between the different styles of calligraphy and the physical builds of the writers. Fat characters known as "ink pigs" tend to be written by someone with a pot belly. On the other hand, skinny and bony characters are likely to be the work of a living skeleton. As an anonymous letter comes almost invariably from some acquaintance of the addressee, and the latter will have little difficulty in recognizing the handwriting of a friend, the sender must figure out a way to conceal his identity. He cannot ask someone else to write the letter for him because, if he does, he will let at least one other person into his secret. Besides, it is hard to find someone of a like mind and a kindred spirit. So he must do his own writing. Writers of anonymous letters (such as kidnappers) in Western countries often cut out the letters they need from a newspaper and paste them together to form the words. This is indeed a very clever method, but it is a regret that the movement to romanize the Chinese language has not yet succeeded. In order to compose a Chinese letter with characters cut out from newspapers, one would have to compile in advance an extensive index. So, the only feasible alternative is for the writer to try as far as possible to change his (or her) handwriting, but that is easier said than done. No one is capable of more tricks than a fairy fox.[16] Yet, no matter how many different shapes it can assume, it can never shed its tail.

---

16 Chinese folklore abounds with stories about fairy foxes, which, like witches, can assume human and other forms.

　　匿名信作家在伸紙吮筆之際也有一番為難，筆跡是一重難關，
中國的書法比任何其他國的文字更容易表現性格。有人寫字勻整如
打字機打出來的，其人必循規蹈矩；有人寫字不分大小一律出格，
其人必張牙舞爪。甚至字體還和人的形體有關，如果字如墨豬，其
人往往似「五百斤油」，如果筆畫乾瘦如柴，其人往往亦似一堆排
骨。匿名信總是熟人寫的，熟人的字跡誰還看不出來？所以寫的人
要費一番思索。匿名信不能託別人寫，因為託別人寫，便至少有一
個人知道了你的姓名，而且也難得找到志同道合的人，所以只好自
己動筆。外國人(如綁票匪)寫匿名信，往往從報紙上剪下應用的字
母，然後拼成字黏上去，此法甚妙，可惜中國字拉丁化運動尚未成
功，從報上剪字便非先編一索引不可。唯一可行的方法是竭力變
更字體。然而談何容易！善變莫如狐，七變八變，總還變不脫那
條尾巴。

A letter composed in the classical style (*wen-yen*) is less likely than one written in the vernacular (*bai-hua*) to leave a telltale clue to its authorship, just as a falsetto in a Chinese opera is harder to identify than a speaking voice. Individuality is significantly reduced by employing literary jargon, while the use of set phrases and classical allusions in combination with literary techniques as exemplified by the *Anthology of the Greatest Classical Writers* will make it extremely difficult to figure out who may have written the letter. (Naturally, if any one of the eight most celebrated writers of the Tang and Song dynasties, such as Han Yu or Liu Zongyuan, had a mind to write an anonymous letter, perhaps he would be induced to employ the "apothegmatic" style.[17]) A person who can write tolerably well may perhaps have to introduce a few intentional errors into the text to throw the hunter off the scent. But such a need will not arise if he chooses to write in the classical style; in that case, even his best effort can only produce a language that is awkward, obscure and unreadable.

The effect of an anonymous letter varies widely, depending on the personality of the person who receives it. It may be compared to a fly that alights on a dish of food. This incident will cause great consternation to a person who habitually sterilizes his chopsticks with rubbing alcohol before using them. He will refuse to touch the contaminated food and order it removed from his table. A person who routinely washes his chopsticks in boiling water will insist that the food be cooked again before he will eat it. But a person who lives in an environment where flies are a common sight will simply whisk the winged pest away. Even if the fly became mixed in the food rather than just alighting on it, he would pick it up and throw it away with no mental reaction other than an annoyance that lasted only a split

---

17 Han Yu (768–824) and Liu Zongyuan (773–819) were two of the most famous poets and essayists of the Tang dynasty. This style, popular in the Song dynasty, was employed to record the lectures of famous philosophers of the time.

文言文比白話文難於令人辨出筆調，等於唱西皮二簧，比說話難於令人辨出嗓音。之乎者也的一來，人味減少了許多，再加上成語典故以及《古文觀止》上所備有的古文筆法，我們便很難推測作者是何許人(當然，如果韓文公或柳子厚等唐宋八大家寫匿名信，一定不用文言，或者要用語錄體罷？)本來文理粗通的人，或者要故意的寫上幾個別字，以便引人的猜測走上歧途。文言根本不必故意往壞裏寫，因為竭力往好裏寫，結果也是免不了拗澀蹩扭。

匿名信的效力之大小，是視收信人性格之不同而大有差異的。譬如一隻蒼蠅落在一碗菜上，在一個用火酒擦筷子的人必定要大驚小怪起來，一定屏去不食，一個用開水洗筷子的人就要主張燒開了再食，但是在司空見慣了的人，不要說蒼蠅落在菜上，就是拌在菜裏，驅開摔去便是，除了一刹那間的厭惡以外，別無其他反應。

second. An anonymous letter can definitely cause such a mild case of nausea, but this effect is by no means limited to anonymous letters. I recall a similar experience I had on a winter night more than a decade ago (in the heyday of the so-çalled proletarian literature). That night, I was sleeping in a garret over the third floor and the telephone on the ground floor was ringing off the hook. I put on my robe, rushed down two flights of stairs and picked up the receiver.

"Yes?"

"I'd like to speak to Mr. So–and–so."

"Speaking."

"So you are Mr. So-and-so?"

"That's right."

Thereupon, the voice at the other end of the line suddenly changed and turned gruff and aggressive.

"You are an S-O-B."

Before I could recover from the shock, the caller banged down his receiver and the telephone went dead. I climbed the stairs back to my room on the third floor, took off my robe and got into bed. It was an unsettling experience to be aroused in the dead of a winter night and rush down and then climb back up two flights of stairs only to be called an ugly name. I remember that, for about an hour, I could not go back to sleep as a result of that incident. Such a telephone call and an anonymous letter produce the same effect, although via two different media: one employs the spoken language while the other uses written words.

There are certain things in this mundane world which one cannot prevent and is reluctant to track down to the source. Anonymous

引人惡心這一點點功效，匿名信是有的，不過又不是匿名信所獨有。記得十幾年前(就是所謂普羅文學鼎盛的那一年)的一個冬夜，我睡在三樓亭子間，樓下電話響得很急，我穿起衣服下樓去接：「找誰？」「我請×××先生說話。」「我就是。」「啊，你就是×××先生嗎？」「是的，我就是。」這時節那方面的聲音變了，變得很粗厲，厲聲罵一句「你是□□□！」正驚愕間，呱啦一聲，寂然無聲了。我再上三層樓，脫衣服，睡覺。在冬天三更半夜上下三層樓挨一句罵，這是令人作嘔的事，我記得我足足為之失眠約一小時！這和匿名信是異趣同工的，不過一個是用語言，一個是用文字。

　　天下事有不可預防不便追究者，如匿名信便是。要預防，很難，除非自己是文盲，並且專結交文盲。要追究，很苦，除非自甘

letters belong to this category. It is extremely difficult to avoid them unless you are illiterate and have only illiterate people for friends. And it takes too much trouble to track down their sources unless you are willing to debase yourself and sink to the level of their senders. Actually, it is not absolutely impossible to trace an anonymous letter to its origin. Comparison of handwriting, like that of fingerprints, is a most convenient method of identification. Once a man, who was vigilant and had an exceptionally good nose, received an anonymous letter. When he opened the letter, he could detect a scent, the sweet smell of some cosmetic used by a lady. Using the technique of a police dog, he was able to trace it all the way to that lady's boudoir. But there is the rub: if a person succeeds in identifying the source of an anonymous letter, what is he going to do about it? Worse still, how can life go on if the sender turns out to be a good friend whom he sees every day? "Every time I went out in the morning," writes Marcus Aurelius, "I would say to myself, 'Today I shall meet an insolent person, an ungrateful person, or a garrulous person. It is only natural and necessary for them to act in that way; and therefore be not surprised.'" This, I believe, is a correct attitude. There exists in this world a type of people who have the need to write anonymous letters, because they, both males and females, are angry with or feel wronged by someone else, but they lack a sufficiently stiff backbone to stand up to him (or her). If they refrain from writing such letters, their pent-up emotions will trigger some biological mutation. For this reason, writing anonymous letters is, to them, something both natural and indispensable, and it should surprise no one.

As to the sender of this anonymous letter, will he not be troubled by his own conscience when he meets me in the future? I believe that definitely he will not be able to look me in the eyes. I believe that he is bound to blush and walk away, or mutter something, or make an attempt at small talk while, at the same time, striving to

暴棄與寫匿名書信者一般見識。其實匿名信的來源不是不可破獲的。核對筆蹟是最方便的法子，猶之核對指紋。有一位細心而嗅覺發達的人曾經在啟開匿名信之後嗅到一股脂粉香，按照警犬追蹤的辦法，他可以一直跟蹤到人家的閨閣。不過問題是，萬一破獲了來源，其將何以善其後？尤其是，萬一證明了那寫信的人是天天見面的一個好朋友，這個世界將如何住得下去？Marcus Aurelius說：「每天早晨我離家時便對自己說：『我今天將要遇見一個傲慢的人，一個忘恩負義的人，一個說話太多的人。這些人之所以要這樣，乃是自然的而且必然的，所以不可驚異。』」我覺得這態度很好。世界上是有一種人要寫匿名信，他或她覺得憤慨委曲，而又沒有一根夠硬的脊椎支持著，如果不寫匿名信，情感受了壓抑，會生出變態，所以寫匿名信是自然的而且必然的，不可驚異。這也就是俗話所說，見怪不怪。

寫匿名信給我的人以後見了我，不難過嗎？我想他一定不敢兩眼正視我，他一定要臊不搭的走開，或是搭趄著扯幾句淡話，同時

maintain his composure and trying not to make me feel that, in some way, he is not his usual self. I am certain that, after writing this anonymous letter, he will spend each day hoping that the letter will produce the effect he desires. The uncertainty as to whether it will or will not produce that effect will keep him in a state of suspense and unease. He who has mailed out an anonymous letter will not be able to sleep like a log throughout the night.

他還要努力鎮定，要使我不感覺他與往常有甚麼不同。他寫過匿名
信後，必定天天期望著他所希冀的效果，究竟有效呢？無效呢？這
將使他惶惑不寧。寫了匿名信的人一定不會一覺睡到大天光的。

The Sixth Human Relationship

The so-called five human relationships are those between ruler and subject, father and son, husband and wife, brothers, and friends. If a sixth is to be added, it should be the relationship between master and servant. This sixth relationship is something from which no one can escape. A head of state, for all the dignity of his office, is a servant of the people. A peddler or porter, despite his lowly station, may act like a master in his own household, where at least his wife and daughters-in-law are supposed to carry out his orders like servants. But, for the purposes of this article, a servant refers to someone who is employed for the sole purpose of providing service in private homes and the term "master" refers to a person who uses money to hire another person or persons to perform household chores at his bidding. Compared to the other five human relationships, it is even more difficult to maintain a good rapport between masters and servants.

In the eyes of the master, a servant is often a "necessary evil", who is indispensable to him, but whose mere sight will incur his displeasure. First, domestic servants, both male and female, are seldom properly clad or shod; some of them may even look unwashed and unkempt, or carry with them an offensive smell of garlic, while others may go barefoot and shirtless and look like nothing but skin and bones, like Mahatma Gandhi. These creatures go about their chores in the various

第六倫

君臣父子夫婦兄弟朋友，是為五倫，如果要添上一個六倫，便應該是主僕。主僕的關係是每個人都不得逃脫的。高貴如一國的元首，他還是人民的公僕，低賤如販夫走卒，他回到家裏，頤指氣使，至少他的妻子媳婦是不免要做奴下奴的。不過我現在所要談的「僕」，是以伺候私人起居為專職的那種僕。所謂「主」，是指用錢雇買人的勞力供其驅使的人而言。主僕這一倫，比前五倫更難敦睦。

在主人的眼裏，僕人往往是一個「必需的罪惡」，沒有他不成，有了他看著討厭。第一，僕人不分男女，衣履難得整齊，或則蓬首垢面，或則蒜臭襲人，有些還跣足赤背，瘦骨嶙嶙，活像甘地先

quarters of a house, but other people tend to look upon them as eyesores. One aesthete (was it Oscar Wilde or Joris-Karl Huysmanns?) came up with a design whereby he would first cover all the walls in his house with wallpaper and then order the servants to wear clothes that matched the wallpaper in color and pattern. In that way the servants would acquire a sort of protective coloration so that their entries and exits would not attract much attention. This may be an apt solution to the problem, but so far very few people have adopted it. Some arrogant and supercilious foreigners living in China, as well as those Chinese who ape them, often dress their domestics in a uniform that makes them look like waiters in Western-style restaurants. On the other hand, bureaucrats in diplomatic missions located in the Legation Quarters of Beijing make their doormen and coachmen wear red-tasseled hats all year around. All these are done for no other purpose than to make the servants appear less objectionable in order to suit their equally, if not more, objectionable taste.

Servants, like their masters, must eat to live and they, as a rule, consume more food than their masters do. This, in the eyes of the masters, must be counted as a very great demerit. Very few masters (and fewer mistresses) would not frown and sicken at the sight of a servant raising a heaped bowl of rice and shoveling the food into his or her mouth. Many of them are puzzled as to why a fellow human being can develop such a capacity for food, once he or she is reduced to the status of a servant.

The demands of a master cannot be easily and fully satisfied and, for that reason, he tends to consider his servants lazy and the work they perform unsatisfactory. The "Articles of Service" by Wang Bao,[18]

---

18 A famous poet and writer and official at the court of Emperor Xuan (73 – 49 B.C.) of the Han dynasty. The "Articles" tells the story of Wang's visit to a friend who

生，也公然升堂入室，誰看著也是不順眼。一位唯美主義者(是王爾德還是優思曼？)曾經設計過，把屋裏四面牆都糊上牆紙，然後令僕人穿上與牆紙同樣顏色同樣花紋的衣裳，於是僕人便有了「保護色」，出入之際，不至引人注意。這是一種辦法，不過尚少有人採用。有些作威作福的旅華外人，以及「二毛子」之類，往往給家裏的僕人穿上制服，像番菜館的侍者似的，東交民巷裏的洋官僚，則一年四季的給看門的趕車的戴上一頂紅纓帽。這種種，無非是想要減少僕人的一些討厭相，以適合他們自己的其實更為可厭的品味而已。

僕人，像主人一樣，要吃飯，而且必然吃的更多。這在主人看來，是僕人很大的一個缺點。僕人早起一碗碰鼻尖的滿碗飯往嘴裏扒的時候，很少主人(尤其是主婦)看著不皺眉的，心痛。很多主人認為是怪事，同樣的是人，何以一旦淪為僕役，便要努力加餐到這種程度。

主人的要求不容易完全滿足，所以僕人總是懶的，總是不能稱意，王褒的〈僮約〉雖是一篇遊戲文字，卻表示出一般人唯恐僕人少

though intended as a *jeu d'esprit*, has the effect of exposing the common practice of drawing up in advance a frightfully long list of chores to be performed by each servant in order to keep the servant occupied all the time. Yet the master in question will not feel satisfied even if the servant agrees to and performs each and every chore required by the articles, because there are bound to be many other chores unforeseen by the master at the signing of the indenture. A short play written in medieval France tells the story of a gentleman who is hiring a servant and who, like Wang Bao, lists in detail all the duties of the servant in a document, which both parties subsequently accept and sign. One day the master falls into the well and cries out for help. The servant slowly takes out the document and says, "*Un moment!* Let me see if there is a provision about rescuing you from the well." I have forgotten how the play ends, but the story shows that people everywhere tend to think and act alike. There is yet another thing that masters require of their servants, that is, to show an absolute obedience similar to that shown by troops to the orders they receive on a battlefield and never to have any ideas of their own. Unfortunately, despite the ordeal of a hard life, servants do tend to keep a trace of individual character. Likewise, since they have been nurtured by their parents and have received a sort of education necessary to the development of their character, they tend to preserve a vestige of human nature. As such, they cannot completely avoid contradicting their masters. Nowadays, very few of them measure up to the ancient yardstick of proper behavior for domestic servants. Indeed, those menservants from Beijing

---

was a widow. When her bondservant acted insolently and refused to go out and buy wine for the guest, the widow became angry. Wang offered to buy the bond, but the servant bade Wang draw up a new service contract, saying that he would perform the duties specified therein. Wang then made a list of about a hundred household chores and showed it to the servant, who broke down in tears and begged the guest to forgive his insolence.

作了事，事前一樁樁的列舉出來，把人嚇倒。如果那個僕人件件應允，件件做到，主人還是不會滿意的，因為主人有許多事是主人自己事前也想不到的。法國中古有一篇短劇，描寫一個人雇用一個僕人，也是做王褒筆意，開列了一篇詳盡的工作大綱，兩相情願，立此為憑。有一天，主人落井，大聲呼援，僕人慢騰騰的取出那篇工作大綱，說：「且慢，等我看看，有沒有救你出井那一項目。」下文怎樣，我不知道，不過可見中西一體，人同此心。主人所要求於僕人的，還有一點，就是絕對服從，不可自做主張，要像軍隊臨陣一般的聽從命令，不幸的是，僕人無論受過怎樣折磨，總還有一點個性存留，他也是父母養育的，所以也受過一點發展個性的教育，因此總還有一點人性的遺留，難免頂撞主人。現在人心不古，僕人的風度之合於古法的已經不多，像北平的男僕，三河縣的女僕，那樣

and maidservants from the nearby Sanhe County—both highly regarded for their polite manners and sense of propriety—may have to be placed like American Indians in reservations to protect them from corruption by bad influences from the outside world. If not, they will become an endangered species.

The key to success in managing servants is to treat them as human beings. In this way, we will not blame them for failing to do anything that is almost humanly impossible and will forgive them for any mistake that all human beings are liable to make. In a letter introducing a servant, the poet Tao Yuanming[19] said to his son, "You must treat this servant well because he, too, is somebody's son." Indeed, these words were spoken with great wisdom. What Sir J. M. Barrie describes in his play *The Admirable Crichton* may also help us understand the quintessence of the relationship between master and servant. Crichton, a servant, is marooned with his master on an uninhabited island following their shipwreck. At first the master cannot forget his superior station. But the posturing of the master soon becomes untenable because the servant is the only one who can chop firewood and hunt for food. As the provider, Crichton gradually becomes the master who gives orders, while his master also undergoes a gradual change, becoming first an assistant, then a servant. This metamorphosis is all too natural, having been brought upon them by circumstances. Eventually, after their rescue and return to civilization, Crichton feels uneasy in his changed condition and voluntarily returns to his former position as servant. On the other hand, his master, having regained the props of his social status, resumes his role as master. The play has a message for us: the relationship between master and servant is not preordained; there may be an exchange of their positions once they are removed from civilization. We need not advocate rebellion against

---

19 Literary name of Tao Qian (365–427), one of the greatest poets of China.

的應對得體，進退有節，大概是要像美洲紅人似的需要特別闢地保
護，勿令沾染外習。否則這一類型是要絕跡於人寰的了。

　　駕馭僕人之道，是有秘訣的，那就是，把他當做人，這樣一
來，凡是人所不容易做到的，我們也就不苛責於他，凡是人所容易
犯的毛病，我們也可加以曲宥。陶淵明介紹一個僕人給他的兒子，
寫信囑咐他說：「彼亦人子也，可善視之。」這真是一大發明！J. M.
Barrie爵士在《可敬愛的克來頓》那一齣戲裏所描寫的，也可使人恍
然於主僕一倫的精義。主僕二人漂海遇險，在一荒島上過活。起初
主人不能忘記他是主人，但是主人的架子不能搭得太久，因為僕人
是唯一能砍柴打獵的人，他是生產者，他漸漸變成了主人，他發號
施令，而主人漸漸變成為一助手，一個奴僕了。這變遷很自然，環
境逼他們如此。後來遇救返回到「文明世界」，那僕人又局促不安起
來，又自甘情願的回到僕人的位置，那主人有所憑藉，又回到主人
的位置了。這齣戲告訴我們，主僕的關係，不是天生成的，離開了
「文明世界」，主僕的位置可能交換。我們固不必主張反抗文明，但

civilization, but we can somehow help to improve the relationship between master and servant by making certain masters realize that they are not born to be masters and that, in terms of practical skills, they may rank far below their servants.

Peace in a family of five generations living under the same roof calls for the utmost forbearance. The relationship between master and servant, though less complicated, also requires a considerable degree of tolerance on both sides. When the cook takes a cut of the daily allowance for food, or the laundry woman appropriates a cake of soap, the master should ask himself, "Is it not true that negotiators for state loans also receive kickbacks?" When a servant becomes wayward and defiant or insolent and surly, the master should ask himself, "Is it not true that sometimes I can do nothing but restrain my anger and keep quiet when my own son talks back to me in a sarcastic manner?" When servants get together in a mixed group to gossip and flirt, the master should ask himself, "Is it not true that sex scandals also abound in the so-called upper stratum of society?" The thought of these questions will calm him and bring peace to his mind and enable him to realize that each of the servants has his or her merits. There is an even greater need for tolerance on the part of the servants. The master is in a sulk because he has lost a lot of money at gambling, or he has been put on the carpet by his boss and has nowhere else to vent his spleen, or did not sleep well last night, or is suffering from dyspepsia.

The "Directions to Servants" written by Jonathan Swift contains the following passage:

> Let it be a constant rule, that no chair, stool, or table, in the servants' hall, or the kitchen, shall have above three legs, which has been the ancient and constant practice in all the families I ever knew, and it is said to be founded upon two reasons: first, to show that servants

是我們如果讓一些主人明白，他不是天生成的主人，講到真實本領他也許比他的僕人矮一大截，這對於改善主僕一倫，也未始沒有助益哩！

五世同堂，乃得力於百忍。主僕相處，雖不及五世，但也需雙方相當的忍。僕人買菜賺錢，洗衣服偷肥皂，這時節主人要想，國家借款不是也有回扣嗎？僕人倔強頂撞傲慢無禮，這時節主人要想，自己的兒子不也是時常反脣相稽，自己也只好忍氣吞聲麼？僕人調笑謔浪，男女混雜，這時節主人要想，所謂上層社會不也有的是桃色案件嗎？肯這樣想便覺心平氣和，便能發現每一個僕人都有他的好處。在僕人一方面，更需要忍。主人發脾氣，那是因為輸了錢，或是受了上司的氣而無處發洩，或是夜裏沒有睡好覺，或是腸胃消化不良。

Swift在他的〈婢僕須知〉一文裏有這樣一段：

> 這應該定為例規，凡下房或廚房裏的桌椅板凳都不得有三條以上的腿。這是古老定例，在我所知道的人家裏都是如此，據說有兩個理由，其一，用以表示僕役都是在桌

are ever in a tottering condition; secondly, it was thought a point of humility that the servants' chairs and tables should have at least one leg fewer than those of their masters. I grant there has been an exception to this rule, with regard to the cook, who, by old custom, was allowed an easy chair to sleep in after dinner; and yet I have seldom seen them with above three legs. Now this epidemic lameness of servants' chairs, is, by philosophers, imputed to two causes, which are observed to make the greatest revolutions in states and empires; I mean love and war. A stool, a chair, or a table, is the first weapon taken up in a general romping or skirmish; and after a peace, the chairs, if they be not very strong, are apt to suffer in the conduct of an amour, the cook being usually fat and heavy, and the butler a little in drink.

The sarcasm of this passage is quite obvious, although it is not fully applicable to our national conditions. In our country, it is true that some chairs for servants have only three legs, but it is also true that many have "above three legs". As an ordinary chair has no more than four legs, the distinction between master and servant is only marginal in this respect. What I deplore is the fact that most servants are probably like Caliban in *The Tempest*, clumsy yet crafty, cowardly yet daring, obedient yet resistant, discontented yet resigned— an embodiment of contradictions in the extreme. In most cases, however, this fault does not lie with the servant. If the world's population were evenly divided between masters and servants, needless to say, the sixth human relationship would have to be readjusted.

兀不定的狀態，其二，算是表示謙卑，僕人用的桌椅比主
人用的至少要缺少一條腿。我承認這裏對於廚娘有一個例
外，她依照舊習慣可以有一把靠手椅備飯後的安息；然而
我也少見有三條以上的腿的。僕人的椅子之發生這種傳染
性跛疾，據哲學家說是由於兩個原因，即造成邦國的最大
革命者：我是指戀愛與戰爭。一條凳，一把椅子，或一張
桌子，在總攻擊或小戰的時候，每被拿來當作兵器；和
平以後，椅子——倘若不是十分結實——在戀愛行為中又
容易受損，因為廚娘大抵為重，而司酒的又總是有點醉
了。

　　這一段諷刺的意義是十分明白的，雖然對我們國情並不甚合。
我們國裏僕人們坐的凳子，固然有只有三條腿的，可是在三條以上
的也甚多。一把普通的椅子最多也不過四條腿，主僕之分在這上面
究竟找不出多大距離，我覺得慘的是，僕人大概永遠像莎士比亞《暴
風雨》中的那個卡力班，又蠢笨，又狡猾，又怯懦，又大膽，又服
從，又反抗，又不知足，又安天命，陷入極端的矛盾。這過錯多半
不在僕人方面。如果這世界上的人，半是主人半是僕，這一倫的關
係之需要調整是不待言的了。

A Cur

When I first arrived in Chongqing, I was lodged in a small, low-lying room, which was made gloomier by the presence of two or three tall and robust plantain trees in front of its only window. In rainy nights, the patter of raindrops on the plantain leaves created a feeling of wretchedness that was almost unbearable. Yet there was a hint of something poetic in that dreary place. Having found a shelter like that in my exile from home, what more could I ask for? My greatest headache, however, was the dog that stood guard outside my room.

The door of my room opened into a hallway that doubled as the dining area for my landlord and his family. And this dog, with its massive head and huge body, was always found crouching under the dining table. My host never had the need to sweep the floor—the dog would lick up the bits of meat and bones, spilled rice and porridge, as well as the droppings of a toddler, that lay scattered on the floor. Should a stranger venture into the hallway, the dog would mistake him for an interloper come to compete for its food and would bare its teeth and snarl and rush at the intruder. In this way, the dog took on the combined duties of janitor and doorman for the house.

"There are three things a gentleman should fear," said Confucius. One of them is a cur. I knew that my life was not in danger, but every time I left or returned to my room, I had to traverse the dog's turf.

狗

　　我初到重慶，住在一間湫隘的小室裏，窗外還有三兩窠肥碩的芭蕉，屋裏益發顯得陰森森的，每逢夜雨，淒慘欲絕。但淒涼中畢竟有些詩意，旅中得此，尚復何求？我所最感苦惱的乃是房門外的那一隻狗。

　　我的房門外是一間穿堂，亦即房東一家老小用膳之地，餐棹底下永遠臥著一條腦滿腸肥的大狗。主人從來沒有掃過地，每餐的殘羹剩飯，骨屑稀粥，以及小兒便溺，全都在地上星羅棋佈著，由那隻大狗來舐得一乾二淨。如果有生人走進，狗便不免有所誤會，以為是要和牠爭食，於是聲色俱厲的猛撲過去。在這一家裏，狗完全擔負了「灑掃應對」的責任。

　　「君子有三畏」，猘犬其一也。我知道性命並無危險，但是每次出來進去總要經過他的防次，言語不通，思想亦異，每次都要引起

Each time, the absence of a common language and the tendency to misjudge each other's purposes would create friction and lead to confrontation. After a while, this situation became a cause of extreme aggravation to me. Meanwhile, I resorted to various strategies. Once I threw the dog a biscuit with the intention to appease it. But, even before finishing the biscuit, the beast seized the moment I turned my back to unlock the door and, without warning, launched a sneak attack directed at my legs. After this incident, I switched to a new strategy, which was founded on the doctrine that "the best defense is offense". I began to take the initiative, using a stick to hit it on the head or on the tail, whichever I caught sight off. In all these skirmishes I never suffered a defeat, neither did my small triumphs add up to a complete victory. Besides, for some time after each battle, my blood vessels remained swollen, making me look totally out of decorum. As a result, whenever I was out, I was afraid to go home; after I had returned to my room, I dared not drink much tea. What troubled me most, however, was not the dog but the attitude of its owner.

If the landlord was present when the dog rushed at me from under the dining table, I would entertain an extravagant hope. Even though the dog was also a higher animal, a mammal among vertebrates, I felt that, after all, the landlord and I had a closer genetic link, at least so in our outward forms, and that I could expect a little help or sympathy from him. But I was wrong. The dog and its owner appeared to take a common stand. My landlord and I, as his tenant, were on opposite sides of a business deal, and he found that a distinction had to be made between a family member and an outsider. I do not mean that my landlord would join his dog to bark at me; they had not yet developed that kind of herd instinct. What I really mean is that my landlord, instead of coming to my rescue, would burst out laughing whenever he saw me in such a plight. With a smile on his face and an unconcealed look of satisfaction, he would call out to his dog, "Are

摩擦,釀成衝突,日久之後真覺厭煩之至。其間曾經謀求種種對策,一度投以餌餅,期收綏靖之效,不料餌餅尚未啖完,乘我返身開鎖之際,無警告的向我的腿部偷襲過來,又一度改取「進攻乃最好之防禦」的方法,轉取主動,見頭打頭,見尾打尾,雖無挫衄,然積小勝終不能成大勝,且轉戰之餘,血脈債張,亦大失體統。因此外出即怵回家,回到房裏又不敢多飲茶。不過使我最難堪的還不是狗,而是他的主人的態度。

狗從棹底下向我撲過來的時候,如果主人在場,我心裏是存著一種奢望的:我覺得狗雖然也是高等動物,脊椎動物哺乳類,然而,究竟,至少在外形上,主人和我是屬於較近似的一類,我希望他給我一些援助或同情。但是我錯了,主客異勢,親疏有別,主人和狗站在同一立場。我並不是說主人也幫著狗猖猖然來對付我,他們尚不至於這樣的合群。我是說主人對我並不解救,看著我的狼狽而闃然噱笑,泛起一種得意之色,面帶著笑容對狗嗔罵幾聲:「小

you crazy, Spotty? Don't you recognize Mr. X?" Though the rebuke was directed at the dog, it was couched in a language I could understand. He seemed to say in an overtone, "I've done my duty of trying to control my dog. So, you shouldn't blame me even if you end up in its stomach." Having said this, he assumed the role of an onlooker, in the manner of a spectator at the Coliseum in Rome watching a Christian gladiator being mauled by a lion. There is a common saying: "Look at the master before you beat the dog." But, in this case, I felt that I had better not look at the master because, if I did, I would get violent and, with my stick, treat the dog to a few more whacks than it deserved.

Later on, I was able to move out of the home of that cur when I followed an order to evacuate to the countryside. I was told that the new tenant of that room was a military officer. When he met with the same treatment by the dog and its owner, he had a better way to deal with them. He took out his service revolver and shot and killed the dog on the spot. When my initial reaction of jubilation was over, I began to visualize the landlord in mourning and could not help feeling compassion for him. It was particularly sad to think that, with no dog to lap up the leavings of meals on the floor, the landlord was now obliged to do the cleaning himself. His feeling of bereavement was not difficult to imagine.

Relocation to the countryside does not mean freedom from the menace of dogs. But strays, being without family connections, are easier to deal with. With the exception of rabid dogs that roam the streets at the time of the year when the rape begins to put out yellow flowers, ordinary strays are shaggy, pitiable creatures that walk with their tails between their legs. Even their barking sounds weak and nervous. On the other hand, kept dogs bark in a garrulous and assertive manner, which sets them apart as a distinct class. Many

花！你昏了？連×先生你都不認識了！」罵的是狗，用的是讓我所能聽懂的語言。那絃外之音是：「我已盡了管束之責了，你如果被狗吃掉莫要怪我。」然後他就像是在羅馬劇場裏看基督徒被猛獸撲食似的作壁上觀。俗語說：「打狗看主人」，我覺得不看主人還好，看了主人我倒要狠狠的再打狗幾棍。

後來我疏散下鄉，遂脫離了這惡犬之家，聽說繼續住那間房的是一位軍人，他也遭遇了狗的同樣的待遇，也遭遇了狗的主人的同樣的待遇，但是他比我有辦法，他拔出槍來把狗當場格斃了，我於稱快之餘，想起那位主人的悲愴，又不能不付予同情了。特別是，殘茶剩飯丟在地下無人舐，主人勢必躬親灑掃，其淒涼是可想而知的。

在鄉下不是沒有犬厄。沒有背景的野犬是容易應付的，除了菜花黃時的瘋犬不計外，普通的野犬都是些不修邊幅的夾尾巴的可憐的東西，就是汪汪的叫起來也是有氣無力的，不像人家豢養的狗那樣振振有詞自成系統。有些人家在門口掛著牌示「內有惡犬」，我覺

homes have put up a sign on their gates, which says: "Beware of the Dog." This, I believe, is a far more humane practice than keeping a cur in ambush behind the door. The other day I had the experience of walking into such an ambush, which caught me completely unprepared and caused me to scream in panic. The master of the house heard the noise and emerged from behind a curtain and, with a smile, invited me into his living room. Then he calmly told me that his dog had recently attacked quite a few people. He gave me this information as an effective solace and I was supposed to consider myself rather fortunate to have escaped unharmed. But I could not help thinking that he might as well keep a tiger in the house and let it devour each visitor who dared to venture into his home. Wouldn't that bring him greater pride and notoriety?

It took me some time to discover the truth. My cottage is not located in a walled enclosure and burglaries have grown rampant in the area. For that reason, my landlord has brought in a dog as a security measure. One day, when the unwary mailman showed up at the door, the dog snarled and attacked him. While the mailman put up a fight in retreat and stumbled along the route of escape, my landlord clapped his hands and laughed heartily. I suddenly saw the light. The sight of somebody in an embarrassing situation always strikes us as funny, and a person being attacked by a dog is no less funny than someone who slips on a banana peel. The purpose of keeping a dog is to see it attack people or at least look as ferocious as a man-eating beast. This may be compared to raising chickens for their eggs. If a dog looks as docile as a cat, dozes away its days in the sun, meows at a visitor and then timidly beats a hasty retreat, I think it will be a shame for its owner and a surprise to the visitors. For that reason, when a dog attacks a visitor, its owner will regard it as properly discharging its duty. On the surface, the owner may be profuse in his apologies, but it gives him a secret pleasure to realize that his dog is not occupying a

得這比門裏埋伏惡犬的人家要忠厚得多。我遇見過埋伏，往往猝不及防，驚惶大呼，主人聞聲搴簾而出，嫣然而笑，肅客入座。從容相告狗在最近咬傷了多少人。這是一種有效的安慰，因為我之未及於難是比較可慶幸的事了。但是我終不明白，他為什麼不索興養一隻虎？來一個吃一個，來兩個吃一雙，豈不是更為體面麼？

這道理我終於明白了。雅舍無圍牆，而盜風熾，於是添置了一隻狗。一旦郵差貿貿然來，狗大咆哮，郵差且戰且走，蹣跚而逸，主人拊掌大笑。我頓有所悟。別人的狼狽永遠是一件可笑的事，被狗所困的人是和踏在香蕉皮上面跌交的人同樣的可笑。養狗的目的就要他咬人，至少作吃人狀。這就是等於養雞是為要他生蛋一樣，假如一隻狗像一隻貓一樣，整天曬太陽睡覺，客人來便咪咪叫兩聲，然後逡巡而去，我想不但主人慚愧，客人也要驚訝。所以狗咬客人，在主人方面認為狗是克盡厥職，表面上儘管對客抱歉，內心裏是有一種愉快，覺得我的這隻狗並非是掛名差事，他守在崗位上

sinecure; instead, it is effectively performing the functions of its post. So the dog gets apparent rebuke but real approbation. And that goes to explain the air of triumph that makes the owner's face glow. Besides, as a rule, a dog does not attack a well-dressed person. In this respect, the master definitely believes that the pet can read his mind. Surely, there are dog owners who do not make it a rule to receive or reject visitors depending on whether they are well or poorly dressed. Regrettably, they cannot possibly explain this to their dogs, which act as their doormen, to prevent them from behaving insolently to their visitors. But, in general, a dog tends to judge a visitor in much the same way as its owner. That is the reason so many people keep dogs.

發揮了作用。所以對狗一面訶責，一面也還要嘉勉。因此臉上纔泛
出那一層得意之色。還有衣裳楚楚的人，狗是不大咬的，這在主人
也不能不有「先獲我心」之感。所可遺憾者，有些主人並不以衣裳取
人，亦並不以衣裳廢人，而這種道理無法通知門上，有時不免要慢
待佳賓。不過就大體論，狗的眼力總是和他的主人差不了多少。所
以，有這樣多的人家都養狗。

Visitors

"None but God and wild beasts love solitude." I have no way of knowing what God loves. Regarding wild beasts, I have been told that most of them live in packs or herds, and few of them are real loners. As for us mortals, it may be assumed that, as long as we are in good health, all of us, without exception, would love to have company at home. Even Henry Thoreau, despite his well-known love for a quiet and secluded life, took pains to provide all sorts of comforts for visitors to his shack in the woods. I often dream of the joyful atmosphere conjured up by the verse, "Amid wind and rain comes an old friend to my door." Imagine that, on a stormy day when you feel lonely and bored, you suddenly hear a visitor knocking on your door. You are thrilled to see an old buddy and hold his hands in yours and chat with him cheerfully and without reservation. Such a visitor need not be a person of refined taste, but at least he must not talk about the ups and downs of commodity prices, or prattle on the ins and outs of politicians, or try to sell me an insurance policy, or persuade me to accept any religion. When a visitor "arrives in high spirits and departs well content", that is truly a joy of life. But on many occasions, visitors can bring us annoyance instead of pleasure.

Very few homes have a gatehouse and fewer homes have unfriendly gatekeepers. Private residences whose entrances are not jealously

客

「只有上帝和野獸纔喜歡孤獨。」上帝吾不得而知之，至於野
獸，則據說成群結黨者多，真正孤獨者少。我們凡人，如果身心健
全，大概沒有不好客的。以歡喜幽獨著名的Thoureau他在樹林裏也
給來客安排得舒舒貼貼。我常幻想著「風雨故人來」的境界，在風颯
颯雨霏霏的時候，心情枯寂百無聊賴，忽然有客款扉，把握言歡，
莫逆於心，來客不必如何風雅，但至少第一不談物價升降，第二不
談宦海浮沉，第三不勸我保險，第四不勸我信教，乘興而來，興盡
即返，這真是人生一樂。但是我們為客所苦的時候也頗不少。

很少的人家有門房，更少的人家有拒人千里之外的閽者，門禁
既不森嚴，來客當然無阻，所以私人居處，等於日夜開放。有時主

guarded become, as it were, open houses around the clock, with nothing there to keep out unwanted visitors. Sometimes the host is on his way to the bathroom when a visitor invites himself into the house. It is too late to avoid the encounter and the situation is too awkward for a proper reception. The host keeps bowing while the visitor stands there transfixed with embarrassment. Sometimes a visitor arrives in the middle of a meal and the host is obliged to follow the example of the ancient Duke of Zhou by repeatedly putting away his dinner plate.[20] But the visitor shows no intention to leave. Only after seeing the visitor to the door is the host able to resume his meal and satisfy his hunger with whatever is left on the table. Sometimes the host has already turned in and has to get up and dress himself hastily in order to receive a visitor. Under such circumstances, the host remains in a state of uncertainty around the clock, not knowing when a visitor may invade his home. As visitors have the initiative, no defense is possible.

People in Western countries seldom receive what we call visitors at home, because they have offices for the conduct of official business and clubs for recreation. Their homes are reserved for family life. Our customs are somewhat different. We may conduct official business, play mahjong, drink tea or chew fat in somebody else's parlor at any hour of the day. Since the host may not put a pincushion on every chair, visitors often feel really at home. There was a time when mandarins strictly observed a custom called "raise the teacup and say good-bye." When the host felt that it was time for a visitor to leave, he would raise his lidded teacup in a pledge to the visitor. Upon seeing this signal, a stocky and well-trained servant in attendance would

---

20 Official title of Ji Dan, who helped his older brother, King Wu (1122–1115 B.C.), found the Zhou dynasty, and who established its political and legal systems. He was so occupied with the affairs of state that he was repeatedly interrupted at his meals.

人方在廁上，客人已經升堂入室，迴避不及，應接無術，主人鞠躬如也，客人呆若木雞。有時主人方在用飯，而高軒賁止，便不能不效周公之「一飯三吐哺」，但是來客並無歸心，只好等送客出門之後再補充些殘羹賸飯，有時主人已經就枕，而不能不倒屣相迎。一天二十四小時之內，不知客人何時入侵，主動在客，防不勝防。

在西洋所謂客者是很希罕的東西。因為他們辦公有辦公的地點，娛樂有娛樂的場所，住家專做住家之用。我們的風俗稍為不同一些。辦公打牌吃茶聊天都可以在人家的客廳裏隨時舉行的。主人既不能在座位上遍置針氈，客人便常有如歸之樂。從前官場習慣，有所謂端茶送客之說，主人覺得客人應該告退的時候，便舉起蓋碗請茶，那時節一位訓練有素的豪僕在旁一眼瞥見，便大叫一聲「送

announce loudly, "See the guest out!" Another servant would raise the door curtain. Under such circumstances, the visitor had no alternative but to take his leave. It is regrettable that this excellent, time-saving practice has fallen into disuse. Besides, it was limited to visits between public officials. Were I to raise my teacup in my small living room and have my wife or my young son cry out: "See the guest out!" I am sure the visitor would suspect that my whole family had gone nuts.

When a visitor outstays his welcome, to get rid of him becomes nearly as difficult as to exorcize an evil spirit. If you sit there without saying a word, he will launch into a lengthy monologue and, like a punctured garbage bag, let out a great deal at the slightest touch. Or he may chain-smoke and listen quietly to the tick-tock of the clock on the wall. If you gave a hint that you have something to do and must go out, he will offer to accompany you on the way. If you ask him if he has any other matter to discuss with you, he will simply tell you that he has only come for a chat. If you give him to understand that you are in the middle of doing something, he will advise you to take a longer break. If you keep filling up his teacup, he will finish one cup after another while repeating the words: "Please don't bother." According to a superstition among our country-folk, when a visitor overstays his welcome, someone in the family may place a broom behind a door and repeatedly stick it with a needle. The visitor will instantly feel a pricking pain in his limbs, which will make him uneasy whether sitting or standing, and he will hurriedly take his leave. Someone has actually tried this trick but pronounced it ineffective.

"Tea, make tea, make good tea; take a seat, please take a seat, please take the seat of honor."[21] When a man of the cloth is such a snob, one

---

21 According to legend, the abbot of a certain Buddhist temple used to signal different treatments for visiting pilgrims of different social positions by ordering

客！」另有人把門簾高高打起，客人除了告辭之外，別無他法。可惜
這種經濟時間的良好習俗，今已不復存在，而且這種辦法也只限於
官場，如果我在我的小小客廳之內端起茶碗，由荊妻稚子在旁嚶然
一聲「送客」，我想客人會要疑心我一家都發瘋了。

客人久坐不去，驅禳至為不易。如果你枯坐不語，他也許發表
長篇獨白，像個垃圾口袋一樣，一碰就洩出一大堆，也許一根一根
的紙煙不斷的吸著，靜聽掛鐘滴答滴答的響。如果你暗示你有事要
走，他也許表示願意陪你一道走。如果你問他有無其他的事情見
教，他也許乾脆告訴你來此只為閒聊天。如果你表示正在為了什麼
事情忙，他會勸你多休息一下。如果你一遍一遍的給他斟茶，他也
許就一碗一碗的喝下去而連聲說「主人別客氣。」鄉間迷信，惡客盤
踞不去時，家人可在門後置一掃帚，用針頻頻刺之，客人便會覺得
有刺股之痛，坐立不安而去。此法有人曾經實驗，據云無效。

「茶，泡茶，泡好茶；坐，請坐，請上坐。」出家人猶如此勢

can imagine how much worse lay people can be. But if you stand in the shoes of a host who is constantly plagued by unwelcome visitors, you will consider it justifiable to offer different kinds of tea and seat to different visitors. It would be inappropriate to offer a cup of choice tea, such as "narcissus" or "cloud and mist", to a visitor who drinks like a fish. On the other hand, a connoisseur who is well versed in the mysteries recorded in the ancient *Book of Tea* will definitely refuse to taste a brew made from powdered or brick tea. The very sight of a large bowl of tea made by adding boiling water to a concentrate and covered with a whitish beer-like froth or a colorful gasoline-like film will definitely turn one's stomach. Likewise, it will hurt a host's feelings when a visitor, unappreciative of the choice tea offered him, gives the cup only a light kiss without leaving a trace on the rim. The tea becomes useless to keep but too good to throw away. For these reasons, visitors are often divided into several categories. Some visitors are to be offered the best tea that is reserved by the host for special occasions. Others are to be served the second best tea, which the host enjoys drinking on ordinary days. Visitors in the third category are to be offered a tea made by adding boiling water to a concentrate, which is kept in ready supply. Those who do not qualify for any of these categories are to be given tea in glasses. With regard to seating, those visitors who are allowed to go straight to the host's study or the hostess' boudoir are honored guests. They are treated with intimacy and considerable respect, as these rooms are usually furnished with a number of pieces of bric-a-brac, yet the host or the hostess feels no need to keep an eye on them. A visitor who enjoys such privileges should have no regret whatsoever. Ranking immediately below these are visitors whom the host may receive in a corridor or on a

---

a novice to "bring tea", "make tea" or "make good tea", and by asking his visitors to "take a seat", "please take a seat" or "please take the seat of honor".

利，在家人更可想而知。但是為了常遭客災的主人設想，茶與座二者常常因客而異，蓋亦有說。夙好牛飲之客，自不便奉以「水仙」「雲霧」，而精研茶經之士，又斷不肯嘗試那「高末」，「茶磚」。茶滷加開水，渾渾滿滿一大盅，上面泛著白沫如啤酒，或漂著油彩如汽油，這固然令人惡心，但是如果名茶一盞，而客人並不欣賞，輕呷一口，盅緣上並不留下芬芳，留之無用，棄之可惜，這也是非常討厭之事。所以客人常被分為若干流品，有能啟用平夙主人自己捨不得飲用的好茶者，有能享受主人自己日常享受的中上茶者，有能大量取用茶滷沖開水者，饗以「玻璃」者是為未入流。至於座處，自以直入主人的書房繡閣者為上賓，因為屋內零星物件必定甚多，而主人略無防閑之意，於親密之中尚含有若干敬意，作客至此，毫無遺憾；次焉者廊前簷下隨處接見，所謂班荊道故，了無痕跡；最下者

covered porch and chat about old days without formality. The lowest rank is reserved for those who are ushered into a parlor that is furnished only with tables and chairs or benches, but nothing else. The host comes out wearing the formal long gown and exchanges greetings with the visitor, both extremely courteous and polite. Those who are kept standing at the service entrance next to the kitchen while they speak with the host or hostess are too lowly to receive any ranking. I regard such discriminatory treatment as inevitable. I do not believe that the Lord of Mengchang[22] treated his three thousand retainers equally.

Human beings are never content. They feel lonely when no one comes to visit them, uneasy or annoyed when they have visitors, deserted and empty when they do the clean-up after the visitors have left. The crux of the problem lies in the qualities of a visitor. If a visitor is a person of good qualities, the host will look forward to his arrival, pray that he will stay after he has arrived, and hope that he will come again after he has left. If a visitor is a person of bad qualities, the host will await his visit with apprehension, worry that he will never leave after he has arrived, and fear that he will come again after he has left. Although it is said that birds of a feather flock together, the visit of an uninvited guest is something very hard to prevent. The following lines depict a scene that, more than anything else, lingers on at the back of my mind. "Waiting at midnight for a visitor, / But the visitor has not yet arrived, / I tapped the table with a *go* stone[23], / And watched a piece of burnt candlewick fall."

---

22 Tian Wen, the Lord of Mengchang, was one of the four great patrons of talent in the period of the Warring States (475–221 B.C.) and was famous for his largess to his thousands of retainers.

23 An ancient board game played by two opponents using small round pieces called stones. The game is called *qi* or *weiqi* in Chinese and *go* in Japanese.

則肅入客廳，屋內只有桌椅板凳，別無長物，主人著長袍而出，寒暄就座，主客均客氣之至。在廚房後門佇立而談者是為未入流。我想此種差別待遇，是無可如何之事，我不相信孟嘗門客三千而待遇平等。

　　人是永遠不知足的。無客時嫌岑寂，有客時嫌煩囂，客走後掃地抹桌又另有一番冷落空虛之感，問題的癥結全在於客的素質，如果素質好，則未來時想他來，既來了想他不走，既走想他再來；如果素質不好，未來時怕他來，既來了怕他不走，既走怕他再來。雖說物以類聚，但不速之客甚難預防。「夜半待客客不至，閒敲碁子落燈花」，那種境界我覺得最足令人低徊。

Handshake

The custom of holding each other's hand as a form of greeting goes back to ancient times. The *History of the Later Han Dynasty*[24] records that: "As children, Ma Yuan and Gongsun Shu[25] lived in the same neighborhood and were good friends. Later, as adults, they continued to hold each other's hands whenever they met, as happily as before." But the handshake that is widely performed nowadays is not an ancient practice. Neither was it a formality prescribed by law or a custom prevailing in those times. Perhaps it did not exist in China before we cut off our queues.[26] Anyway, we cannot cite the hand-holding act between the two ancient friends mentioned above as clear evidence that this form of greeting has long existed in China.

Now that we have developed a tolerance even for Western-style suits and leather shoes, there is certainly no need for us to be opposed to such a simple and easy social gesture as handshaking. Yet, there are

---

24 Written by Fan Ye, a famous historian in the Song dynasty (420–479).

25 Ma Yuan was a great general and military strategist. Gongsun Shu was a warlord and the self-proclaimed king of Shu until he was defeated and killed by the troops of Emperor Guangwu (A.D. 25–58) of the Later Han dynasty. `

26 That is, after the revolution of 1911. Throughout the Qing dynasty (1644–1911), every man and boy in China was required by law to wear a queue, a custom introduced by their Manchu rulers.

握　手

　　握手之事，古已有之，《後漢書》：「馬援與公孫述少同里閭相善，以為既至常握手，如平生歡。」但是現下通行的握手，並非古禮，既無明文規定，亦無此種習俗。大概還是薙了小辮以後的事，我們不能說馬援和公孫述握過手便認為是過去有此禮節的明證。

　　西裝革履我們都可以忍受，簡便易行而且惠而不費的握手我們

a few kinds of people who may give you a painful feeling when you shake their hands.

First, you will not enjoy shaking the hand of a person who is, or considers himself, a political bigwig. He will stand there, with his chest out, his hand extended and his eyes turned to the sky. When you step forward to grasp his hand, his fingers remain rigidly unbent; he will not shake your hand but wait for you to initiate the shaking. You have no way of knowing in advance that he is so anxious to conserve his energy and are therefore highly excited to approach him and shake his hand. You end up holding a stiff and unresponsive hand and bringing on yourself a cold snub. Even then, you must quickly release your hold and withdraw your hand because, at the very moment, he has already turned to the next person in line, ready to hold out his big hand for the other person to shake—not to shake, but to touch. The only proper way to deal with such a bigwig is that, instead of shaking his hand, you simply stick yours out as if you are ready for a "low five", while waiting to see who will strike first.

But too much is as bad as too little. Another type of person will grab your fingers and give them a ferocious squeeze, causing an excruciating pain that goes all the way to your vital organs. Were it not accompanied by words of greeting and a smile, you would think that he meant to engage you in a match of wrist wrestling. A person of this type usually has staying power. Once you have fallen into his grip, don't even think about freeing yourself from it. If he is a good friend who has not seen you for a long time and cannot control his emotions at such a meeting, I believe that you will be willing to forgive him in spite of the pain he is causing to your knuckles. But people who give you the fiercest grips in handshaking are usually your most casual acquaintances. When he applies pressure to you, he intends to give you the illusion that he regards you as a special friend. Actually,

當然無需反對。不過有幾種人，若和他握手，會感覺痛苦。

第一是做大官或自以為做大官者，那隻手不好握。他常常挺著胸膛，伸出一隻巨靈之掌，兩眼望青天，等你趁上去握的時候，他的手仍是直僵的伸著，他並不握，他等著你來握。你事前不知道他是如此愛惜氣力，所以不免要熱心的迎上去握，結果是孤掌難鳴，冷淬淬的討一場沒趣。而且你還要及早罷手，趕快撒手，因為這時候他的身體已轉向另一個人去，他預備把那巨靈之掌給另一個人去握——不是握，是摸。對付這樣的人只有一個辦法，便是，你也伸出一隻巨靈之掌，你也別握，和他作「打花巴掌」狀，看誰先握誰！

另一種人過猶不及。他握著你的四根手指，惡狠狠的一擠，使你痛澈肺腑，如果沒有寒喧笑語偕以俱來，你會誤以為他是要和你角力。此種人通常有耐久力，你入了他的掌握，休想逃脫出來。如果你和他很有交情，久別重逢，情不自禁，你的關節雖然痛些，我相信你會原諒他的。不過通常握手用力最大者，往往交情最淺。他是要在向你使壓力的時候使你發生一種錯覺，以為此人遇我特善。

he has the same hard grip for all the hands he shakes without respect to the persons. If he is a former secretary in a government agency, he will shake your hand while, at the same time, giving you a hefty slap on the shoulder and saying, "Hello, how you doin'?"

Based on the sense of touch alone, one might say in general that handshaking is seldom a pleasant experience. After all, beautiful hands with slender fingers "as smooth as bamboo shoots in spring" are very rare in the world and the chance of shaking such a hand is even more remote. The hands we usually shake are as coarse to the touch as winter or dehydrated bamboo shoots; some are rougher than a bear's paws, despite the nail polish that often embellishes them. Equally unforgettable is the hand of Uriah Heep in Dickens' *David Copperfield*— always moist and cold, so that one has the feeling of holding five eels when shaking his hand. It does not matter much if the hand you shake is a little dirty, since you have no time to examine it before shaking it. You should only shun a clammy hand, because it would be rude to wipe your hand right after shaking it, and even ruder to offer the other person something to wipe his hand with before allowing him to shake yours.

"There is one thing which men do standing, women do sitting down and dogs do by raising a leg." That thing is—handshaking. I have not yet had the experience of shaking hands with a dog and have no way of knowing if a dog's paw is fat or bony, if its grip is tight or loose. I might as well not talk about it. But men shake hands in a way different from women, who do not have to stand up or remove their gloves while they perform this ritual. This definitely violates the principle of equality between the sexes. Yet I am not aware of any initiative being taken by the feminists to rectify it. A Western lady will hold out her hand, but etiquette allows a man to take only the tips, about one or two inches, of her fingers and hold them only for a second.

其實他是握了誰的手都是一樣賣力的。如果此人曾在某機關做過幹事之類，必能一面握手，一面在你的肩頭重重的拍一下子，「哈嘍，哈嘍，怎樣好？」

單就握手時的觸覺而論，大概愉快時也就不多。春筍般的纖纖玉指，世上本來少有，更難得一握，我們常握的倒是些冬筍或筍乾之類，雖然上面更常有蔻丹的點綴，乾倒還不如熊掌。迭更斯的《大衛高拍菲爾》裏的烏利亞，他的手也是令人不能忘的，永遠是濕津津的冷冰冰的，握上去像是五條鱔魚。手髒一點無妨，因為握前無暇檢驗，惟獨帶液體的手不好握，因為事後不便即揩，事前更不便先給他揩。

「有一椿事，男人站著做，女人坐著做，狗翹起一條腿兒做。」這椿事是——握手。和狗行握手禮，我尚無經驗，不知狗爪是肥是瘦，亦不知狗爪是鬆是緊，姑置不論。男女握手之法不同。女人握手無需起身，亦無需脫手套，殊失平等之旨，尚未聞婦女運動者倡議糾正。在外國，女人伸出手來，男人照例只握手尖，約一英吋至

We Chinese seem less restrictive on this score and allow greater laxity in respect of both the time and the space allowed.

When friends meet, a handshake is but a natural way to show their pleasure at seeing each other. They may even show this pleasure in any more affectionate way. As long as this is done by mutual consent, it is no concern of others. But such pleasure is not to be found at a big party. On such an occasion, all the guests sit in a circle and, in such a situation, the handshake has to be performed *en bloc*. You are expected to press the flesh of each and every one present, including those whose appearances are detestable, those whose conversation is boring, and those whose noses you want very much to flatten with a punch of your fist in order to vent some of your pent-up anger. Under such circumstances, I consider the act of shaking hands a torture.

In *Hamlet*, Polonius admonishes his son, "But do not dull thy palm with entertainment / Of each new-hatched, unfleg'd comrade." Indeed, we should take great care of our palms.

二英吋，稍握即罷，這一點在我們中國好像禁忌少些，時間空間的限制都不甚嚴。

朋友相見，握手言歡，本是很自然的事，有甚於握手者，亦未曾不可，只要雙方同意，與人無涉。惟獨大庭廣眾之下，賓客環坐，握手勢必普遍舉行，面目可憎者，語言無味者，想飽以老拳尚不足以洩忿者，都要一一親炙，皮肉相接，在這種情形之下握手，我覺得是一種刑罰。

《哈姆雷特》中波婁尼阿斯誡其子曰：「不要為了應酬每一個新交而磨粗了你的手掌。」我們是要愛惜我們的手掌。

The Game of Chess[27]

There is a kind of chess player I hate most to play against and that is a man with absolute self-control. Even when you wipe out half of his troops or capture one of his rooks, he will maintain his composure, cool his spleen and keep his temper, as if nothing could irritate him, and thereby rob you of the pleasure of playing the game. A gentleman should hold himself above strife in all things—except in a game of chess. When you put your opponent in a big fix, you can see blue veins standing out on his temples and beads of perspiration appearing on his forehead. He puts on a long face or a rueful smile, or purses his lips into a grimace, or tweaks his ears and scratches his cheeks, or utters a loud cry, or moans and groans, or mutters some words of regret, or lets out an endless string of hiccups, while his face turns scarlet. In addition to these, he may exhibit other signs of anxiety. At this moment you may conserve your energy and light a cigarette or take a sip from your teacup, and quietly enjoy seeing your opponent in a state of anguish. This, I think, is more or less like the pleasure felt by a hunter when he has cornered his game after a chase. From this I

---

27 The game described in this article is *xiangqi*, or Chinese chess, which shares a common origin with the Western chess. To facilitate understanding by Western readers, the English names of the chessmen are consistently used here to substitute for the Chinese terms in the original text.

下　棋

　　有一種人我最不喜歡和他下棋，那便是太有涵養的人。殺死他一大塊，或是抽了他一個車，他神色自若，不動火，不生氣，好像是無關痛癢，使得你覺得索然寡味。君子無所爭，下棋卻是要爭的。當你給對方一個嚴重威脅的時候，對方的頭上青筋暴露，黃豆般的汗珠一顆顆的在額上陳列出來，或哭喪著臉作慘笑，或咕嘟著嘴作吃屎狀，或抓耳撓腮，或大叫一聲，或長吁短嘆，或自怨自艾口中念念有詞，或一串串的噎膈打個不休，或紅頭漲臉如關公，種種現象，不一而足，這時節你「行有餘力」便可以點起一枝煙，或啜一碗茶，靜靜的欣賞對方的苦悶的象徵。我想獵人困逐一隻野兔的時候，其愉快大概略相彷彿。因此我悟出一點道理，和人下棋的時

have learned a secret. In a game of chess, you should stop at nothing in order to harass your opponent if you have a chance. When it is you who are being harassed, you should try by all means to look unconcerned. Now that you cannot actively cause pain to your opponent, you can only try passively to reduce his pleasure.

From time immemorial, chess has always been associated with gambling, both falling into the category of games of chance. Playing chess is sometimes regarded as only slightly better than "keeping the stomach full and the mind idle". Although chess involves only a minor skill, it is a litmus test of a player's character. There is a story about a slowpoke in a game of chess. Faced with a threat from a bishop of his opponent, he wondered whether he should move the queen's knight or the king's knight. After deliberating for half an hour, he still could not make up his mind, thus forcing his impatient opponent to give up and concede the game to him. There are indeed chess players of such a phlegmatic disposition who will ponder before each move and grow more and more deliberate as the game gets underway. I often think that, if such a person could join the fabled race between the hare and the turtle, he would also come out the winner. On the other hand, there are also impatient people who play a chess game as if they were running a race. They plunk down their men on the board hastily and thoughtlessly. In doing so, they merely follow their routine of "keeping the stomach full and the mind idle". Conflict is inevitable in a game of chess, but the scope of conflict may be large or small. Some players are extremely calculating and will seek small gains only to suffer big losses, while others will ignore small setbacks and keep their eyes on the entire field. Some players will meet each other head on for a life-and-death combat at close quarters, while others will arrange their troops in different battle formations and confront each other with equal strength. Some players are determined to kill all the enemy troops, sparing none, while others are bold and reckless and will not stop

候，如果有機會使對方受窘，當然無所不用其極，如果被對方所
窘，便努力作出不介意狀，因為既不能積極的給對方以苦痛，只好
消極的減少對方的樂趣。

自古博弈並稱，全是屬於賭的一類，而且只是比「飽食終日無所
用心」略勝一籌而已。不過弈雖小術，亦可以觀人，相傳有慢性人，
見對方走當頭炮，便左思右想，不知是跳左邊的馬好，還是跳右邊
的馬好，想了半個鐘頭而遲遲不決，急得對方拱手認輸。是有這樣
的慢性人，每一著都要考慮，而且是加慢的考慮，我常想這種人如
加入龜兔競賽，也必定可以獲勝。也有性急的人，下棋如賽跑，劈
劈拍拍，草草了事，這仍就是飽食終日無所用心的一貫作風。下棋
不能無爭，爭的範圍有大有小，有斤斤計較而因小失大者，有不拘
小節而眼觀全局者，有短兵相接作生死鬪者，有各自為戰而旗鼓相
當者，有趕盡殺絕一步不讓者，有好勇鬪狠同歸於盡者，有一面下

until both camps end in common ruin. Some players will accompany each of their moves with a verbal attack, but the worst occurs when the scope of conflict extends beyond the chessboard and the opponents end up exchanging blows and kicks. Once two people sat down for a game of chess. After a long while when no sound was heard coming from the room where the game was being played, someone opened the door to look in, but found the room empty. Actually, the players were wrestling each other behind the door, with one riding on top of the other and trying to pry the other player's mouth open in order to retrieve his rook. The other player dared not utter a sound because he would then have to open his mouth. If he opened his mouth, the first player would be able to retrieve his rook. If the first player retrieved the rook, he would surely retract his false move. If the false move were retracted, the second player could not win the game. Such a serious attitude reveals a childlike naivety that is endearing in adults. I once saw two such players at a chess game. When the game started, they were seated in their chairs, appearing relaxed and unconstrained, like a pair of immortal fairies. After a while, when the game grew tense, both players rose to their feet, resembling two combatants with their daggers drawn or, rather, two quails ready for a fight. Eventually, both jumped onto the table when the game reached its decisive stage.

Li Liweng[28] says in his *Random Thoughts at a Leisure Hour* that chess players do not derive as much pleasure from the game as onlookers, because an onlooker does not worry about who will win or lose. It is indeed a real pleasure to watch a game of chess, just as one would enjoy watching a bullfight, a cockfight, or a fight between two crickets. But the spectator of a game of chess has a peculiar problem, as it is a painful experience for him to remain silent when he feels an unbearable itch in his throat, which can be relieved only by spitting out the words

---

28 Literary name of Li Yu. See footnote 2.

棋一面誚罵者，但最不幸的是爭的範圍超出了棋盤，而拳足交加。有下象棋者，久而無聲響，排闥視之，闃不見人，原來他們是在門後角裏扭做一團，一個人騎在另一個人的身上，在他的口裏挖車呢。被挖者不敢出聲，出聲則口張，口張則車被挖回，挖回則必悔棋，悔棋則不得勝，這種認真的態度憨得可愛。我曾見過二人手談，起先是坐著，神情瀟灑，望之如神仙中人，俄而棋勢吃緊，兩人都站起來了，劍拔弩張，如鬪鵪鶉，最後到了生死關頭，兩個人跳到棹上去了！

　　笠翁《閒情偶寄》說奕棋不如觀棋，因觀者無得失心，觀棋是有趣的事，如看鬪牛、鬪雞、鬪蟋蟀一般，但是觀棋也有難過處，觀棋不語是一種痛苦。喉間硬是癢得出奇，思一吐為快。看見一個人

in his mouth. It is next to impossible for him to keep quiet when he sees a chess player about to fall into a trap. If his warning turns out to be correct, one of the players will hate him for it and silently dub him "an ass with a big mouth". Nor will the other player show any appreciation; instead, he will say to himself, "Do I need anyone to tell me I should make this move?" If his warning proves to be wrong, he will be jeered at and called an idiot by both opponents. However, if he holds his breath and says nothing, he is likely to get sick. That is why an onlooker, even after taking a box on the ear, will rub his burning cheek, while he continues to cry out: "Watch your rook! Watch your rook!"

Chess is intended merely as a pastime. The reason why so many people are never tired of this game is that, in a way, it caters to the combative instinct of the human race, although it is a game that involves a battle of wits rather than of physical strength. This explains why young villagers and old peasants, who have no quarrel with the world, will sit under a horizontal trellis for squash vines or beanstalks and spend their long day facing each other across a chessboard. This also explains why members of the leisured class will gather in an urban teahouse to amuse themselves with a game of chess, as if saying that, "If they do not devote themselves to such a useless undertaking, how can they go through such a tedious life?" Prominent politicians, who have reluctantly retired from public life and still yearn for action but have nowhere to go to exercise their talents, can only play chess as a pastime in their remaining years. For them, playing chess is but a way to sublimate their "surplus energy". Human beings will always fight or engage in a contest of wits and intrigues. Instead of fighting each other for power and profit, they should strive to secure a few more positions on the chessboard. Instead of swindling and bluffing, they should try to capture a rook on the chessboard. A writer of the Song dynasty took note of the following anecdote:

要入陷阱而不作聲是幾乎不可能的事，如果説得中肯，其中一個人要厭恨你，暗暗的罵一聲：「多嘴驢！」另一個人也不感激你，心想「難道我還不曉得這樣走！」如果説得不中肯，兩個人要一齊嗤之以鼻：「無見識奴！」如果根本不説，憋在心裏，受病。所以有人於挨了一個耳光之後還要撫著熱辣辣的嘴巴大呼：「要抽車，要抽車！」

　　下棋只是為了消遣，其所以能使這樣多人嗜此不疲者，是因為它頗合於人類好鬬的本能，這是一種「鬬智不鬬力」的遊戲。所以瓜棚豆架之下，與世無爭的村夫野老不免一枰相對，消此永晝；鬧市茶寮之中，常有有閒階級的人士下棋消遣，「不為無益之事，何以遣此有涯之生？」宦海裏翻過身最後退隱東山的大人先生們，髀肉復生，而英雄無用武之地，也只好閒來對弈，了此殘生，下棋全是「賸餘精力」的發洩。人總是要鬬的，總是要鈎心鬬角的和人爭逐的。與其和人爭權奪利，還不如在棋盤上多佔幾個官，與其招搖撞騙，還不如在棋盤上抽上一車。宋人筆記曾載有一段故事：

Deputy Prime Minister Li Na was a person with a quick temper but a great lover of the game of chess. When he played, he made each of his moves with perfect composure and extreme deliberation. Every time he lost his temper, someone in his family would secretly place a chess set before him. As soon as he saw it, his face would light up and he would begin to set up the pieces on the board, completely oblivious of the cause of his anger. (*Nanbu Xinshu*)[29]

I cannot say if the game of chess can or cannot exert such a benign influence on a person's temperament. But it is a fact that certain people will ignore a life-threatening situation when they are in the middle of such a game. One day, two of my friends were so absorbed in a game that their composure remained unruffled when the air-raid siren wailed. Very soon, bombs began to fall, causing the chessmen to bounce on the board and the roof tiles to fly in all directions. The lesser devotee of the two turned pale and jumped to his feet. His opponent grabbed him by the arm and said, "If you go, you lose." This is indeed a bona fide aficionado of the game.

---

29 Written by Qian Xibai, a writer of the Song dynasty. It is a collection of anecdotes about famous persons of the Tang dynasty (618–907) and the subsequent period known as the Five Dynasties (907–960).

李訥僕射，性卞急，酷好弈棋，每下子安詳，極於寬緩，往往躁怒作，家人輩則密以弈具陳於前，訥睹，便忻然改容，以取其子布弄，都忘其恚矣。(《南部新書》)

下棋，有沒有這樣陶冶性情之功，我不敢說，不過有人下起棋來確實是把性命都可置諸度外。我有兩個朋友下棋，警報作，不動聲色，俄而彈落，棋子被震得在盤上跳盪，屋瓦亂飛，其中一位棋癮較小者變色而起，被對方一把拉住，「你走！那就算是你輸了」。此公深得棋中之趣。

Haggling

For more than thirty years an ancient apothecary named Han Kang[30] gathered medicinal herbs from remote mountains and sold them in the marketplace in Chang'an,[31] never asking two prices for the same article. This does not mean, however, that the prices of his commodities remained unchanged for all those years. It only means that he never lied to his customers, and this idiosyncrasy of his was enough to win him a place among the famous recluses whose lives are recorded in the official *History of the Later Han Dynasty*.[32] Yet, this is no proof that the absence of haggling in business transactions has been a traditional virtue among us Chinese since ancient times. Rather, it proves that buyers and sellers through the ages have always had the need to haggle over prices and that, in this regard, Han Kang was so conspicuous an exception that he is immortalized in history. In fact, not only has he become a celebrity in history, his name was already a household word in his lifetime. Once a woman came to him to buy some medicinal herbs. When he maintained his price and refused to give a discount, the female patron lost her temper and said to him,

30 He is said to have lived at the time of Emperor Huan (A.D.147–168) of the Han dynasty.
31 Chang'an was the capital city of the Han dynasty.
32 See footnote 24.

講　價

　　韓康采藥名山，賣於長安市，三十餘年，口不二價。這並不是說三十餘年物價沒有波動，這是說他三十餘年沒有要過一次謊，就憑這一點怪脾氣他的大名便入了《後漢書》的〈逸民列傳〉。這並不證明買賣東西無需講價是我們古已有之的固有道德，這只證明自古以來買賣東西就得要價還價，出了一位韓康，便是人瑞，便可以名垂青史了。韓康不但在歷史上留下了佳話，在當時也是頗為著名的。一個女子向他買藥，他守價不移，硬是沒得少，女子大怒，說：「難

"Do you think you are Han Kang that you won't even take off a cent?" Han Kang had wanted to live in obscurity. Now that even an ordinary woman had heard about him, he became afraid and fled to the mountains. Throughout history it is extremely rare that a seller would refuse to haggle. But we must not forget that this apothecary was a member of an illustrious family and not a tradesman by birth. If he had been a businessman "seeking a ten percent profit margin", would he not have welcomed an opportunity to increase that margin to twenty or thirty percent?

In former days, some stores maintained their policy of offering genuine products at fair prices. A few among them even proudly put up gold-character shop signs bearing such mottoes as "Our prices are not negotiable" or "We won't even lie to young or old customers". These stores saw no need to hold big sales or hire street bands to advertise their wares. Customers came on their own initiative. Today, this practice seems to be going steadily out of fashion. Nor are young and old customers easily deceived. Besides, most vendors and buyers today are mobile and there are no longer shoppers who can be called regular customers. A customer will not feel satisfied without haggling and a storekeeper will not look friendly without giving twenty or thirty percent discounts. Yet, as soon as a transaction is completed, the customer will feel cheated. In a world of mutual deception, haggling has become a necessary phase in any business dealing. In any case, "the seller will ask sky-high prices; the buyer will make rock-bottom offers." The more skillful player will win the game.

When I buy something, I seldom come away without paying a higher price than other people. There exists in the world a kind of person who likes to come to your house for a cost-of-living survey. Such a visitor will examine everything in your home and ask how much you paid for it. He or she will pester you with endless questions

道你是韓康，一個錢沒得少？」韓康本欲避名，現在小女子都知道他的大名，嚇得披髮入山。賣東西不講價，自古以來，是多麼難得！我們還不要忘記韓康「家世著姓」，本不是商人，如果是個「逐什一之利」的，有機會能得什二什三時豈不更妙？

從前有些店舖講究貨真價實，「言不二價」「童叟無欺」的金字招牌偶然還可以很驕傲的懸掛起來，不必大減價雇吹鼓手，主顧自然上門。這種事似乎漸漸少了。童叟根本也不見得好欺侮，而且買賣大半是流動的，無所謂主顧，不講價還是不過癮，不七折八扣顯着買賣不和氣，交易一成買者就又會覺得上當。在爾虞我詐的情形之下，講價便成為交易的必經階段，反正是「漫天要價，就地還錢」。看看誰有本事誰討便宜。

我買東西很少的時候能不比別人的貴。世界上有一種人，喜歡到人家裏面調查物價，看看你家裏有什麼東西都要打聽一下是用什

unless you have put a price label on every article. The visitor has a most effective way of dampening my spirits. Sometimes he will shake his head "like a rattle" to indicate that I have been taken to the cleaners—even after I have withheld the real price and, in a lie to him as well as to myself, told him I only paid half of its real cost, just to put him off. I submit to the fact that some people are particularly adept at bargaining. They have a politician's cheek, a diplomat's glib tongue, a killer's nerve and an angler's patience. Since they are as hard as rock or steel and as tough as cowhide, they are able to wear out the most tenacious shopkeeper. I have humbly sought their advice, and it appears that the art of haggling may be reduced to the following rules:

First, never reveal your real interest. When you step into a store, look around to find out what are *not* available there and ask for them, so as to make the salesperson feel humbled and put him a little out of countenance from the outset. After that, mention casually the thing you are really looking for. The salesperson, recovering from his initial dejection, is naturally elated to be able to show you the merchandise he has in stock, and the asking price will definitely be reasonable. Even if you happen to see something you really like, do not cry out as if you had discovered a priceless treasure. Instead, act as if nothing had happened and look indifferent. Return to that article only after you have inquired about the prices of many other things. Otherwise, your rashness will alert him and he will treat that article as a rare commodity and ask an exorbitant price.

Second, criticize mercilessly. As a sweet melon will have a bitter stem, nothing is perfect under the sun. When you hold the merchandise in your hand, instead of hastening to show your admiration, try first to find its blemishes, go to great lengths in your criticism and point out as many faults as you can. Even if a certain article is really flawless, there is yet no arguing about taste. If the thing is red, you

麼價錢買的，除非你在每一事物上都粘上一個紙籤標明價格，否則將不勝其囉唆。最掃興的是，我已經把真的價錢瞞起，自欺欺人的只說了一半的價錢來搪塞他，他有時還會把頭搖得像個「波浪鼓」似的，表示你上了瞞天的大當！我承認，有些人是特別的善於講價，他有政治家的臉皮，外交家的嘴巴，殺人的膽量，釣魚的耐心，堅如鐵石，韌似牛皮，所以他能壓倒那待價而沽的商人。我嘗虛心請教，大概歸納起來講價的藝術不外下列諸端：

第一，要不動聲色。進得店來，看準了他沒有什麼你就要什麼，使得他顯著寒傖，先有幾分慚愧。然後無精打采的道出你所真心要買的東西，夥計於氣餒之餘，自然歡天喜地的捧出他的貨色，價錢根本不會太高。如果偶然發現一項心愛的東西，也不可失聲大叫，如獲異寶，必要行若無事，淡然處之，於打聽許多種物價之後，隨意問詢及之，否則你打草驚蛇，他便奇貨可居了。

第二，要無情的批評。甘瓜苦蒂，天下物無全美。你把貨物捧在手裏，不忙鑒賞，先求其疵繆之所在，不厭其詳的批評一番，盡量的道出它的缺點。有些物事，本是無懈可擊的，但是「嗜好不能爭

prefer it white. If it is big, you prefer it small. In short, you must condemn it as having too many defects and therefore worthless. All the while the salesperson's face will change from red to white and from white to red again. He may even look a little offended, but his confidence sags and the price now has room for negotiation, naturally. Since you are buying the article against your inclination and taste, how can he remain unyielding with regard to the price?

Third, bargain ruthlessly. Let us assume that, ever since the escape of Han Kang into the mountains, every businessman is a liar. Whatever the asking price, make sure you cut it in half. You will need a measure of courage and callousness to make such an offer and must be prepared to see a nasty look on the salesperson's face. But a human face is highly changeable. You need only raise your offer a little higher and his gloomy face will immediately light up like a burst of sunshine from behind dark clouds and reveal the hint of a smile. This is a most critical moment and involves a contest of patience. Whoever lacks patience loses the contest. While he continues to knock down his price one cent at a time, you will continue to raise your bid in response.

Fourth, have the courage to return. If a deal cannot be struck, you have no choice but to walk away. Perhaps he will call you back before you have taken a few steps. If he does not, you must have the courage to return on your own account. Do not feel piqued. Do not insist that "your honor permits no looking back and your strategy rules out turning around". When you reach this stage of bargaining, you have touched the bottom.

This secret formula for successful bargaining is easy to learn but hard to practice, and that is why I have so far been unable to use it. I worry about the loss of time. I worry about the possibility of hurting someone's feelings. If my neck thickens and my face turns red in the course of haggling, I will suffer physical injury. If the same changes occur on the other person, I will suffer mental pain. To avoid these,

辯」，你這東西是紅的，我偏喜歡白的，你這東西是大的，我偏喜歡小的。總之，是要把東西褒貶得一文不值缺點百出，這時候夥計的臉上也許要一塊紅一塊白的不大好看，但是他的心裏軟了，價錢上自然有了商量的餘地，我在委曲遷就的情形之下來買東西，你在價錢上還能不讓步麼？

第三，要狠心還價。先假設，自從韓康入山之後每個商人都是說謊的。不管價錢多高，攔腰一砍。這需要一點膽量，要狠得下心，說得出口，要準備看一副嘴臉。人的臉是最容易變的，用不了加多少錢，那副愁雲慘霧的苦臉立刻開霽，露出一縷春風。但這是最緊要的時候，這是耐心的比賽，誰性急誰失敗，他一文一文的減，你就一文一文的加。

第四，要有反顧的勇氣。交易實在不成，只好掉頭而去，也許走不了好遠，他會請你回來，如果他不請你回來，你自己要有回來的勇氣，不能負氣，不能講究「義不反顧，計不旋踵」。講價到了這個地步，也就山窮水盡了。

這一套講價的秘訣，知易行難，所以我始終未能運用。我怕費功夫，我怕傷和氣，如果我粗脖子紅臉，我身體受傷，如果他粗脖

I have learned to console myself by keeping in mind the favorite saying of Zheng Banqiao:[33] "It is very hard to play the fool."

The ancient book entitled *Huainan Zi*[34] specifically mentions "the existence of a Kingdom of Gentlefolk in the East", but I have failed to locate it on any map. *The Classic of Mountains and Seas*[35] also records that "the men in the Kingdom of Gentlefolk wear gowns, hats and swords; they will rather concede than contend." Only the novel *Jinghua Yuan*[36] provides a little information about that kingdom in the following episode: The buyer said to the seller, "Your merchandise is of such excellent quality and yet you ask so low a price for it. How can I have an easy conscience if I buy it? Please raise the price. Only then can I agree to the deal. If you insist on making such a concession, I will take it that you do not really want to sell it." "How can I not welcome your kind patronage?" replied the seller. "I already feel ashamed for having asked such a high price. I am surprised to hear you say, instead, that my merchandise is of excellent quality and that the price is too low. How can I not feel even more ashamed of myself? Besides, the prices of my merchandise are by no means non-negotiable; in fact, there is a considerable profit margin for bargaining." Judging from this episode, even the business transactions in the Kingdom of Gentlefolk were not based on fixed and non-negotiable prices; they too involved haggling. The parties did not try to avoid bargaining, nor could they complete a deal before they had wasted much breath. Is there any country where one can buy things without haggling?

---

33 See footnote 13.

34 A Taoist classic edited by Liu An (179–122 B.C.), Prince of Huainan and grandson of Emperor Gaozu, the founder of the Han dynasty.

35 In Chinese, *Shan-hai Jing*, an ancient book on geography, traditionally attributed to Emperor Yu (? 2205–? 2197 B.C.), the founder of the Xia dynasty.

36 Or *The Legend of the Goddess of Flowers*, a novel written by Li Ruzhen during the reign of Emperor Qianlong (1736–1796).

子紅臉,我精神上難過,我聊以解嘲的方法是記起鄭板橋愛寫的那四個大字:「難得糊塗」。

《淮南子》明明的記載著:「東方有君子之國」,但是我在地圖上卻找不到。《山海經》裏也記載著:「君子國衣冠帶劍,其人好讓不爭。」但只有《鏡花緣》給君子國透露了一點消息。買物的人說:「老兄如此高貨,卻討恁般賤價,教小弟買去,如何能安?務求將價加增,方好遵教。若再過謙,那是有意不肯賞光交易了。」賣物的人說:「既承照顧,敢不仰體?但適才妄討大價,已覺厚顏,不意老兄反說貨高價賤,豈不更教小弟慚愧?況敝貨並非『言無二價』,其中頗有虛頭。」照這樣講來,君子國交易並非言無二價,也還是要講價的,也並非不爭,也還有要費口舌唾液的。什麼樣的國家,才能

As far as haggling is concerned, I believe that it is more in line with human instinct to fight for one's own rather than somebody else's profit.

Someone has taught me the secret of hiring a rickshaw: When you see only one rickshaw waiting at a street corner and its puller has a healthy color and appears to be well-fed, ignore him. If you find half a dozen rickshaws waiting and their pullers all looking shabby and hungry, they will flock to your call and compete for your patronage by charging unusually low fares. This advice reveals one of the many facets of human nature—cruelty.

買東西不講價呢？我想與其講價而為對方爭利，不如講價而為自己爭利，比較的合於人類本能。

　　有人傳授給我在街頭雇車的秘訣：街頭孤另另的一輛車，車夫紅光滿面鼓腹而遊的樣子，切莫睬他，如果三五成群鳩形鵠面，你一聲吆喝便會蜂湧而來，競相延攬，車價會特別低廉。在這裏我們發現人性的一面——殘忍。

Haircut

Getting a haircut is by no means a pleasant experience. Anyone who has had a bad tooth extracted by a dentist will get the jitters when he sees a barber's chair, because there is some likeness between these two kinds of chair. Although we do not expect the chairs in a barbershop to be made of sandalwood with mother-of-pearl inlay, or in the style of Louis Quatorze armchairs, they should at least be less ugly than they usually are. The seat is neither round nor square and is so rigid and uncomfortable that, when you recline on it, you feel as though you are lying on an operating table. The itinerant barber, with his tools and his furniture—which he carries around on a shoulder pole—is an even more scary sight. On top of his tool cabinet stands a slender flagpole, which was originally used to display a human head.[37]

But a haircut is a necessary evil. "A gentleman should dress himself properly and attach proper importance to his appearance. Is it necessary for a person to look unkempt and unwashed before he can be regarded as wise?" A haircut is a necessary step to improve a

---

37 Following their conquest of China, the Manchu rulers ordered all the males of the Han nationality, on pain of death, to adopt the Manchurian tonsure and queue. Itinerant barbers were sent out everywhere to implement that edict and the soldiers who accompanied them were given the power to execute any nonconformist on the spot, and hung his head on such a flagpole. Cf. footnote 26.

理　髮

　　理髮不是一件愉快事。讓牙醫拔過牙的人，望見理髮的那張椅子就會怵怵不安，兩種椅子很有點相像。我們並不希望理髮店的椅子都是檀木螺鈿，或是路易十四式，但至少不應該那樣的醜，方不方圓不圓的，死橛橛硬幫幫的，使你感覺到坐上去就要受人割宰的樣子。門口擔挑的剃頭挑兒，更嚇人，豎著的一根小小的旂杆，那原是為掛人頭的。

　　但是理髮是一種必不可免的麻煩。「君子整其衣冠，尊其瞻視，何必蓬頭垢面，然後為賢？」理髮亦是觀瞻所繫。印度錫克族，向來

man's appearance. The Sikhs of India never cut their hair or shave their faces. This custom is based on their belief that "the human body, including the hair that covers it, is inherited from one's parents and must never be mutilated." That is why the face of every Sikh man lies mostly hidden under a mop of hair. As this is the custom of the land, it will not cause anyone to turn his head. But this will not do in our country. If your hair is disheveled and unkempt, someone will suspect that you are in mourning or have just got out of jail. But the hair on the face is a greater problem. If you grow a mustache or a beard, it hardly matters even though you may not have a lot of hair either on your upper lip or on your chin. As long as you have some hair around your mouth, you will command respect. If your face shows a patch of blue skin after a close shave, people will also find you respectable. But a stubbly growth on your face, measuring two or three millimeters in length and sticking out like an animal's bristles, or a hedgehog's spines, or stubble on a cut paddy field, will discourage intimacy. Lu Zhishen[38] "always had a short growth of beard on his cheeks that made him look extremely forbidding", and that was half the reason why people were afraid of him. Zhong Kui's mustache and beard radiated like a porcupine's quills, making him look exactly what a gobbler of ghosts should be like.[39] Since we have no desire either to terrify people or to gobble ghosts and must always try to look like civilized men, we have no choice but to make regular visits to the barber's.

---

38 Lu Da, alias Lu Zhishen, is one of the 108 fictional outlaws portrayed in *Shuihu Zhuan* (or *The Legend of the Water Margin*), a popular novel written by Shi Nai'an and Lo Guanzhong in the late fourteenth century. The principal characters were outlaws who rebelled against the oppressive authorities, robbed and killed corrupt officials and helped the poor.

39 In Chinese legend, Zhong Kui is a petty god who destroys demons by eating them and whose picture is often posted on the walls or doors of houses to ward off evil spirits.

是不剪髮不剃鬚的，那是「受諸父母不敢毀傷」的意思，所以一個個
的都是滿頭滿臉毛毿毿的，滔滔皆是，不以為怪。在我們的社會
裏，就不行了，如果你鬈髰著頭髮，就會有人疑心你是在丁憂，或
是才從監獄裏出來。髭鬚是更討厭的東西，如果蓄留起來，七根朝
上八根朝下都沒有關係，嘴上有毛受人尊敬，如果刮得光光的露出
一塊青皮，也行，也受人尊敬，惟獨不長不短的三兩分長的髭鬚，
如鬃鬣，如刺蝟，如刈後的稻稈，看起來令人不敢親近，魯智深「腮
邊新剃暴長短鬚戲戲的好慘瀨人」，所以人先有五分怕他。鍾馗鬚髯
如戟，是一副啖鬼之相。我們既不想嚇人，又不欲啖鬼，而且不敢
不以君子自勉，如何能不常到理髮店去？

There is nothing in the profession of barbers that does not deserve our respect. Like executioners and butchers, barbers are trained professionals in the service of mankind. Moreover, barbers look particularly respectable in their Western-style suits,[40] which may be regarded as a distinguishing mark of the Chinese elite. Suppose you have a friend who is an executioner. Whenever he meets you, he will silently observe your neck while trying to figure out where his axe should most properly fall. In doing so, he is merely following his professional instinct. As soon as you settle down into his chair, your barber will stretch his arms and roll up his sleeves while examining the hair on your head, without taking the slightest interest in the person to whom the hair belongs. Then he will throw a sheet of white silk over your body. This sheet may not have been newly washed and often has stains on it that resemble the markings on a kind of rice paper called "tiger skin".[41] Next, he will wrap a cloth band around your neck and pull it really tight—but, of course, not tight enough to choke the life out of you. If it were his own neck, he would probably not apply so much strength. In principle, hair is to be cut, but a barber inevitably combines cutting with plucking and tearing. The most appropriate form of protest you can make is to frown and grimace into the mirror before you and hope that he will notice your complaint. A man's head is attached to his neck in such a way as to allow it to turn with considerable freedom, but there are a few angles to which the head cannot freely turn. It seems that a barber seldom takes this limitation into account. He always finds your head in an improper position and keeps twisting it back and forth so that it will lend itself

---

40 Chinese barbers in the big cities wore Western suits as their uniforms in the 1930s and 1940s, a time when most men in that country still preferred the traditional long gown (*changpao*).

41 A special rice paper with patchy markings highly prized by professional Chinese painters and calligraphers.

　　理髮匠並沒有令人應該不敬重的地方，和劊子手屠戶同樣的是一種為人群服務的職業，而且理髮匠特別顯得高尚，那一身西裝便可以說是高等華人的標幟。如果你交一個劊子手朋友，他一見到你就會相度你的脖頸，何處下刀相宜，這是他的職業使然。理髮匠俟你坐定之後，便伸胳臂挽袖相度你那一腦袋的毛髮，對於毛髮所依附的人並無興趣。一塊白綢布往你身上一罩，不見得是新洗的，往往是斑斑點點的如虎皮宣。隨後是一根布條在咽喉處一勒。當然不會致命，不過箍得也就夠緊，如果是自己的頸子大概捨不得用那樣大的力。頭髮是以剪為原則，但是附帶著生薅硬拔的卻也不免，最適當的抗議是對著那面鏡子獰眉皺眼的做個鬼臉，而且希望他能看見。人的頭生在頸上，本來是可以相當的旋轉自如的，但是也有幾個角度是不大方便的，理髮匠似乎不大顧慮到這一點，他總覺得你的腦袋的姿勢不對，把你的頭扳過來扭過去，以求適合他的刀剪。

to the workings of his tools. I suspect that barbers have all taken muscle-building lessons. How else can they have developed such strong wrists and biceps?

A huge mirror is usually installed in front of a barber's chair, this with good reason. The idea is not to allow you to admire yourself but rather to let you see what the barber is doing to your head, since no one thinks lightly of his own head. If you wear eyeglasses, as soon as they are removed, everything appears in a blur and your vision becomes limited. In particular, when a razor or a pair of scissors is being wielded about you, you hold your body as stiff as if in rigor mortis. You dare not make any random move, and regret that you cannot even steal a glance at the patron to your left or the one to your right. When the patron to your left reclines in the chair while receiving a shave, which produces a noise that suggests the sound of a lawn mower, you will assume that the patron is a man. You may be wrong, because that patron may turn out to be a lady. When the patron to your right is being sprayed with eau-de-cologne or moisturized with some facial cream, you will assume that the patron is a lady. You may be wrong again, because the patron may turn out to be a gentleman. For that reason, you may as well close your eyes and spare yourself an unpleasant sight. At this moment, the best way is to sit idly and with resignation.

By comparison, the most pleasant experience in the process of a haircut is the shampoo. The thick liquid soap poured onto your hair feels as refreshing as the ceremonial ghee or clarified butter used in the Buddhist form of baptism.[42] Then the barber begins to scratch and massage your scalp with his fingers, which feel as sharp as an eagle's claw. What is tantalizing is that, when your scalp begins to hurt, the itchiest spot in the southeastern corner remains untouched. While your

---

42 This ceremony is performed either to impart wisdom or remove worries.

我疑心理髮匠許都是孔武有力的，不然腕臂間怎有那樣大的力氣？

椅子前面豎起的一面大鏡子是頗有道理的，倒不是為了可以顧影自憐，其妙在可以知道理髮匠是在怎樣收拾你的腦袋，人對於自己的腦袋沒有不關心的。戴眼鏡的朋友摘下眼鏡，一片模糊，所見亦屬有限。尤其是在刀剪幌動之際，呆坐如僵屍，輕易不敢動彈，對於左右坐著的鄰客無從瞻仰，是一憾事。左邊客人在挺著身子刮臉，聲如割草，你以為必是一個大漢，其實未必然，也許是個女客；右邊客人在噴香水擦雪花，你以為必是佳麗，其實亦未必然，也許是個男子。所以不看也罷，看了怪不舒服。最好是廢然枯坐。

其中比較最愉快的一段經驗是洗頭。濃厚的肥皂汁滴在頭上，如醍醐灌頂，用十指在頭上搔抓，雖然不是麻姑，卻也手似鳥爪。令人著急的是頭皮已然搔得清痛，而東南角上一塊最癢的地方始終

hair is being rinsed, you cannot prevent water from getting into your ears. However, when you consider that your daily wash is probably limited to your face proper, leaving out all the outlying areas, you will regard such a thorough ablution as quite a memorable event that occurs only at infrequent intervals. Drying one's hair with an electric blower is, however, quite an ordeal, because the gadget produces one moment a cool breeze and the next a stream of air that is unbearably hot, as if it were a form of torture.

The most unbearable part of the process is shaving. All the while a large, extremely sharp blade is gliding over your throat, your eyelids and your earlobes, you can only close your eyes and hold your breath. Robert Lynd wrote in "A Sermon on Shaving":

> As the razor touched my face, I was not always free from such apprehensive thoughts as: "Suppose the barber should suddenly go mad?" Luckily, the barber never did, but I have known other and comparable perils. There was that little French barber, for instance, who shaved me during a thunderstorm and who sprang into the air at every flash of lightning. There was also the drunken barber who felt for my cheek with the razor as a drunken man reaches out for something and misses it. Having at last brought the razor down on my face, he leaned on it to steady himself, and, by leaning hard, even succeeded in shaving a certain patch on my right jaw. I did not dare so much as to utter a word of protest while the razor was on my skin. Even a whisper, I felt, might unnerve and overbalance the man, and my jugular would be severed before he knew he had done it. No sooner, however, was the razor temporarily withdrawn from my face—*reculer pour mieux sauter* is, I think, the way the French describe it—than in a nightmare voice I gasped out: "No more. No more. That will do, thank you!" ...

不曾搔到。用水沖洗的時候,難免不汎濫入耳,但念平凤盥洗大概是以臉上本部為限,邊遠陬隅輒弗能屆,如今痛加滌盪,亦是難得的盛舉。電器吹風,卻不好受,時而涼颸習習,時而夾上一股熱流,熱不可當,好像是一種刑罰。

最令人難堪的是刮臉。一把大刀鋒利無比,在你的喉頭上眼皮上耳邊上,滑來滑去,你只能瞑目屏息,捏一把汗。Robert Lynd 寫過一篇〈關於刮臉的講道〉,他說:

> 當剃刀觸到我的臉上,我不免有這樣的念頭:「假使理髮匠忽然瘋狂了呢?」很幸運的,理髮匠從未發瘋狂過,但我遭遇過別種差不多的危險。例如,有一個矮小的法國理髮匠在雷雨中給我刮臉,電光一閃,他就跳得好老高。還有一個喝醉了的理髮匠,舉著剃刀找我的臉,像個醉漢的樣子伸手去一摸卻摸了個空。最後把剃刀落在我的臉上了,他卻靠在那裏鎮定一下,靠得太重了些,居然把我的下頰右方刮下了一塊鬍鬚,刀還在我的皮上,我連抗議一聲都不敢。就是小聲說一句,我覺得,都會使他喪膽而失去平衡,我的頸靜脈也許要在他不知不覺間被他割斷,後來剃刀暫時離開我的臉了,大概就是法國人所謂 *reculer pour mieux sauter* (退回去以便再向前撲) 我趁勢立刻用夢魘的聲音叫起來:「別刮了,別刮了,夠了,謝謝你」……

Terrifying experiences such as these are far from common. But anyone who is in the middle of a shave when he suddenly recalls the funny story told by a Chinese stand-up comedian cannot help feeling his heartbeat quicken. According to that comedian, apprentice barbers traditionally use fuzz-covered winter melons to hone their shaving skills. Whenever they have some other business to attend to, they will stick their razors into the melons and walk away. After they have completed their apprenticeship and become journeyman barbers, they often mistake a human head for a melon. Yet, the danger inherent in shaving is only a secondary concern to me. The most abominable practice is that the barber, after giving you the shave, will fondle your cheeks with impunity. After suffering this indignity, you still have to pay him.

這樣的怕人的經驗並不多有。不過任何人都要心悸，如果在刮臉時想起相聲裏的那段笑話，據說理髮匠學徒的時候是用一個帶茸毛的冬瓜來做試驗的，有事走開的時候便把刀向瓜上一剁，後來出師服務，常常錯認人頭仍是那個冬瓜。刮臉的危險還在其次，最可惡的是他在刮後用手毫無忌憚的在你臉上摸，摸完之後你還得給他錢！

Birds

I love birds.

I used to see people carrying birds in cages or on their arms when they took to the streets for a stroll early in the morning (now the number of such people of leisure has dwindled). What caught my attention then was, however, not the leisurely manner of those people but the misery of their birds. Sometimes the falcons on their arms wore leather hoods over their heads. Those birds, with roughened feathers and curled-up and motionless bodies, had completely lost the dignified and majestic look they had once possessed. The cagelings kept behind bars all year round were even worse off. You might say that they were very "well-treated", enjoying an endless supply of food and drink and, during the winter, the comfort of cotton-padded jackets that were pulled over their cages to keep out the cold. But, if they ever tried to "ride the wind and soar into the sky", they could only hurt themselves by bumping their heads against the latticed wall. A bird in such a situation is, I think, only a little less miserable than a fly caught on flypaper and is slightly happier than its cousins that reside in a specimen room.

I did not begin to like birds until I went to Sichuan. At dawn outside my window, there was a chorus of birds—not the sparrow's chirps or the crow's caws, but loud and clear songs. Some sang in drawn-out

鳥

我愛鳥。

從前我常見提籠架鳥的人，清早在街上蹓躂（現在這樣有閒的人少了）。我感覺興味的不是那人的悠閒，卻是那鳥的苦悶。胳膊上架著的鷹，有時頭上蒙著一塊皮子，羽翮不整的蜷伏著不動，哪裏有半點瞵視昂藏的神氣？籠子裏的鳥更不用説，常年的關在柵欄裏，飲啄倒是方便，冬天還有遮風的棉罩，十分的「優待」，但是如果想要「摶扶搖而直上」，便要撞頭碰壁。鳥到了這種地步，我想它的苦悶，大概是僅次於黏在膠紙上的蒼蠅，它的快樂，大概是僅優於在標本室裏住著罷？

我開始欣賞鳥，是在四川。黎明時，窗外是一片鳥囀，不是吱吱喳喳的麻雀，不是呱呱噪啼的烏鴉，那一片聲音是清脆的，是嘹

trills of six or seven notes; others in single-note squeals that were full and mellow rather than monotonous; now solo, now in unison, but all combined to produce the harmonious effect of a symphony. I cannot tell on how many spring dawns I was awakened from my dreams by such avian music. When the sun rose high in the sky and the marketplace began to bubble with noises, the birds would fall silent, making me wonder where they had gone. I had to wait until long after nightfall to be able to hear again the cries of the cuckoo that sounded now afar, now near, each more urgent than the one before and as mournful as a dirge. On hearing these nocturnal calls, an exile from home like me could not help feeling unspeakable misery.

In the daytime, I did not hear the birds sing but I could see their physical forms. Of all living things in the world, none is more exquisite in shape than a bird. There were so many kinds of nameless little birds leaping up and down in the trees, some with long, trailing tails; others with long, slender bills that pointed upward. Some sported a colorful patch on their breasts; others only momentarily displayed a riot of color on their plumage when they take flight. Almost without exception, the bodies of birds were dainty yet buxom, lean but not scraggy, plump but not bloated. Indeed, the addition or reduction of a jot in weight would make them too fat or too thin. They performed avian gymnastics with such agility that they seemed to have springs in their legs. The sight of them—perching on lofty twigs and surveying the world around them in the breeze—provided such a keen delight that hit me like a stab to my heart. Startled by something unknown to me, they would suddenly flap their wings and fly away without looking back or lingering about and, in an instant, vanish like a rainbow, leaving me with only a feeling of infinite bewilderment and loss. Sometimes I spotted a lone heron standing motionless in a rice paddy, with one leg curled up and its neck drawn in. Sometimes I saw "a column of herons flying toward the blue sky" against a background of purple

亮的，有的一聲長叫，包括著六七個音階，有的只是一個聲音，圓潤而不覺其單調，有時是獨奏，有時是合唱，簡直是一派和諧的交響樂。不知有多少個春天的早晨，這樣的鳥聲把我從夢境喚起。等到旭日高升，市聲鼎沸，鳥就沉默了，不知到哪裏去了。一直等到夜晚，才又聽到杜鵑叫，由遠叫到近，由近叫到遠，一聲急似一聲，竟是淒絕的哀樂。客夜聞此，説不出的酸楚！

　　在白晝，聽不到鳥鳴，但是看得見鳥的形體。世界上的生物，沒有比鳥更俊俏的。多少樣不知名的小鳥，在枝頭跳躍，有的曳著長長的尾巴，有的翹著尖尖的長喙，有的是胸襟上帶著一塊照眼的顏色，有的是飛起來的時候才閃露一下斑斕的花彩。幾乎沒有例外的，鳥的身軀都是玲瓏飽滿的，細瘦而不乾癟，豐腴而不臃腫，真是減一分則太瘦，增一分則太肥那樣的穠纖合度，跳盪得那樣輕靈，腳上像是有彈簧。看它高踞枝頭，臨風顧盼——好銳利的喜悦刺上我的心頭。不知是什麼東西驚動它了，它倏的振翅飛去，它不回顧，它不徘徊，它像虹似的一下就消逝了，它留下的是無限的迷惘。有時候稻田裏佇立著一隻白鷺，拳著一條腿，縮著頸子，有時候「一行白鷺上青天」，背後還襯著黛青的山色和釉綠的梯田。就是

mountains and glaze-green terraced fields. Even the chick-snatching kite that screeches and wheels in the sky had a majestic form that was to me a source of delight.

I love the shapes and sounds of birds, and this in a most simple way. But I do not have any illusions about them. Someone I know heard the cry of the cuckoo for the first time and got so excited that he could not sleep a wink all night. He thought about the legend of Du Yu or King Wangdi,[43] then about the blood-spitting bird and finally about nostalgia, and he felt deeply touched by the immensely poetic quality of the bird's call. I told him that the truth was quite different. The cuckoo is actually a rather robust bird, much bigger and stronger than other birds in general. It has a flat bill and is not particularly noted for its beauty. It never bothers to build its own nest but, taking advantage of its physical bulk and strength, lays its egg in someone else's nest—if the nest is already crowded, it will rudely push out one of the eggs already there—and leaves the brooding responsibility to the host. When this hatchling became full-fledged, it will appropriate the nest to itself. After hearing what I said, my friend could no longer entertain any poetic feeling for this tyrannical and ruthless bird. I believe that Keats' nightingale and Shelley's skylark were likewise products of the poets' imaginations and had nothing to do with any real bird.

Birds do not always bring us joy; sometimes they also bring us

---

43 Du Yu was the original name of King Wangdi of the state of Shu, whose territory comprised the present-day Chengdu region in Sichuan province. According to legend, the king had an affair with the wife of his prime minister, whom he had sent to deal with disasters caused by floods. When the secret liaison became known, the king abdicated his throne in favor of his prime minister and went into exile. When he died, his spirit changed into a cuckoo and returned to his city. The bird continued to cry until it began to cough up blood. The mournful call of the bird is believed to make travelers homesick.

抓小雞的鳶鷹，啾啾的叫著，在天空盤旋，也有令人喜悅的一種雄姿。

我愛鳥的聲音鳥的形體，這愛好是很單純的，我對鳥並不存任何幻想。有人初聞杜鵑，興奮的一夜不能睡，一時想到「杜宇」「望帝」，一時又想到啼血，想到客愁，覺得有無限詩意。我曾告訴他事實上全不是這樣的。杜鵑原是很健壯的一種鳥，比一般的鳥魁梧得多，扁嘴大口，並不特別美，而且自己不知構巢，依仗體壯力大，硬把卵下在別個的巢裏，如果巢裏已有了夠多的卵，便不客氣的給擠落下去，孵育的責任由別個代負了，孵出來之後，羽毛漸豐，就可把巢據為己有。那人聽了我的話之後，對於這豪橫無情的鳥，再也不能幻出什麼詩意出來了。我想濟慈的〈夜鶯〉，雪萊的〈雲雀〉，還不都是詩人自我的幻想，與鳥何干？

鳥並不永久的給人喜悅，有時也給人悲苦。詩人哈代在一首詩

sorrow. Thomas Hardy tells such a story in a poem. On one Christmas Eve, he had a sparkling fire over the hearth and a sumptuous dinner on the table. He was preparing to spend a happy evening when suddenly he noticed, in the beautiful snow scene outside the window, a little bird huddled up on a barren twig and pecking at a lone frozen berry. Overcome by the cold of the winter wind, the bird fell to the ground and died and rolled itself into a snowball. The poet exclaimed, "Bird, you do not give me a happy evening." I, too, had a similar experience. One day, while I was sitting in a room with double-paned windows in Manchuria, I suddenly saw a house sparrow in a tree. It was trembling, hopping and trying to brace itself while at the same time pecking at a dried leaf. I could see that its plumage was particularly long and ruffled, resembling the traditional coir rain cape worn by Chinese farmers. In an instant, the bird made me think of a group of poor people in shabby and bloated clothes rummaging on a garbage dump. These people and the bird looked nearly identical in profile. I was so fully absorbed in that thought that I had no time to mourn the fate of the poor and lonely sparrow.

Since I left Sichuan, I have hardly ever again seen the gymnastics of such a variety of birds or heard their melodious songs. Only at dawn, when smoke begins to issue from the kitchen, can I see a group of house sparrows huddling for warmth around the stovepipe under the eaves. At other times, I can still see through the window paper the silhouette of a sparrow curled up on the lattice. I have no idea where the magpies have gone into hiding. And pigeons with whistles are now seldom seen wheeling in the sky. On occasion at dusk, I still hear the raucous calls of jackdaws perching on an old tree. At night I still hear the eerie hooting of the barn owl that sounds like a cross between laughing and crying. Other than these, what have caught my eye, though only occasionally, are little birds imprisoned in their cages, but I cannot bear to look at them.

裏說，他在聖誕的前夕，爐裏燃著熊熊的火，滿室生春，桌上擺著豐盛的筵席，準備著過一個普天同慶的夜晚，驀然看見在窗外一片美麗的雪景當中，有一隻小鳥踟躕縮縮的在寒枝的梢頭踞立，正在啄食一顆殘餘的僵凍的果兒，禁不住那料峭的寒風，栽倒地上死了，滾成一個雪團！詩人感謂曰：「鳥！你連這一個快樂的夜晚都不給我！」我也有過一次類似經驗，在東北的一間雙重玻璃窗的屋裏，忽然看見枝頭有一隻麻雀，戰慄的跳動抖擻著，在啄食一塊乾枯的葉子。但是我發現那麻雀的羽毛特別的長，而且是蓬鬆戟張著的：像是披著一件簑衣，立刻使人聯想到那垃圾堆上的大羣襤褸而臃腫的人，那形容是一模一樣的。那孤苦伶仃的麻雀，也就不暇令人哀了。

自從離開四川以後，不再容易看見那樣多型類的鳥的跳盪，也不再容易聽到那樣悅耳的鳥鳴。只是清早遇到煙突冒煙的時候，一群麻雀擠在簷下的煙突旁邊取煖，隔著窗紙有時還能看見伏在窗檻上的雀兒的映影。喜鵲不知逃到哪裏去了。帶哨子的鴿子也很少看見在天空打旋。黃昏時偶爾還聽見寒鴉在古木上鼓噪，入夜也還能聽見那像哭又像笑的鴟梟的怪叫。再令人觸目的就是那些偶然一見的囚在籠裏的小鳥兒了，但是我不忍看。

Poverty

Man is born poor and naked, bringing with him nothing but a mouthful of milk.[44] No one comes into this world with a coin in each hand. It is only after a period of growth that social distinctions begin to emerge gradually among children. Some become "golden branches and jade leaves",[45] while others become "bags of mixed flour".[46] But, taken as a whole, most children at that age, rich or poor, still tumble in dust and mud and wipe their noses with their sleeves. In my day, the number of toys owned by the average child was quite limited, but they inevitably included a piggy bank. Most of these toy banks were made of baked clay and were as crude as artifacts from an ancient Pottery Age. They came in all sizes; some even had a green glaze on them. A few were in the shape of a safe and were made of iron sheets. Their purpose was to warn children of the need to save money as an insurance against poverty in bad times. At that age we were already under the darkening clouds of poverty. We were talked into dropping the few silver coins we managed to get as presents from our elders on New Year's Eve into piggy banks. That was an act we regretted as soon as it was done, but it was almost impossible to get the coins out

44 That is, the milky fluid commonly found in the mouth of a newborn baby.

45 This refers to members of a royal or noble family.

46 A mixture of corn and soybean flour, a staple among the poor.

窮

　　人生下來就是窮的，除了帶來一口奶之外，赤條條的，一無所有，誰手裏也沒有握著兩個錢。在稍稍長大一點，階級漸漸顯露，有的是金枝玉葉，有的是「雜和麵口袋」。但是就大體而論，還是泥巴裏打滾袖口上抹鼻涕的居多。兒童玩具本是少得可憐，而大概其中總還免不了一具「撲滿」，瓦做的，像是陶器時代的出品，大的小的掛綠釉的都有，間或也有形如保險箱，有鐵製的，這種玩具的用意就是警告孩子們，有錢要積蓄起來，免得在饑荒的時候受窮，窮的陰影在這時候就已罩住了我們！好容易過年賺來幾塊壓歲錢，都被騙弄丟在裏面了，丟進去就後悔，想從縫裏倒出來是萬難，用小刀撥也是枉然。積蓄是稍微有一點，窮還是窮。而且事實證明，凡是積在撲滿裏的錢，除了自己早早下手摔破的以外，大概後來就不

through the slot and all attempts to pry them out with a penknife proved fruitless. Despite the small savings we had accumulated, we remained poor as ever. And it is a belief borne out by fact that, unless we took action soon enough to break the piggy banks ourselves, the money we kept in them would in the end disappear mysteriously, hardly ever fulfilling its purpose of helping us meet our emergency needs. As we grew older, we began to feel a stronger urge to spend money. Our mouths watered at the sight of anything tasty, but we were always broke. On such an occasion we really wanted to start an October Revolution. Children of rich families were no exceptions. They wore expensive clothes, but they still regretted that they could not inherit their family fortunes sooner. At this age they had the keenest feeling for poverty, even though they had not yet any real knowledge of it. After attaining adulthood, a person begins to face the problem of feeding hungry mouths, his own as well as those of his dependents. If he is not sufficiently thick-skinned and hard-hearted, and if his ancestors have all been honest though well-educated people, he can never dream of freeing himself from the grip of poverty in his lifetime. His life will be a story of struggle against poverty and, whether he succeeds or fails, this life-long battle is bound to be extremely bloody. Blessed is he who need not struggle against poverty or, if he does, still has a little time left for some other pursuits.

But poverty is a relative term. Some people never stop complaining about being poor. Today they will take out an advance on their salaries and tomorrow they will raise a loan, both involving large amounts of money. And then they will point to a patch on their clothes or a small split in their leather shoes as hard evidence of their poverty. This is to achieve opulence through poverty, similar to the rhetorical device of achieving emphasis by means of understatement. Others make it a rule to live within their means and have no difficulty keeping the wolf from the door. However, they are worried that they will not have

知怎樣就沒有了，很少能在日後發生什麼救苦救難的功效。等到再稍稍長大一點，用錢的慾望更大，看見甚麼都要流涎，手裏偏偏是空空如也，那時候真想來一個十月革命。就是富家子也是一樣，儘管是綺襦紈袴，他還是恨繼承開始太晚。這時候他最感覺窮，雖然他還沒認識窮。人在成年之後，開始面對著餬口問題，不但餬自己的口，還要餬附屬人員的口，如果臉皮欠厚心地欠薄，再加上祖上是「忠厚傳家詩書繼世」的話，他這一生就休想能離開窮的掌握，人的一生，就是和窮掙扎的歷史。和窮掙扎一生，無論勝利或失敗，都是慘。能不和窮掙扎，或於掙扎之餘還有點閒工夫做些別的事，那人是有福了。

　　所謂窮，也是比較而言。有人天天喊窮，不是今天透支，就是明天舉債，數目大得都驚人，然後指著身上衣服的一塊補綻或是皮鞋上的一條小小裂縫做為他窮的鐵證。這是寓闊於窮，文章中的反

enough funds to send their children abroad for advanced study and, for that reason, have fallen into a state of self-induced poverty psychosis. A man may be regarded as really close to the poverty line if the seat of his pants has worn thin, then out, then been carefully darned, then backed by a big patch and secured with concentric circles of close stitching, which make it look like a target for archers. (Strange to say, a worn-out seat of pants is always the first sign of poverty!) This rule, however, does not always apply, because poverty knows no limit. "While snowflakes fall helter-skelter, / In a firewood shed I take shelter. / How can the poor survive, I wonder."[47] In the eyes of the poor there are always those who are even worse off.

Poverty has its advantages, however. A man in easy circumstances relies on too many external trappings and embellishments, which tend to conceal his true identity. As a result, other people will fail to discern his real character and will often form inaccurate (mainly favorable) opinions about him, and sometimes it is easy for him to forget who he is. This is not the case with a poor man, whose shabby clothes are like a house with open windows, which enable people to see its contents. His house may be just a hovel in which the signs of poverty are everywhere, but one can easily see that it is the home of a real man. The poorer a man is, the more he needs to rely on his real qualities without recourse to dissembling or trickery. He who lives in poverty also lives in leisure. He has few visitors and fewer job-seekers. Obituary notices and invitations to parties seldom arrive in his mailbox. His time is his own. A poor man has an open heart; there is no barrier between him and other poor people. That is why such a person is likely to be most generous. He has very little money in reserve, not enough to buy a house or a piece of land. Since it cannot buy him luxuries but is enough to keep hunger from his door, he may as well

---

47 From a beggar's cant.

襯法。也有人量入為出，溫飽無虞，可是又擔心他的孩子將來自費留學的經費沒有著落，於是於自我麻醉中陷入於窮的心理狀態。若是西裝褲的後方越磨越薄，由薄而破，由破而織，由織而補上一大塊布，細針密縫，老遠的看上去像是一個圓圓的箭靶，（說也奇怪，人窮是先從褲子破起！）那麼，這個人可是真有些近於窮了。但是也不然，窮無止境。「大雪紛紛落，我往柴火垜，看你們窮人怎麼過！」窮人眼裏還有更窮的人。

　　窮也有好處。在優裕環境裏生活著的人，外加的裝飾與舖排太多，可以把他的本來面目掩沒無遺，不但別人認不清他真的面目，往往對他發生誤會（多半往好的方面誤會）就是自己也容易忘記自己是誰。窮人則不然，他的襤褸的衣裳等於是開著許多窗戶，可以令人窺見他的內容，他的蓽門蓬戶，儘管是窮氣冒三尺，卻容易令人發見裏面有一個人。人越窮，越靠他本身的成色，其中毫無夾帶藏掖。人窮還可落個清閒，既少「車馬駐江干」，更不會有人來求謀事，訃聞請箋都不會常常上門，他的時間是他自己的。窮人的心是赤裸的，和別的窮人之間沒有隔閡，所以窮人才最慷慨。金錯囊中

be liberal with it and enjoy a moment's satisfaction from his own generosity. From this comes the expression "a poor man with an open hand". We have witnessed two brothers in a wealthy family cut a dining table in two when the time comes to divide the family estate, but we have never seen two beggars fight over half a bowl of leftovers.

It is a natural phenomenon that a person who is poor is treated with disdain. Is it not the case that dogs will reserve their loudest barks for people in tatters? Poverty tends to make a person draw in his neck, hunch his shoulders and hang his head. His hair and beard seem to grow faster than usual. He walks timidly in the street, keeping close to the wall. He may not be a thief, but he looks very much like one. Appearing in this manner, he is rebuffed wherever he turns. As a result, a poor person tends to develop a natural resistance, called "priggery". Poverty, once compounded with priggery, is no longer something to be ashamed of. Never mind how shabby he may look; he never tries to excel in the world of fashion anyway, as a man should be different from a clotheshorse. Never mind how empty his pocket may be; he will have no ill-gotten gains. Never mind how long he has been unemployed; there are certain jobs that he will never take. With these in mind, he feels a hot stream of moral force rising from his pubic region, which automatically straightens his back, pushes out his chest and enables him to swagger with courage and pride. In the eyes of other people, he may be like a tile beneath a toilet—stinking and hard. Yet, by relying on this force, a poor person may cherish great ambitions and a commoner may stand up to a member of the royalty. Seen in this light, priggery may not be an entirely negative quality in a poor person; rather, it is a necessity. And a poor person cannot persevere without the support of priggery.

所餘無幾，買房置地都不夠，反正是吃不飽餓不死，落得來個爽快，求片刻的快意。此之謂「窮大手」。我們看見過富家弟兄析產的時候把一張八仙桌子劈開成兩半，不曾看見兩個窮人搶食半盂殘羹賸飯。

窮時受人白眼是件常事，狗不也是專愛對著鶉衣百結的人汪汪嗎？人窮則頸易縮，肩易聳，頭易垂，鬚髮許是特別長得快，擦著牆邊逡巡而過，不是賊也像是賊。以這種姿態出現，到處受窘。所以人窮則往往自然的有一種抵抗力出現，是名曰：酸。窮一經酸化，便不復是怕見人的東西。別看我衣履不整，我本來不以衣履見長！人和衣服架子本來是應該有分別的。別看我囊中羞澀，我有所不取；別看我落魄無聊，我有所不為，這樣一想，一股浩然之氣火辣辣的從丹田升起，腰板自然挺直，胸膛自然凸出，裏裏嘯傲，無往不宜。在別人的眼裏，他是一塊茅廁磚──臭而且硬，可是，人窮而不志短者以此，布衣之士而可以傲王侯者亦以此，所以窮酸亦不可厚非，他不得不如此。窮若沒有酸支持著，它不能持久。

Yang Xiong[48] wrote an ode entitled "The Banishment of Poverty."
Han Yu[49] wrote "Goodbye to Poverty", an essay in prose. Both authors
boldly and resolutely announced their decisions to severe their
relationship with Poverty, but Poverty was able to persuade them
to reverse their decisions. They changed countenance, begged him to
forgive them their mistake and offered him the seat of honor. This was
an altered form of priggery. If they could banish Poverty or ask him to
leave, why would they not do it gladly? Since Poverty could not be
banished or asked to leave, they had to put up with him and keep his
company. Poverty is not a crime; neither is it a virtue, so it is not
something to brag about, let alone a source of pride. The best model
among the poor must be Yan Hui,[51] who dwelled in a back alley and
lived on "a bowl of rice and a scoop of water", but he was always happy
and content. It is certainly very nice to be happy and content, but it is
not particularly nice to live on a bowl of rice and a scoop of water. As a
result of malnutrition, he died prematurely at the age of thirty-two.
Confucius said: "One can find happiness even when he lives on coarse
food and water and sleeps with his own elbow for a pillow." This is all
right as a metaphor. Taken literally, it cannot be a prescription for a
healthy way of life.

---

48 Yang Xiong (53 B.C.–A.D. 18), a poet of the Han dynasty especially known for
his *fu* or odes.

49 Han Yu (678–824), a master of Chinese prose and outstanding poet of the Tang
dynasty.

51 The most gifted among Confucius' disciples.

揚雄有逐貧之賦，韓愈有送窮之文，理直氣壯的要與貧窮絕緣，反倒被窮鬼說服，改容謝過肅之上座，這也是酸極一種變化。貧而能逐，窮而能送，何樂而不為？逐也逐不掉，送也送不走，只好硬著頭皮甘與窮鬼為伍。窮不是罪過，但也究竟不是美德，值不得誇耀，更不足以傲人。典型的窮人該是顏回，一簞食，一瓢飲，在陋巷，不改其樂。不改其樂當然是很好，簞食瓢飲究竟不大好，營養不足，所以顏回活到三十二歲短命死矣。孔子所說「飯疏食飲水，曲肱而枕之，樂亦在其中矣。」譬喻則可，當真如此就嫌其不大衛生。

蔣舍小品續集

From A Cottager's Sketchbook, Part 2

Things Old

"I love everything old: old friends, old times, old manners, old books, old wine; and I believe, Dorothy, you'll own I have been pretty fond of an old wife." So says Mr. Hardcastle, the old-fashioned, antiquated gentleman in Oliver Goldsmith's famous play *She Stoops to Conquer*. His wife Dorothy is more than a little pleased by these words, which show that the lewd old man is still fond of her, but not without feeling a little cross, because that statement ends with a reminder of her age. There is nothing wrong in the first part of this declaration, since it deals with his personal preferences, which are nobody else's business. And, in fact, this predilection is shared by many other people, who attach greater value to all things old and who believe that, besides friends, times, manners, books and wine, there are countless other things that improve with age. For this reason, certain people have copied down the first part of this famous declaration in black letters and have it framed and hung on the wall, as if to declare war on those who are fond of getting rid of the old to make way for the new.

There is a common saying: "Friends are best when old; clothes are best when new." Yet things such as clothes are most comfortable when old. A new suit or dress makes its wearer cautious and reluctant to sit down anywhere or lean against anything. I have seen people who focus their attention on the front creases on the legs of their new

舊

「我愛一切舊的東西——老朋友，舊時代，舊習慣，古書，陳釀；而且我相信，陶樂賽，你一定也承認我一向是很喜歡一位老妻。」這是高爾斯密的名劇《委曲求全》(She Stoops to Conquer) 中那位守舊的老頭兒哈德卡索先生說的話。他的夫人陶樂賽聽了這句話，心裏有一點高興，這風流的老頭子還是喜歡她，但是也不是沒有一點慍意，因為這一句話的後半段說穿了她的老。這句話的前半段沒有毛病，他個人有此癖好，干別人什麼事？而且事實上有很多人頗具同感，也覺得一切東西都是舊的好，除了朋友、時代、習慣、書、酒之外，有數不盡的事物都是越老越古越舊越陳越好。所以有人把這半句名言用花體正楷字母抄了下來，裝在玻璃框裏，掛在牆上，那意思好像是在向喜歡除舊佈新的人挑戰。

俗語說，「人不如故，衣不如新」。其實，衣着之類還是舊的舒適。新裝上身之後，東也不敢坐，西也不敢靠，戰戰兢兢。我看見過有人全神貫注在他的新西裝褲管上的那一條直線，坐下之後第一樁事便是用手在膝蓋處提動幾下，生恐膝部把他的筆直的褲管撐得

pants. The first thing they do after sitting down is to pinch those pant legs at the knees and pull them up a few times for fear that their knees would ruin the ramrod creases and cause two pockets to be formed in those places. When people are reduced to such a state, what pleasures can they enjoy in life? Have you seen snapshots of Albert Einstein? Those pictures show him always wearing the same loose, shabby, unbuttoned jacket, which must have had quite a number of holes burned by cigarette ashes, not to mention sweat and grease stains. But he was perhaps wearing exactly that shabby piece of garment when his mind made leisurely voyages into outer space. The following story appears in *Shishuo Xinyu*[51]: Huan Chong, a general in charge of the imperial horses and chariots in the Jin dynasty, had a strong dislike of new clothes. One day, after taking a bath, he was presented with new clothes, which his wife had deliberately ordered for him. The general was very angry and ordered his servant to take them away. His wife sent them back and asked the servant to relay the question to the general: "How can clothes become old if they have not once been new?" The general chuckled and put them on. In fact, the general might have yielded too readily to persuasion. Instead, he should have asked in return, "Why should I need new clothes, as long as my old clothes are still wearable?" But he gave in with a chuckle, perhaps just to preserve domestic peace. I have not yet witnessed an example of "trimming the head to fit the hat", but there has been an abundance of cases which are tantamount to "cutting the feet to fit the shoes" . The kinds of shoes worn by people in general have been designed with very little regard to the fact that each foot has five toes. Wearers of these shoes may not have to cut their feet literally, but I dare say their toes definitely lack *lebensraum*. There are people who firmly

---

51 A collection of anecdotes about famous personages in China during the period from the first to the fourth century, edited by Liu Yiqing (403–444), a writer and administrator in the state of Song during the period of the Southern Dynasty.

變成了口袋。人生至此，還有什麼趣味可說！看見過愛因斯坦的小
照麼？他總是披着那一件敞着領口胸懷的鬆鬆大大的破夾克，上面
少不了煙灰燒出的小洞，更不會沒有一片片的汗斑油漬，但是他在
這件破舊衣裳遮蓋之下優哉遊哉的神遊於太虛之表。《世說新語》記
載着：「桓車騎不好着新衣，浴後婦故進新衣與，車騎大怒，催使持
去，婦更持還，傳語云，『衣不經新，何由得故？』桓公大笑着之。」
桓沖真是好說話，他應該說：「有舊衣可着，何用新為？」也許他是
為了保持閫內安寧，所以才一笑置之。「殺頭而便冠」的事情，我還
沒有見過；但是「削足而適履」的行為，則頗多類似的例證。一般人
穿的鞋，其製作設計很少有顧到一隻腳是有五個趾頭的，穿這樣的
鞋雖然無需「削」足，但是我敢說五個腳趾絕對缺乏生存的空間。有

believe that new shoes are uncomfortable and old shoes are not to be discarded.

Jin Shengtan[52] listed the completion of a new house as one of the "thirty-three happy moments" of his life. That may well be a happy moment in one's life, but people will be turned off by the sight of the small trees and the new walls, which are typical of the homes of the *nouveaux riches*. "To have centuries-old sprawling trees, you must first find and plant inches-long winter roots." But then you will have a very long wait. A building must be given sufficient time to age before it can charm us with its "shady trees and singing birds" and please our eyes with its "steps tinged green with moss and curtains turned blue by the reflection of the grass." In a Western-style garden, the lawn must be mown and the trees must be trimmed at regular intervals and care must be taken to keep things fresh and sparkling. Chinese gardening obviously follows quite different principles. Even for an imperial estate, apart from the usual pavilions and terraces with painted rafters and carved beams, a "solitary retreat" or "natural garden" must be included in the plan in order to give the place a hint of antiquity and desolation. As for an institution of higher learning, how can it be called a top-notch college if the walls of its buildings are not covered with perennial ivy and the bases of those walls are not overgrown with age-old moss?

We love old things, often because each of them has a history and can conjure up memories. Take the solar calendar for example. Even though it is the calendar we have officially adopted, yet the lunar calendar has not fallen completely into disuse among the populace. As a result, we have two New Years to celebrate, and only on the

---

52 Literary name of Jin Wei (1608–1661), a satirical writer and annotator of the late Ming dynasty executed for his rejection of the new Manchu rulers.

人硬是覺得，新鞋不好穿，敝屣不可棄。

「新屋落成」金聖嘆列為「不亦快哉」之一，快哉儘管快哉，隨後那「樹小牆新」的一段暴發氣象卻是令人難堪。「欲存老蓋千年意，為覓霜根數寸栽」，但是需要等待多久！一棟建築要等到相當破舊，才能有「樹林陰翳，鳥聲上下」之趣，才能有「苔痕上階綠，草色入簾青」之樂。西洋的庭園，不時的要剪草，要修樹，要打扮得新鮮耀眼，我們的園藝的標準顯然的有些不同，即使是帝王之家的園囿也要在亭閣樓台畫棟雕樑之外安排一個「濠濮間」「諧趣園」，表示一點點陳舊古老的蕭瑟之氣。至於講學的上庠，要是牆上沒有多年蔓生的常春藤，基腳上沒有遠年積留的苔蘚，那還能算是第一流麼？

舊的事物之所以可愛，往往是因為它有內容，能喚起人的回憶。例如陽曆儘管是我們正式採用的曆法，在民間則陰曆仍不能廢，每年要過兩個新年，而且只有在舊年才有「新桃換舊符」。明知

occasion of the lunar New Year do we put up new "spring couplets"[53] to replace the old ones as a ritual marking the transition from the old to the new year. We are fully aware that Taiwan is located in a subtropical zone, but we cannot do away with the tradition of using fire and smoke to produce cured meats that often have a cadaverous smell. Dragon boats and *zongzi*[54] are surely indispensable for the Dragon Boat Festival.[55] Yet how many people still give their thoughts to Qu Yuan, the famous aristocrat and poet of the kingdom of Chu, who displayed his talent and sang his own praises, but suffered injustices and finally drowned himself in the Miluo River? Is this not done merely to preserve an old custom rather than commemorate a historic event? The customs of viewing the full moon on the Mid-Autumn Festival[56] and of climbing a mountain on the Double Ninth Festival[57] are events that people celebrate with sustained interest every year. To certain people, even the *laba* porridge[58] is an unforgettable tradition. As to bric-a-brac, it goes without saying that the older it is, the greater its value. A ceramic teapot made in Yixing and engraved with a motto or

---

53 Congratulatory verses written on strips of red paper and pasted to the opposite sides of an entrance.

54 Sweet rice dumplings wrapped in bamboo leaves and cooked in boiling water.

55 An annual festival observed on the fifth day of the fifth lunar month. Qu Yuan (343–? 277 B.C.) was once a trusted minister of the king of Chu but lost the royal favor after being maligned by his political rivals and was banished from the court. He went into exile to escape persecution. Overcome by anguish, he drowned himself in the Miluo River. Dragon boats have developed from the original flotilla of boats dispatched down the river to search for his body. According to legend, his ghost appeared to some local people in their dreams with a request for food which, the ghosts said, must be wrapped in leaves to avoid interception by river monsters.

56 Celebrated on the fifteenth day of the eighth lunar month.

57 Celebrated on the ninth day of the ninth lunar month.

58 Porridge made from rice, nuts and preserved fruits and served on the eighth day of the twelfth lunar month.

地處亞熱帶，仍然未能免俗要煙薰火燎的製造常常帶有屍味的臘肉。端午的龍舟粽子是不可少的，有幾個人想到那「露才揚己怨懟沉江」的屈大夫？還不是舊俗相因虛應故事？中秋賞月，重九登高，永遠一年一度的引起人們的不可磨滅的興味。甚至臘八的那一鍋粥，都有人難以忘懷。至於供個人賞玩的東西，當然是越舊越有意義。

verse composed by Chen Mansheng,[59] has a natural elegance about it, even if it shows signs of wear. Paintings by Yuan artists mounted on multicolored silk or books printed by the Song publishing houses and bound in gold-speckled paper can give their viewers the delusion of traveling backward in time and keeping company with the ancients. I have an old coin which bears the inscription "for circulation in Lin'an prefecture[60] and valued at three hundred cash." While toying with the coin, I cannot help associating it with the Song courtiers who fled across the Yangtze to resettle in the South and regaled themselves with song and dance shows at the West Lake. I also have two walnuts, which my grandfather used to squeeze and click like castanets in his hand. My father inherited them and carried on this ritual for a few more decades. As a result, the walnuts have become smooth and ruddy like chalcedony. It is now my turn to work and play them. Since coming into my possession, they have had several close calls of being cracked open by my grandchildren to satisfy their craving for the kernels. Each family, even a family in reduced circumstances, has a few old things that are worth showing to visitors, and that should not be a surprise to anyone. The same can be said of countries. Many an ancient country in decline still has a number of relics which inspire wonder, admiration, adoration and sighs.

True, old things have many nostalgic values, but there are also many things in human life that call for constant renovation. We may feel free to love and marvel at ancient statues and cultural relics, yet we cannot dwell forever in the realm of beautiful memories but must return to the real world. In a museum, we have before us sacrificial vessels of the Shang and Zhou dynasties, and books, paintings and ceramics dating back to the Song, Yuan and Ming periods. But, as soon

---

59 A well-known pottery designer of the Qing dynasty.
60 Lin'an, now Hangzhou, was the capital of the Southern Song dynasty.

一把宜興砂壺，上面有陳曼生製銘鐫句，縱然破舊，氣味自然高雅。「樗蒲錦背元人畫，金粟箋裝宋版書」，更是足以使人超然遠舉，與古人遊。我有古錢一枚，「臨安府行用，準參百文省」，把玩之餘不能不聯想到南渡諸公之觀賞西湖歌舞。我有胡桃一對，祖父常常放在手裏揉動，噶咯噶咯的作響，後來又在我父親手裏揉動，也噶咯噶咯的響了幾十年，圓滑紅潤，有如玉髓，真是先人手澤，現在輪到我手裏噶咯噶咯的響了，好幾次險些兒被我的兒孫輩敲碎取出桃仁來了！每一個破落戶都可以拿出幾件舊東西來，這是不足為奇的事。國家亦然。多少衰敗的古國都有不少的古物，可以令人驚羨，欣賞，感慨，唏噓！

舊的東西之可留戀的地方固然很多，人生之應該日新又新的地方亦復不少。對於舊日的典章文物我們儘管歡喜讚嘆，可是我們不能永遠盤桓在美好的記憶境界裏，我們還是要回到這個現實的地面上來。在博物館裏我們面對商周的吉金，宋元明的書畫瓷器，可是

as we emerge from it with tired and aching legs, we have to deal with the reality of over-crowded buses, ugly street posters and glass tumblers that are used indiscriminately for all kinds of beverage.

Old things are generally likable, but old diseases should not be allowed to recur. Such old things as parochial arrogance, the vestiges of slavery, the evils of sloth and selfishness, the ugly ways of mammonism and profiteering, the skewed and morbid esthetic concepts, as well as countless other faults and ills, are the sooner rid of the better. An old disease may go away, only to be succeeded by a new one, yet this is still better than having both at the same time. The worst scenario is that our traditionalists are simply cultural necrophiles and our avant-gardists are but cultural dilettantes. In that case, we will lose the old as well as the new.

溜瘦雙腿走出門外便立刻要面對擠死人的公共汽車，醜惡的市招，和各種飲料一律通用的玻璃杯！

　　舊的東西大抵可愛，惟舊病不可復發。諸如夜郎自大的脾氣，奴隸制度的殘餘，懶惰自私的惡習，蠅營狗苟的醜態，畸形病態的審美觀念，以及罄竹難書的諸般病症，皆以早去為宜。舊病才去，可能新病又來，然而總比舊疴新恙一時併發要好一些。最可怕的是，倡言守舊，其實只是迷戀骸骨；唯新是鶩，其實只是摭拾皮毛，那便是新舊之間兩俱失之了。

On Taking Baths

Who on earth has never taken a bath? In China, a "baby bath party" is held on the third day after a child is born. On such an occasion, the child is placed in a tub full of scented hot water, accompanied by an array of goodies and money gifts and surrounded by a crowd of relatives and family friends who watch the baby being given his first ablution. No one, of course, can recall his or her own experience with the "baby bath". The notorious An Lushan was perhaps the only "baby" to have any recollection of such an experience when Yang Yuhuan, the imperial consort, had him wrapped in giant-sized brocade swaddling clothes for such a bath.[61] But I believe that he probably had something else on his mind on that occasion.

When a child gets a little older, he or she is regularly made to sit in a tub for a bath administered by the mother, an experience the child

---

61 Yang Yuhuan (719–756) was the favorite consort of Emperor Xuanzong. An Lushan (703–757) was a military governor of Turkic descent and a favorite of the emperor and his consort. In an act of buffoonery aimed at ingratiating himself, An acknowledged the beautiful imperial consort as his "mother" and was given his "baby bath party" in the women's quarters at the palace three days after his birthday. Soon after that he started a rebellion, forcing the emperor to flee the capital. and, on his way into exile, to order Yang executed . An was eventually defeated by the royal troops and murdered by his own son.

洗　澡

　　誰沒有洗過澡！生下來第三天，就有「洗兒會」，熱騰騰的一盆香湯，還有果子綵錢，親朋圍繞着看你洗澡。「洗三」的滋味如何，沒有人能夠記得。被楊貴妃用錦繡大襁褓裹起來的安祿山也許能體會一點點「洗三」的滋味，不過我想當時祿兒必定別有心事在。

　　稍為長大一點，被母親按在盆裏洗澡永遠是終身不忘的經驗。

will never forget. The harder the child tries to keep out soap water, the more likely it is that soap water will get into the corners of the eyes. The armpits are ticklish spots, so are the sides, but the base of the neck is the part of the body most sensitive to the touch. If the child does not stop giggling or wriggling like a piece of twisted malt candy, a slap is certain to fall on the head or on the face, and sometimes it really hurts.

After growing up, a person begins to realize that taking a bath to clean the dirt and filth on the body is, after all, a pleasurable human experience. But not everybody thinks so. When I was a middle school student, my school was equipped with bathing facilities, which, though simple and crude, had an abundant supply of hot and cold water. Still, the administration found it necessary to lay down a strict rule requiring each student to take at least one bath every three days. This was similar, but not identical, to a rule in the civil code promulgated by public authorities during the Han dynasty, which provided that "government officials may be excused from work once every five days in order for them to take a bath." This "bath day" meant a day off, but to bathe or not to bathe was a decision left entirely to each official. On the other hand, it was compulsory at my school to take a bath every three days, and this rule was supplemented by clearly defined penalties. The bathhouse kept an attendance register. The names of three-time violators would be posted on the bulletin board. For repeated violators who refused to repent, a time would be appointed for the enforcement of the rule under the supervision of an appointed administrator. As far as I know, there were quite a number of students who signed the register but did not take a bath. This practice was similar to forgery, yet the school never for once published the names of violators, let alone ordered them actually to strip and bathe under the eyes of the supervisor. So the rule finally became a dead letter.

越怕肥皂水流進眼裏，肥皂水越愛往眼角裏鑽。胳肢窩怕癢，兩肋
也怕癢，頸子底下尤其怕癢，如果咯咯大笑把身子弄成扭股糖似
的，就會順手一巴掌沒頭沒臉的拍了下來，有時候還真有一點痛。

　　成年之後，應該知道澡雪垢滓乃人生一樂，但亦不盡然。我讀
中學的時候，學校有洗澡的設備，雖是因陋就簡，冷熱水卻甚充
分。但是學校仍須嚴格規定，至少每三天必須洗澡一次。這規定比
起漢律「吏五日得一休沐」意義大不相同。五日一休沐，是放假一
天，沐不沐還不是在你自己。學校規定三日一洗澡是強迫性的，而
且還有懲罰的辦法，洗澡室備有簽到簿，三次不洗澡者公佈名單，
仍不悔悔者則指定時間派員監視強制執行。以我所知，不洗澡而簽
名者大有人在，儼如偽造文書；從未見有名單公佈，更未見有人在
眾目睽睽之下袒裼裸裎，法令徒成具文。

We Chinese have always treated bathing as a major event. There is an ancient tradition requiring courtiers to bathe before going to court and priests to fast and bathe before offering sacrifices to the gods. To Zeng Dian,[62] bathing in the Yihe[63] was the most joyful event of his life. It is precisely because bathing is treated as a major event that we have apparently failed to make it a part of our daily lives . As late as in the Tang dynasty, there were still people who "spent three years in mourning and self-mortification without taking a single bath". The story of Wang Meng,[64] who had the habit of searching his own body for lice while engaged in a conversation, was a sufficient proof that he rarely took a bath. A poem by the famous Tang poet Bai Juyi[65] contains the following lines: "When I took a bath this morning, / I found my body rather weak and thin." To him, a bath was an event that called for its celebration in verse.

Old-style homes, even great mansions with large estates, are seldom equipped with bathrooms *per se*. Occupants of such a home will be happy as long as there is a large wooden vat with hot water for one person to squat and splash in. Streets in Beijing used to be lined with public bathhouses whose "pools are heated before the cocks crow and whose halls are packed with customers at sunrise." And there were other public bathhouses, with such names as "Western Peace", that were said to be slightly better. Most people, however, shunned the public bathhouses, not because they, like Mi Fei,[66] had an obsession

---

62 Zeng Dian was one of Confucius' disciples.

63 A river originating in Shandong and flowing through Jiangsu before emptying into the Yellow Sea.

64 Wang Meng (325–376) was a great military strategist and man of learning in the Jin dynasty.

65 Also Pai Chu-I (772–846), alias Bai Letian and Bai Xiangshan, was one of the best known poets of China.

66 See footnote 1.

　　我們中國人一向是把洗澡當做一件大事的。自古就有沐浴而朝，齋戒沐浴以祀上帝的說法。曾點的生平快事是「浴於沂」。唯因其為大事，似乎未能視為日常生活的一部分。到了唐朝，還有人「居喪毀慕，三年不澡沐」。晉朝的王猛捫蝨而談，更是經常不洗澡的明證。白居易詩「今朝一澡濯，衰瘦頗有餘」，洗一回澡居然有詩以紀之的價值。

　　舊式人家，儘管是深宅大院，很少有特闢浴室的。一隻大木盆，能蹲踞其中，把浴湯潑濺滿地，便可以稱心如意了。在北平，街上有的是「金雞未唱湯先熱，紅日東昇客滿堂」的澡堂，也有所謂高級一些的如「西昇平」，但是很多人都不敢問津，倒不一定是如米芾之「好潔成癖至不與人同巾器」，也不是怕進去被人偷走了褲子，實在是因為醫藥費用太大。「早晨皮包水，晚上水包皮」，怕的是水

with hygiene and refused to share towels or tubs with others, or because they worried that, while they were bathing, somebody might make away with their clothes. They did so because they did not wish to incur enormous medical expenses. It was a common saying: "In the morning, I put water into my body. In the evening, I put my body in water."[67] They worried that they might get into something else besides bath water; they might even get something in their skin. It was common knowledge that bathhouses in certain cities provided many services, such as a wet-towel rubdown, back or feet massage, pedicure, haircut, refreshments, beds for a nap or more than a nap, and all other conveniences. However, people who were more cautious than others would just look at them and walk away. They would rather go home to squat in those wooden vats and make do with them.

The bathroom in a modern home is indeed an amenity. The only regret is that this amenity is a westernized feature rather than an indigenous invention of China. But we should not allow this to affect our national self-confidence. The habit among people in Western countries of having two ablutions every day, namely, a shower in the morning and another at night, is a relatively recent thing. The splendid public baths built by order of Emperor Caracalla of Rome, each capable of accommodating up to sixteen thousand bathers at the same time, are now merely a historical legend. Those bathhouses have long been reduced to ruins as a result of invasions by barbarians. The ascetic leanings among early Christians also helped to break the good bathing habit. The clerics of the Middle Ages paid scant attention to personal cleanliness. Perhaps because they upheld the belief that "Rather than bathe in water, one should bathe in virtue" (words inscribed on a soap dish belonging to Fu Xuan[68]). Even in modern

---

67 That is, by going to the teahouse in the morning and to the bathhouse in the evening.

68 Fu Xuan (217–278) was a great thinker and scholar of the Jin dynasty.

不僅包皮，還可能有點什麼東西進入皮裏面去。明知道有些城市的
澡堂裏面可以搓澡，敲背，捏足，修腳，理髮，吃東西，高枕而
眠，甚而至於不僅是高枕而眠，一律都非常方便，有些膽小的人還
是望望然去之，寧可回到家裏去蹲踞在那一隻大木盆裏將就將就。

　　近代的家庭洗澡間當然是令人稱便，可惜頗有「西化」之嫌，非
我國之所固有。不過我們也無需過於自餒，西洋人之早雨浴晚雨浴
一天瀏洗兩回，也只是很晚近的事。羅馬皇帝喀拉凱拉之廣造宏麗
的公共浴室容納一萬六千人同時入浴，那只是歷史上的美談。那些
浴室早已由於蠻人入侵而淪為廢墟，早期基督教的禁慾趨向又把沐
浴的美德破壞無遺。在中古期間的僧侶是不大注意他們的肉體上的
清潔的。「與其澡於水，寧澡於德」(傅玄澡盤銘) 大概是他們所信奉

times European convents still kept some of their medieval ways. Novices were allowed to bathe only once every two weeks. On such an occasion they were required to bring with them calf-length robes to use as bathing suits and to follow a special procedure to undress so as to prevent them from seeing their own bodies. In the Victorian era, the "Saturday night bath" was a routine activity in the life of ordinary folks. All the other days of the week were probably "unpropitious for bathing".

Similarly, Buddhist monks in China had their own rules on bathing. The reader is referred to Section 6 of *Baizhang Qinggui*,[69] which contains the following instruction to the monks: "Spread out your bundle and place the accessories to one side. Unbutton your upper garment. Take off your underpants before you remove your robe, then use a towel to wrap around your body. Only then may you put on your bathing skirt and fold up your trousers before putting them in the bundle." The rules did not specify the proper interval between baths, but, judging from the steps strictly prescribed for undressing, the intention might well have been the same as that of the medieval Christian church, although a different approach was adopted.

There are occasions when a person must go naked; taking a bath is one of them. It may not be an act of great impropriety if, after taking a bath, the bather should cast an admiring glance at his or her own body, as long as it is done in a proper place and for a very short time. If nakedness is to be condemned as an evil, what good is it when a person behaves like a beast in human clothes?

---

69 Or the *Rules of the Mount Baizhang Monastery*.

的道理。歐洲近代的修女學校還留有一些中古遺風,女生們隔兩個星期纔能洗澡一次,而且在洗的時候還要攜帶一件長達膝部以下的長袍作為浴衣,脫衣服的時候還有一套特殊技術,不可使自己看到自己的身體!英國維多利亞時代之「星期六晚的洗澡」是一般人民經常有的生活項目之一。平常的日子大概都是「不宜沐浴」。

我國的佛教僧侶也有關於沐浴的規定,請看《百丈清規‧六》:「展浴袱取出浴具於一邊,解上衣,未卸直裰,先脫下面裙裳,以腳布圍身,方可繫浴裙,將裩袴捲摺納袱內」。雖未明言隔多久洗一次,看那脫衣層次規定之嚴,其用心與中古基督教會殆異趣同工。

在某些情形之下裸體運動是有其必要的,洗澡即其一也。在短短一段時間內,在一個適當的地方,即使於洗濯之餘觀賞一下原來屬於自己的肉體,亦無傷大雅。若說赤身裸體便是邪惡,那麼衣冠禽獸又好在哪裏?

According to The *Book of Rites*[70] (in the chapter on conduct becoming to a follower of Confucius), "a Confucian scholar must bathe both in water and in virtue." In my opinion, a person should maintain a clean body and a clean mind, and the two should be parallel rather than mutually exclusive.

---

70 Chinese title *Li Ji*, one of the five Confucian classics. The work treats such subjects as royal regulations, rites, ritual objects and sacrifices, education and music.

　　《禮》(「儒行云」)：「儒有澡身而浴德」。我看人的身與心應該都
保持清潔，而且並行不悖。

Trees

Almost every home in Beijing has a few trees of a considerable size. A huge Chinese locust tree is a standard fixture in a front yard. Such a tree keeps the entire courtyard under its umbrage and casts its shadows on the windows. In June and July, its foliage is dotted with profuse panicles of yellowish flowers. All this adds to the homey atmosphere of the house, although one may be bothered occasionally by the green-colored worms dangling on filaments from the tree, which may cling to your hair and your face if you are not too careful. Chinese locust trees have very long lives, and it is said that some of the locust trees planted in the Tang dynasty have survived to this day. The trunk of such a tree, with its tangles and snarls, has the peculiar air of an old and ugly but, nonetheless, proud person. A home with such a tree in its front yard is safe from at least one of the three sneers usually directed at the home of a *nouveau riche*: small trees, new walls, and contemporary paintings.[71] Traditionally there should be an elm in the backyard, because its Chinese name, pronounced *yu*, is homonymous with the Chinese word for "surplus". Except for its propitious name, the elm has hardly anything about it that is particularly likable. All year round there is a constant scattering of multicolored caterpillars from its branches. Cakes made from elm-seeds taste awful. As for the side

---

71 That is, instead of the works of old masters.

樹

　　北平的人家差不多家家都有幾棵相當大的樹。前院一棵大槐樹是很平常的，槐蔭滿庭，槐影臨窗，到了六七月間槐黃滿樹，使得家像一個家，雖然樹上不時的由一根細絲吊下一條綠顏色的肉蟲子，不當心就要黏得滿頭滿臉。槐樹壽命很長，有人說唐槐到現在還有生存在世上的，這種樹的樹幹就有一種糾繞蟠屈的姿態，自有一股老醜而並不自嫌的神氣，有這樣一棵矗立在前庭，至少可以把「樹小牆新畫不古」的譏誚免除三分之一。後院照例應該有一棵榆樹，榆與餘同音，示有餘之意，否則榆樹沒有什麼特別值得令人喜愛的地方，成年的往下灑落五顏六色的毛毛蟲，榆錢作糕也並不好吃。至於邊旁胯院裏，則只有棗樹的分，「葉小如鼠耳」，到處生些

courtyard, it is a proper place to grow a jujube tree whose tiny leaves resemble rat's ears and whose trunk, branches and foliage crawl with small caterpillars that have a grotesque shape and give a harmful sting. The jujube fruit serves no other purpose than to make a paste that is used as a cake filling. It will cause diarrhea if eaten raw. For that reason, the owner of such a tree will not bother to stop the children and old women in the neighborhood from hitting and thrashing it with long poles to steal its fruit. Four potted pomegranate trees are traditionally placed at the center of the courtyard to serve as a backdrop for the fish tank under an awning.

My old home had a number of other trees. There were in the east courtyard a persimmon tree and a black date palm, of which the former had an annual yield of between one and two hundred persimmons of the taller variety. The four midget crab apple trees in front of the roofed second gate looked extremely gorgeous in bloom. Four lilacs took up half the space of the west courtyard. In the backyard stood a Chinese toon and a cayenne pepper tree. The young leaves of both trees were excellent condiments respectively for braised yellow croaker and tofu salad. A grapevine trellis stood in the shade of an elm, and each year care was taken to have a dead cat buried near the root of the grapevine (provided that a dead cat was available). An earlier home of mine boasted even more trees: peach, plum, walnut and apricot trees, wisteria vines, pines, willows—you name it. Because of this, I have since my childhood developed a special affection for trees. I used to look at the trees and indulge in various fantasies. I felt that, even though they could not talk or understand words, they too were subject to the cycle of birth, age, sickness and death; they too grew and withered and knew how to propagate; and they should be considered "sentient" beings.

Trees vary widely in shape and bearing. Some are tall and erect

怪模怪樣的能刺傷人的小毛蟲。棗實只合作棗泥餡子，生吃在肚裏就要拉棗醬，所以左鄰右舍的孩子老嫗任意撲打也就算了。院子中央的四盆石榴樹，那是給天棚魚缸做陪襯的。

我家裏還有些別的樹。東院裏有一棵柿子樹，每年結一二百個高莊柿子，還有一棵黑棗。垂花門前有四棵西府海棠，艷麗到極點。西院有四棵紫丁香，佔了半個院子。後院有一棵香椿和一棵胡椒，椿芽椒芽成了燒黃魚和拌豆腐的最好的佐料。榆樹底下有一個葡萄架，年年在樹根左近要埋一隻死貓（如果有死貓可得）。在從前的一處家園裏，還有更多的樹，桃、李、胡桃、杏、梨、籐蘿、松、柳，無不俱備。因此，我從小就對於樹存有偏愛。我嘗面對着樹生出許多非非之想，覺得樹雖不能言，不解語，可是它也有生老病死，它也有榮枯，它也曉得傳宗接代，它也應該算是「有情」。

樹的姿態各個不同。亭亭玉立者有之，矮墩墩的有之，有張牙

and some are thick and stumpy. Some brandish their arms menacingly and some stoop like hunchbacks. Some bristle like warriors with swords and spears and some sway gently and rhythmically like dancers in the wind. Each has its own style. I imagine that a tree must be happy when it is caressed by warm breezes and starts leafing and budding. It must be proud when it is fully decked out in clusters of colorful blossoms that attract bees and butterflies. It might feel a little distressed to see its fallen petals lying on the ground in complete disorder. It must be a little saddened by the thought of old age when it is fully laden with fruit. Likewise, I imagine that a tree might feel a terrible itch when its trunk is crawling with ants and that it, too, may feel greatly annoyed by the cicadas that shriek loudly amid its twigs and foliage. In short, trees are living creatures, only they cannot walk; they remain where they have taken root and never experience the plight of displacement or exile.

When I was little, I heard many lectures by famous persons. One of the speakers was a sort of "military governor" or the like, who lectured on "the philosophy of human life". I remember only one thing from that lecture. "Plants," the speaker said, "have roots that extend downward. Beasts carry their heads on a level with their bodies. Human beings stand erect, with their heads on top." To my young mind, that sounded like an important discovery, perhaps even an entirely new theory of evolution. No wonder that man is the wisest of all creatures. Unlike human beings, trees stand upside down. A person carries his head on top, so "the pure *qi* (or life force) rises upward, while the turbid *qi* goes down." Eminent Buddhist monks either sit or stand when they meditate and refuse to lie down to sleep. When their ends come, they insist on dying in a sitting posture.

Many poets through the ages have refused to accept this view, however. They have not looked down upon trees at all. In his poem

舞爪者，有佝僂其背者，有戟劍森森者，有搖曳生姿者，各極其致。我想樹沐浴在熏風之中，抽芽放蕊，它必有一番愉快的心情。等到花簇簇，錦簇簇，滿枝頭紅紅綠綠的時候，招蜂引蝶，自又有一番得意。落英繽紛的時候可能有一點傷感，結實纍纍的時候又會有一點遲暮之思。我又揣想，螞蟻在樹幹上爬，可能會覺得癢癢出溜的；蟬在枝葉間高歌，也可能會覺得聒噪不堪。總之，樹是活的，只是不會走路，根扎在那裏便住在那裏，永遠沒有顛沛流離之苦。

小時候聽「名人演講」，有一次是一位什麼「都督」之類的角色講演「人生哲學」，我只記得其中一點點，他說：「植物的根是向下伸，獸畜的頭是和身軀平的，人是立起來的，他的頭是在最上端。」我當時覺得這是一大發現，也許是生物進化論的又一嶄新的說法。怪不得人為萬物之靈，原來他和樹比較起來是本末倒置的。人的頭高高在上，所以「清氣上昇，濁氣下降」。有道行的人，有坐禪，有立禪，不肯倒頭大睡，最後還要講究坐化。

可是歷來有不少詩人並不這樣想，他們一點也不鄙視樹。美國的佛洛斯特有一首詩，名〈我的窗前樹〉，他說他看出樹與人早晚是

entitled "Tree at My Window", Robert Frost says: he can see that the tree and he himself would sooner or later meet the same fate and fall down; the only difference is—the tree's head is concerned with outer, while the poet's is concerned with inner, weather. Another poet named Joyce Kilmer has written a famous poem called "Trees". Some critics have referred to the poem as doggerel, but I do not think it is that bad. On the contrary, the final lines ("Poems are made by fools like me, / But only God can make a tree.") make a rather good point. People prattle about their creative power but have yet to achieve anything that is really outstanding. Can people create a tree? Trees, no less than human beings, are God's creation. During a recent trip to the Ali Mountains,[72] I saw the so-called "sacred tree", a Chinese cypress growing by the roadside and believed to be some three-thousand years old. The tree has indeed reached a venerable age, but that is insignificant when compared to the ancient Chinese toon mentioned by Chuangtzu, which "had eight-thousand years for spring and another eight-thousand years for autumn." The tree I saw appeared as withered as a shriveled carcass, and there was nothing sacred about it. I consider it a myth that a dead tree can revive and bloom again. I cannot help being saddened by the thought: "As are trees, so are human beings, only worse."

What I saw on the Ali Mountains were wide expanses of densely grown primeval forests, nothing but towering trees with green, luxuriant foliage, quite different in bearing from all the trees I had seen elsewhere. The cypresses around the parks and temples in Beijing, as well as the so-called General Zhang's cypresses[73] that line the road to Zitong in Sichuan and form what is known as "the blue clouds vista"

---

72 The highest mountain range in central Taiwan.
73 These trees are fabled to have been planted by Zhang Fei, a third-century general whose troops were stationed in the area.

同一命運的，都要倒下去，只有一點不同，樹擔心的是外在的險厄，人煩慮的是內心的風波。又有一位詩人名Kilmer，他有一首著名的小詩——〈樹〉，有人批評說那首詩是「壞詩」，我倒不覺得怎樣壞，相反的，「詩是像我這樣的傻瓜做的，只有上帝才能造出一棵樹」，這兩行詩頗有一點意思。人沒有什麼了不起，侈言創造，你能造出一棵樹來麼？樹和人，都是上帝的創造。最近我到阿里山去遊玩，路邊見到那株「神木」，據說有三千年了，比起莊子所說的「以八千歲為春，以八千歲為秋」的上古大椿還差一大截子，總算有一把年紀，可是看那一副形容枯槁的樣子，只是一具枯骸，何神之有！我不相信「枯樹生華」那一套。我只能生出「樹猶如此，人何以堪」的感想。

　　我看見阿里山上的原始森林，一片片，黑壓壓，全是參天大樹，鬱鬱葱葱。但與我從前在別處所見的樹木氣象不同。北平公園大廟裏的柏，以及梓橦道上的所謂張飛柏，號稱「翠雲廊」，都沒有

are not nearly as tall and straight. The "greeter pines" on the Huang Mountains[74] are worse. These pine trees, with their crooked trunks and twisted branches, are nothing but giant-sized bonsai. The trees on the Ali Mountains are predominantly Chinese cypresses, all of which are as straight as a ramrod and will make excellent telephone poles. Surely, they have no style to speak of, but they impart a feeling of wilderness and desolation that is unique to a primeval forest. For people who have been cooped up in the cities, a visit to such a virgin forest will allow them to catch some smell of "the noble savage" and set their minds free.

---

74 A mountain range in Anhui province, known for its natural beauty.

這裏的樹那麼直那麼高。像黃山的迎客松，屈鐵交柯，就更不用提，那簡直是放大了的盆景。這裏的樹大部分是檜木，全是筆直的，上好的電線桿子材料。姿態是談不到，可是自有一種榛莽未除入眼荒寒的原始山林的意境。局促在城市裏的人走到原始森林裏來，可以嗅到「高貴的野蠻人」的味道，令人精神上得到解放。

Reading Paintings

The poet Yuan Mei said in his *Suiyuan Shihua*:[75] "Artists have advocated the idea of reading paintings. I would say that what one can read is not a painting, but rather the poetry in it." This remark shows great insight. To read means to peruse, and perusal is only possible when it involves language and words. So how can one read a painting? Reading a painting must therefore mean perusing the poetry in the painting.

Poetry and painting are two distinct types that differ in object, medium, mode and other respects. But the confusion of types dates back to ancient times and the expression *Ut pictura poesis* ("As is a painting, so is a poem.") has long since become a famous dictum in art criticism. We Chinese have likewise spoken approvingly of the Tang poet-artist Wang Wei (a.k.a. Wang Mojie) in particular, claiming that "there is poetry in his paintings and paintings in his poetry." In the end, poetry and painting have their respective domains. When we read a poem, we can enjoy its description of scenery, which is said to be "as vivid as in a painting". But the highest ground of poetry lies elsewhere and its emphasis is on human perception and sentiment. Although what we call poetic sentiment, poetic charm and poetic

75 Yuan Mei (1716–1797) was a pre-eminent poet and literary critic. *Suiyuan Shihua* is a collection of his commentaries on poetry.

讀　畫

　　《隨園詩話》：「畫家有讀畫之說，余謂畫無可讀者，讀其詩也。」隨園老人這句話是有見地的。讀是讀誦之意，必有文章詞句然後方可讀誦，畫如何可讀？所以讀畫云者，應該是讀誦畫中之詩。

　　詩與畫是兩個類型，在對象、工具、手法、各方面均不相同。但是類型的混淆，古已有之。在西洋，所謂 *Ut pictura poesis*，「詩既如此，畫亦同然」，早已成為藝術批評上的一句名言。我們中國也特別稱道王摩詰的「畫中有詩，詩中有畫」。究竟詩與畫是各有領域的。我們讀一首詩，可以欣賞其中的景物的描寫，所謂「歷歷如繪」。但詩之極致究竟別有所在，其着重點在於人的概念與情感。所謂詩意、詩趣、詩境，雖然多少有些抽象，究竟是以語言文字來表

atmosphere are more or less abstractions, yet words and language remain the most appropriate medium for expressing them. When we look at a painting, we may enjoy the poetic charm that lies hidden in it, but not all paintings have poetic charm, and the principal function of a painting is the portrayal of an image or images. When we say we read a painting, we are in fact looking for poetry in that painting.

The smile of Mona Lisa was a beautiful, sweet and charming smile, but we cannot ask why she was smiling or what she was smiling at. Many people have tried to solve the riddle behind that smile, but it is much ado about nothing. Some people would have us believe that she was smiling because she had just found out that she was pregnant and that smile symbolized female pride and contentment. Others would ask, "How do you know that she was smiling because she had just found out she was pregnant? She might have been smiling because she had just found out that she was *not* pregnant." We will never get any wiser if we continue to read the painting in that manner. An insinuating smile can only be understood tacitly; it cannot be put into words. Paintings like the "Mona Lisa" may contain something mystical that lends itself to speculation. Other paintings, such as George Watts' "Hope" which portrays a woman straddling the earth and playing on a lute with a broken string, may possess some symbolic meanings to be discovered. But in "Las dos hermanas" by Joaquin Sorolla, what is there to read except the glaring sunlight? Also, in the "Child with a Broken Hat" by Thomas Sully, which depicts a child wearing a worn-out hat, what is there to read except the contrasting light and shade on that innocent and naive face? As for a still life by William Chase, it may show only two dead fish with upturned white bellies on a plate and may have even less to speak of.

Perhaps Chinese paintings provide a slightly greater measure of poetic sentiment. Chinese landscapes are given such captions as

達最為適宜。我們看一幅畫，可以欣賞其中所蘊藏的詩的情趣，但是並非所有的畫都有詩的情趣，而且畫的主要的功用是在描繪一個意象。我們説讀畫，實在是在畫裏尋詩。

「摩娜麗莎」的微笑，即是微笑，笑得美，笑得甜，笑得有味道，但是我們無法追問她為什麼笑，她笑的是什麼。儘管有許多人在猜這個微笑的謎，其實都是多此一舉。有人以為她是因為發現自己懷孕了而微笑，那微笑代表女性的驕傲與滿足。有人説：「怎見得她是因為發覺懷孕而微笑呢？也許她是因為發覺並未懷孕而微笑呢？」這樣的讀下去，是讀不出所以然來的。會心的微笑，只能心領神會，非文章詞句所能表達。像「摩娜麗莎」這樣的畫，還有一些奧秘的意味可供揣測，此外像Watts的「希望」，畫的是一個女人跨在地球上彈着一隻斷了絃的琴，也還有一點象徵的意思可資領會，但是Sorolla的「二姊妹」，除了耀眼的陽光之外還有什麼詩可讀？再如Sully的「戴破帽子的孩子」，畫的是一個孩子頭上頂着一個破帽子，除了那天真無邪的臉上的光線掩映之外還有什麼詩可讀？至於Chase的一幅「靜物」，可能只是兩條死魚翻着白肚子躺在盤上，更沒有什麼可説的了。

也許中國畫裏的詩意較多一點。畫山水不是「春山煙雨」，就是

"Spring Mountains in Misty Rain", or "Trees on a Riverbank in Mist", or "Journey through a Forest in Clouds", or "Boat Returning to Shore in Spring". A look at these captions will fill one's heart with poetic sentiment. This is particularly true with the works of writer-painters, who were completely out of step with their times and who revealed in their landscapes their yearning for a reclusive and transcendental existence. As a result, the poetic atmosphere embodied in such landscape paintings has come to mirror most perfectly the moral quality of Chinese artists. Even small-sized flower-and-plant paintings, such as the works of Li Futang and Xu Qingteng,[76] show a vibrant and unrestrained spirit.

Despite the fact that poetry already exists in paintings, certain Chinese artists have felt compelled to inscribe poems or verses on their works, lest their poetic sentiment be not sufficiently evident. Since the Song dynasty, this has become a familiar and widely accepted practice, even to the extent that sometimes a Chinese painting without an inscription in verse may appear incomplete. Chinese ideograms have their own artistic appeal and, if properly inscribed, may not be offensive to the sight. But this practice cannot be applied with equal success to Western-style paintings. It would be unthinkable to inscribe a poem on "The Gleaners" using a quill. The practice of adding poems and verses to a painting indicates at least that words are needed to express the poetic sentiment in that painting. A Chinese ink-wash painting, done in bold strokes and depicting two celery cabbages, demonstrates the artist's mastery of the ink-wash technique as evidenced by his skillful arrangement of various shades of black ink. But in one corner of that painting the artist added the following words:

---

76 Li Chan, alias Li Futang, was a seventeenth-century poet, painter and
    calligrapher. Xu Wei (1521–1593), alias Xu Qingteng, was a major artist and
    calligrapher of the Ming dynasty.

「江皋煙樹」，不是「雲林行旅」，就是「春浦帆歸」，只看畫題，就會覺得詩意盎然。尤其是文人畫家，一肚皮不合時宜，在山水畫中寄託了隱逸超俗的思想，所以山水畫的境界成了中國畫家人格之最完美的反映。即使是小幅的花卉，像李復堂徐青籐的作品，也有一股豪邁瀟灑之氣躍然紙上。

畫中已經有詩，有些畫家還怕詩意不夠明顯，在畫面上更題上或多或少的詩詞字句。自宋以後，這已成了大家所習慣接受的形式，有時候畫上無字反倒覺得缺點什麼。中國字本身有其藝術價值，若是題寫得當，也不難看。西洋畫無此便利，「拾穗人」上面若是用鵝翎管寫上一首詩，那就不堪設想。在畫上題詩，至少說明了一點，畫裏面的詩意有用文字表達的必要。一幅酣暢的潑墨畫，畫着有兩棵大白菜，墨色濃淡之間充分表示了畫家筆下控制水墨的技

"Indispensable for my palate; undesirable for my complexion."[77] As a result, the painting takes on an extra meaning. In addition to being a work of art, it has become an illustration of the artist's concept of moral values. A painting of a plum tree done in Chinese ink by Jin Dongxin[78] displays his lavish use of tortuous strokes in a way that suggests the great seal script in Chinese calligraphy in combination with thin, kinky lines resembling coiled wires. This technique gives the subject an air of aloofness that is suggestive of an emaciated but proud man. But nearly one half of the space in that painting is taken up by the following inscription: "Sitting by a bright window, I had to warm my fingers with my own breath before I could start painting these few sprays of a plum tree. Yet, it was better to spend my time this way than merely playing with cats and dogs..."[79] With these words, our attention is suddenly shifted from the twigs and buds on the painting to the poor but proud artist. A painting should be capable of expressing by itself what the artist wishes to express without recourse to words. Sometimes, the practice of adding an inscription to a painting makes it no longer purely a work of art.

In my opinion, one cannot comprehend the highest achievement of a painting by "reading" it. Reading is invariably associated with language and words and accomplished via a thinking process. On the other hand, the beauty and charm of a painting appeal directly and intuitively to the mind of its viewer. A painting gives the viewer a sort of mental enjoyment that is beyond words. He will miss the mark if he tries to put it into words.

---

77 This is a hint at "the famished looks of a vegetarian", which is based on the common belief that a pallid complexion usually results from a poor, meatless diet.

78 Literary name of Jin Nong (1687–1764), a famous painter of the Qing dynasty.

79 The cats and dogs here seem to allude to people of no account or boon companions.

巧，但是畫面的一角題了一行大字：「不可無此味，不可有此色」，這張畫的意味不同了，由純粹的畫變成了一幅具有道德價值的概念的插圖。金冬心的一幅墨梅，篆籀縱橫，密圈鐵線，清癯高傲之氣撲人眉宇，但是半幅之地題了這樣的詞句：「晴窗呵凍，寫寒梅數枝，勝似與貓兒狗兒盤桓也……」，頓使我們的注意力由斜枝細蕊轉移到那個清高的畫士。畫的本身應該能夠表現畫家所要表現的東西，不需另假文字為之說明，題畫的辦法有時使畫不復成為純粹的畫。

我想畫的最高境界不是可以讀得懂的，一說到讀便牽涉到文章詞句，便要透過思想的程序，而畫的美妙處在於透過視覺而直訴諸人的心靈。畫給人的一種心靈上的享受，不可言說，說便不着。

Walking Sticks

In ancient Greece there was a sphinx in Thebes, which would stop all passers-by, put a riddle to them and devour them when they could not give the correct answer. The riddle was: What animal walks first with four legs, then two legs and finally three legs, and the more legs it uses in walking, the weaker it will be? It seems that all ancient Greeks were inept at solving riddles and they had to wait until Oedipus came along and gave the right answer, thus causing the monster to kill itself. And the correct answer is man, as a child goes on all fours, an adult walks erect on two legs, and an old man can walk only with a staff, which functions as a third leg. A walking staff is therefore a symbol of old age.

Walking staffs have been in use in China from time immemorial. The *Book of Rites*[80] (in the chapter on the regulations of state) contains the following rules: "A quinquagenarian may walk with a staff at home. A sexagenarian may do so within his village. A septuagenarian may do so within his state. An octogenarian may do so at the king's court. In the case of a nonagenarian, the king should visit him at his house, bringing along delicacies, in order to seek his advice." In ancient times, people began to weaken physically at fifty. Only when they

---

80 See footnote 70.

手　杖

　　古希臘底比斯有一個女首獅身的怪物，攔阻過路行人說謎語，猜不出的便要被吃掉，謎語是：「什麼東西走路用四條腿，用兩條腿，用三條腿，走路時腿越多越軟弱？」古希臘的人好像是都不善猜謎，要等到埃迪帕斯纔揭開謎底，使得那怪物自殺而死。謎底是：「人。」嬰兒滿地爬，用四條腿，長大成了兩腿豎立，等到年老杖而能行，豈不是三條腿了麼？一根杖是老年人的標記。

　　杖這種東西，我們古已有之。《禮記·王制》：「五十杖於家，六十杖於鄉，七十杖於國，八十杖於朝，九十者，天子欲有問焉，則就其室，以珍從。」古人五十始衰，所以到了五十纔可以用杖，未五

had reached that age were they allowed to use walking staffs, and not a day sooner. I have seen many an elderly person whose body has a permanent stoop, as if constantly bowing, which makes him or her look very much like a question mark (?). Without the staff, he or she would certainly lose balance.

Walking staffs are intended to lend support to the old or the weak, but they have also become an ornamental accessory. The following incident is recorded in The *Book of Rites* (in the chapter entitled "Tan Gong"): "Confucius rose early for a promenade outside the gate. He walked with his hands folded behind his back and his staff trailing on the ground." On that occasion, his staff obviously did not fulfill the function of "giving support to the old or the weak", but helped to portray vividly the leisurely manners of the sage. Chinese landscape paintings may show mountains totally devoid of human figures. If there are human figures, they are most likely to be elderly persons equipped with walking staffs, either trudging along a footpath or pausing for a view of the mountains. It would be impossible to make them look antiquated without those walking staffs. If a human figure in a painting is not antiquated, the landscape is bound to lose much of its charm. Du Fu[81] laments in a poem: "I am over fifty now; my life without success; / Tomorrow, with a staff, I will go to watch the clouds." The poet was full of grievances, and on the eve of a trip to the hills to watch the clouds, he reminded himself to bring along his staff, which was made from the stem of goosefoot. Even more notorious is the story of Ruan Xiu, who led a carefree, bohemian life during the Jin dynasty. He would tie his purse to the top of his walking staff when he went to a cantina to get himself drunk. In this way, he made his walking staff perform an additional function.

---

81 Du Fu (712–770), formerly spelled Tu Fu, is generally considered the greatest Chinese poet.

十者不得執也。我看見過不止一位老者，經常佝僂着身子，鞠躬如也，真像是一個疑問符號（？）的樣子，若不是手裏拄着一根杖，必定會失去重心。

杖所以扶衰弱，但是也成了風雅的一種裝飾品，「孔子蚤作，負手曳杖，逍遙於門」，《禮記・檀弓》明明有此記載，手負在背後，杖拖在地上，顯然這杖沒有發生扶衰濟弱的作用，但是把逍遙的神情烘托得躍然紙上。我們中國的山水畫可以空山不見人，如果有人，多半也是扶着一根拐杖的老者，或者行道上，或是佇立看山，若沒有那一根杖便無法形容其老，人不老，山水都要減色。杜甫詩：「年過半百不稱意，明日看雲還杖藜。」這位杜陵野老滿腹牢騷，準備明天上山看雲的時候也沒有忘記帶一根藜杖。豁達恣放的阮脩就更不必說，他把錢掛在杖頭上到酒店去酣飲，那杖的用途更是推而廣之的了。

In the olden days, whether in China or elsewhere, a walking staff came to about a person's height or slightly longer. What we Chinese call a *guaizhang* used to have a Y-shaped top that resembled a goat's head with horns. For that reason, it was also called a *yangzhang* (goat staff). When using the staff for support, one would place his grip somewhere above its mid-point. The same applied to a *khakkara* (a crosier-like metal staff) carried by a *bhiksu* (Buddhist mendicant monk) and equipped with metal rings, which jangled when shaken. Formerly, a European pilgrim on his way to visit the Holy Land in Jerusalem could not do without a giant scallop shell used as a hat and a walking staff, also of considerable length. The walking stick we see today is rather a short rod, which a person can hold under his arm when he walks, or use to draw a circle in the air or tap the ground, or hang on his forearm by its hook. It is a modern product of the West. When it was first introduced into China, it was called *si-ti-ke* (stick) for lack of a better name in Chinese. A walking stick lacks the elegance of a walking staff, but it is the only proper accessory for a man wearing a Western-style suit and a pair of leather shoes.

The best walking staffs were made of bamboo. In his *Book on Bamboo*, Dai Kaizhi[82] points out that "as material for walking staffs, there is no better bamboo than that grown in Qiongzhou (an area in Sichuan), whose unusual, knotty appearance resembles artwork." But good bamboo walking staffs are not limited to those produced in Sichuan. A staff should be regarded as of top quality as long as it is hard and straight, smooth and lustrous. In his "Homecoming Song", Tao Yuanming[83] looked forward to the innocent pleasure of "sauntering aimlessly with a *fulao*". And *fulao* (literally, "support for old age") is another name for walking staff. The advantage of a bamboo walking

---

82 A scholar of the Jin dynasty (265–411).

83 See foot note 19.

從前的杖，無分中外，都有一人來高。我們中國的所謂「拐杖」，杖首如羊角，所以亦稱丫杖，手扶的時候只能握在杖的中上部分。就是乞食僧所用「振時作錫錫聲」的所謂「錫杖」也是如此。從前歐洲人到耶路撒冷去拜謁聖地的香客，少不得一頂海扇壳帽，一根拐杖，那杖也是很長的。我們現在所見的手杖，短短一橛，走起路來可以夾在腋下，可以在半空中劃圓圈，可以滴滴嘟嘟的點地作響，也可以把杖的彎頸掛在臂上，這乃是近代西洋產品，初入中土的時候，無以名之，名之為「斯提克」。「斯提克」並不及拐杖之雅，不過西裝革履也只好配以斯提克。

杖以竹製為上品，戴凱之《竹譜》云：「竹之堪杖，莫尚於筇，礛䃴不凡，狀若人工。」筇杖不必一定要是四川出品，凡是堅實直挺而色澤滑潤者皆是上選。陶淵明〈歸去來辭〉所謂「策扶老以流憩」，「扶老」即是筇杖的別稱。筇杖妙在微有彈性，扶上去顫巍巍的，好像是扶在小丫鬟的肩膀上。重量輕當然也是優點。葛藤作杖

stick lies in its resilience. When you lean on it, it will yield slightly, making you feel as if you are leaning on the shoulder of a young maid. Of course, its lightness is also a plus. For the same reason, the kudzu vine also makes excellent walking sticks. Those made from the heartwood of the Chinese cypress that grows on the Ali Mountains[84] look quite nice despite their knotty appearance, but they feel too light in the hand and produce too crisp a sound when they hit the ground. Other walking sticks, whether made of wood or metal, I seldom find to my liking. But the worst ones are those made glossy with lacquer, or garish with mother-of-pearl inlay.

I love walking sticks. I was barely thirty years old when I first arrived in Qingdao. My friends there all carried walking sticks, and the sight of them was enough to make my heart stir. I enjoyed using a stick to walk up or down slopes, and this eventually became a habit, to the extent that every time I left home, I never forgot to bring along my walking stick. I needed it to traverse difficult paths and repel dogs. I did not have the heart to throw away a walking stick no matter how old or worn it might have become, nor did I envy anybody else for his walking stick. Now I have passed the age required for using a walking staff in the village and may, with a staff and even a *patra* (alms-bowl), take a leisurely walk in front of the city gate in the manner of Confucius. The walking staff owned by King Wu of the Zhou dynasty[85] bore the following inscription: "Alas! Anger leads one into danger; desire leads one astray from the right course; wealth and power cause friends to forget each other." I have no need for such an inscription. My walking stick bears only stains of dust from the road and dew from the grass.

---

84 See footnote 72.

85 King Wu (1122–1115 B.C.) was considered by Confucius as one of the best models for a ruler.

亦佳，也是基於同樣的理由。阿里山的檜木心所製杖，疙瘩嚕囌的
樣子並不難看，只是拿在手裏輕飄飄，碰在地上聲音太脆。其他木
製的，鐵製的都難有令人滿意的。而最惡劣的莫過於油漆賊亮，甚
而至於嵌上螺鈿，斑斕燿目。

我愛手杖。我纔三十歲的時候，初到青島，朋友們都是人手一
杖，我亦見獵心喜。出門上下山坡，扶杖別有風趣，久之養成習
慣，一起身便不能忘記手仗。行險路時要用它，打狗也要用它。一
根手杖無論多麼敝舊亦不忍輕易棄置，而且我也從不羨慕別人的手
杖。如今，我已經過了杖鄉之年，一杖一鉢，正堪效法孔子之逍遙
於門。武王杖銘曰：「惡乎危於忿懥，惡乎失道於嗜慾，惡乎相忘於
富貴！」我不需要這樣的銘，我的杖上只沾有路上的塵土和草葉上的
露珠。

Toothpicks

In the preface to his novel *The Legend of the Water Margin*,[86] Shi Nai'an described one of his daily routines as "eating dishes of food, then chewing an osier stick". What he called "chewing an osier stick" actually means using a toothpick to clean his teeth after a meal. An eminent monk of the Jin dynasty named Faxian went to the "Western Regions"[87] to seek the truth (*dharma*). In his *Journey to the Land of the Buddha*, he related that "the Buddha once chewed an osier twig at a place on the eastern side of the road leading to the southern gate of the state of Satya. Then he stuck the twig into the ground, whereupon it started to grow..." The word "chewing" used here should be understood as a mistranslation of the word "whittling". The expression "chewing an osier twig" certainly did not mean literally to put a twig in one's mouth and nibble on it. While it is quite all right to chew a betel nut after a meal, no one will chew a piece of wood after satisfying his hunger. This expression was borrowed incorrectly from the story of the Buddha and actually meant cleaning the teeth with a toothpick. The use of an

---

86 See footnote 38.

87 The term *xiyu* or "Western Regions", first used in the Han dynasty, loosely applied to the vast areas west of China, including what are now India, Iran and Asia Minor. In a narrower sense, it referred to regions west of the Gate of Yumen in Gansu province, including what is now Xinjiang and parts of Central Asia.

牙　籤

　　施耐庵《水滸》序有「進盤殽，嚼楊木」一語，所謂「嚼楊木」就是飯後用牙籤剔牙的意思。晉高僧法顯求法西域，著《佛國記》，有云：「沙祇國南門道東佛在此嚼楊枝，刺土中即生……」這個「嚼」字當作「削」解。「嚼楊木」當然不是把一根楊木放在嘴裏咀嚼。飯後嚼一塊檳榔還可以，誰也不會吃飽了之後嚼木頭。「嚼楊木」是借用「嚼楊枝」語，謂取一根牙籤剔牙。楊枝淨齒是西域風俗，所以在中文裏也借用佛書上的名詞。《隋書‧真臘傳》：「每旦澡洗，以楊枝淨齒，

osier stick to clean the teeth was a custom in the "Western Regions" and this expression was borrowed originally from some Buddhist text. The *History of the Sui Dynasty* (in the chapter on the people of Chenla[88]) contains the following passage: "They take a bath each morning, clean their teeth with osier sticks, then read aloud the sutras and spells. They bathe again before each meal, pick their teeth again with osier sticks after the meal and continue to read the sutras and spells." One can see from this account that it was an established practice among the people of Chenla to pick their teeth with osier sticks both before reading the sutras and after eating a meal.

Out of curiosity I looked up this expression in the English translation of *Shuihu Zhuan* by Pearl S. Buck.[89] I found that she had rendered this point in a rather peculiar way: "Take food, chew a bit of this or that." Measured by the criteria of accuracy, readability and elegance, this is obviously an unfaithful translation.

When a piece of meat, a bone or any food particle gets stuck between two teeth, it is our nature and instinct to want to remove it, and we cannot be happy until it is gone. I do not understand why such a teeth-cleaning device had to wait until the mid-fifth century to be invented in the "Western Regions" and then introduced into China. We Chinese, who invented the compass, gunpowder and the art of printing, were unable to conceive the idea of cleaning the teeth with a toothpick.

People in the West began to use toothpicks at a much later date. In the late sixteenth century, people in England still regarded a toothpick as a novelty, and only a well-traveled fop would hold a toothpick

---

88 Chenla was a Cambodian state which flourished from the sixth to the eighth centuries.

89 The title given to this translation is *All Men Are Brothers*.

讀誦經咒。又澡灑乃食,食罷,還用楊枝淨齒,又讀經咒。」可見他
們的規矩在唸經前和食後都要楊枝淨齒。

為了好奇,翻閱賽珍珠女士譯的《水滸傳》,她的這一句的譯文
甚為奇特:"Take food, chew a bit of this or that." 我們若是把這句
譯文還原,便成了「進食,嚼一點這個又嚼一點那個。」衡以信達雅
之義,顯然不信。

牙縫裏塞上一絲肉,一根刺,或任何殘膏膩馥,我們都會自動
的本能的思除之而後快。我不了解為什麼這淨齒的工具須要等到五
世紀中由西域發明然後才得傳入中土。我們發明了羅盤火藥印刷
術,沒能發明用牙籤剔牙!

西洋人使用牙籤更是晚近的事。英國到了十六世紀末年還把牙
籤當做一件希奇的東西,只有在海外遊歷過的花花大少纔口裏銜着

in his mouth and swagger around in the street, causing passers-by to raise their eyebrows. Toothpicks were probably introduced into England via Italy, where their origin has been traced back to Asia. Presumably some traders had traveled from Venice to the Near East or even the Far East and brought these teeth-cleaning tools back to Europe. The following line appears in Shakespeare's *Much Ado about Nothing*: "I will fetch you a toothpicker now from the furthest inch of Asia." He mentions toothpicks again in three or four other plays as the mark of a traveler. Sir Thomas Overbury, an essayist famous for his "characters", was a contemporary of Shakespeare. In a character sketch called "The Traveler", he observes that "his [the traveler's] toothpick is a major trait of him." From this we can see that three hundred years ago ordinary people in Europe did not pick their teeth. It was not considered a problem when all the crevices between the teeth were filled to capacity with food residue. On the other hand, people who picked their teeth after meals were frowned upon as affected and conceited.

Older people in China often speak of themselves with great humility, saying that they are "like horses that grow only in the number of teeth."[90] In reality, human beings compare unfavorably with horses. When people reach a certain age, their teeth become loose and are eventually lost. At least, gaps begin to appear between the teeth, causing them to look like a bad hand of mahjong that is made up of such incomplete suits as 1, 3, 5 or 2, 4, 6, with many missing pieces in between. That is the time of life when toothpicks become indispensable. Some toothpicks are made of ivory or silver; some have sharp points, flat bodies or even hooks. All these may look good, but are useless. The most common toothpicks are made from bamboo, hard and sharp, brittle and harmful to the gum. Of all the toothpicks I have

---

90 That is, rather than in learning and wisdom.

一根牙籤招搖過市，行人為之側目。大概牙籤是從意大利傳入英國的，而追究根源，又是從亞洲傳到意大利的，想來是貿易商人由威尼斯到近東以至遠東把這淨齒之具帶到歐洲。莎士比亞的《無事自擾》有這樣的句子：「我願從亞洲之最遠的地帶給你取一根牙籤。」此外在其他三四齣戲裏也都提到牙籤，認為那是「旅行家」的標記。以描述人物著名的散文家Overbury，也是莎士比亞同時代的人，在他的一篇〈旅行家〉裏也說：「他的牙籤乃是他的一項主要的特點。」可見三百年前西洋的平常人是不剔牙的。藏垢納污到了飽和點之後也就不成問題。倒是飯後在齒頰之間橫剔豎抉的人，顯着矯揉造作，自命不凡！

　　人自謙年長曰馬齒徒增，其實人不如馬，人到了年紀便要齒牙搖落，至少也是齒牙之間發生罅隙，有如一把爛牌，不是一三五，就是二四六，中間儘是嵌張！這時節便需要牙籤，有象牙質的，有銀質的，有尖的，有扁的，還有帶彎鈎的，都中看不中用。普通的是竹質的，質堅而銳，易折，易傷牙齦。我個人經驗中所使用過

used in my life, the best were those reserved for the private dining rooms at the Zhimeizhai Restaurant in Beijing. It was an established practice in the restaurant business in Beijing that, at the end of a party, a dish of betel nuts was routinely served, with a bunch of toothpicks placed on the side. Both were paid for by the waiter out of his own pocket and had nothing to do with the management. Those toothpicks were specially designed for that restaurant and were distinguishable by a number of characteristics. The first was their length, about that of a fountain pen, which enabled them to be held in the same manner as one would hold a Chinese writing brush, and to reach even the innermost crevices of the mouth. The second characteristic was their flexibility, because they were made from the best willow wands. These toothpicks, being tough and yet pliant, could be flexed to get into all the nooks and crannies. Taiwan also produces a kind of toothpick that is made of white willow wood, but it is a pity they are not long enough or sharp enough. I really miss the toothpicks of Zhimeizhai, and especially Mr. Chu Renyi. Mr. Chu had worked his way up from waiter to become eventually the general manager of that restaurant (and he used to give me a large bunch of such toothpicks free).

There are things that everybody does but that should not be done openly in the presence of other people. Of course, this rule varies according to the customs and practices of different countries. For example, tooth-picking is an ungraceful act, in which a person holds his blood-red mouth wide open and, with his eyebrows knitted and his eyelids contorted, proceeds to dig, scratch, pick and delve the periodontal crevices, creating a sight that is offensive to the eye of the beholder. Even if he cups his hand over his mouth while doing this, he cannot reduce much of his ugliness because, as the saying goes, "the more one tries to hide, the more one is exposed." If a person walks proudly in public while holding a toothpick between his lips even after he has done the picking, we can only marvel at his silliness.

的牙籤最理想的莫過於從前北平致美齋路西雅座所預備的那種牙籤。北平飯館的規矩，飯後照例有一碟檳榔荳蔻，外帶牙籤，這是由堂倌預備的，與櫃上無涉。致美齋的牙籤是特製的，其特點第一是長，約有自來水筆那樣長，拿在手中可以擺出搦毛筆管的姿勢，在口腔裏到處探鑽無遠弗屆，第二是質韌，是真正最好的楊柳枝作的，拐彎抹角的地方都可以照顧得到，有剛柔相濟之妙。現在台灣也有一種白柳木的牙籤，但嫌其不夠長，頭上不夠尖。如今想起致美齋的牙籤，尤其想起當初在致美齋作堂倌後來作了大掌櫃的初仁義先生 (他常常送一大包牙籤給我)，不勝惆悵！

有些事是人人都作的，但不可當着人的面前公然作之。這當然也是要看各國的風俗習慣。例如牙籤的使用，其狀不雅，裂着血盆大口，獰眉皺眼，擿之，摳之，攢之，抉之，使旁觀的人不快。縱然手搭涼棚放在嘴邊，仍是欲蓋彌張，減少不了多少醜態。至於已經剔牙竣事而仍然叼着一根牙籤昂然邁步於大庭廣眾之間者，我們只能佩服他的天真。

Sleep

Sleep is undeniably an important part of a person's life, since we normally sleep eight hours a day, which accounts for one-third of a day's time, and that means a third of our lifetime is spent "on a pillow in deep and sweet slumber". Yet sleep is something one does as naturally as eating and sex and apparently requires no careful preparation. When a person is physically tired, he has only to rest his head on a pillow and close his eyes in order to be transported to the realm of Morpheus.

We take inspiration from the legend of a heroic warrior[91] who would "rise on hearing the cock's crow at midnight to practice swordsmanship." But we also take delight in the story of Chen Xiyi,[92] who lived in the era of the Five Dynasties and chose sleep as a form of reclusive living. Tradition has it that "his naps lasted for months and his sleeps lasted for years at a time", yet no one ever suspected him of suffering from sleeping sickness. But no ordinary person is capable of such long periods of sleep. Our traditional values tend to discourage people from setting aside too much time for sleep. Long, long ago, a student who slept in the daytime was branded by Confucius as uneducable. Because of this, we who live in a subtropical zone

---

91 An allusion to Zu Ti (266–321), a general in the Jin dynasty.
92 Literary name of Chen Tuan (?–989), a Taoist mystic and recluse.

睡

　　我們每天睡眠八小時，便佔去一天的三分之一，一生之中三分之一的時間於「一枕黑甜」之中度過，睡不能不算是人生一件大事。可是人在筋骨疲勞之後，眼皮一垂，枕中自有乾坤，其事乃如食色一般的自然，好像是不需措意。

　　豪傑之士有「聞午夜荒雞起舞」者，說起來令人神往，但是五代時之陳希夷，居然隱於睡，據說「小則亙月，大則幾年，方一覺」，沒有人疑其為有睡病，而且傳為美談。這樣的大量睡眠，非常人之所能。我們的傳統的看法，大抵是不鼓勵人多睡覺。晝寢的人早已被孔老夫子斥為不可造就。使得我們居住在亞熱帶的人午後小憩（西

cannot take an afternoon nap (known to the Spaniards as *siesta*) without feeling a little ashamed. In the Late Han dynasty, a schoolmaster named Bian Xiaoxian, who fell asleep in class, was ridiculed by his pupils in a song: "Bian Xiaoxian / Has a big tummy. / He reads no book / And is always sleepy." In the *Commandments for the Laity*, the Buddha particularly singles out "fondness for sleep" as an obstacle in the pursuit of *paramitas*.[93] It is very easy indeed for a person to hit the sack and fall asleep and stay in bed long after sunrise. It is harder for him to push away his blanket as soon as he wakes up, jump out of the soft, warm bed and get on his feet, at least physically.

Nevertheless, one always needs a proper amount of sleep. In my opinion, the lack of sleep is the greater of two evils. There is a saying: "Sleep is the second course of nature", that is, the main or most sumptuous course provided for us by nature. All our physical and mental fatigue is completely purged in this process of quasi-death. Traffic accidents are often caused by drivers who fall asleep at the wheel. Some employees at government offices look ghastly pale, arrogant and rude and this, too, is often attributable to a lack of sleep, which can cause dizziness or headaches and an enormous volume of pent-up steam. In such a condition, how can they manage to light up their faces with a radiant smile, which only a human being is capable of doing? To those in powerful positions, sleep should be a matter of even greater concern. Only God knows what disastrous mistakes they are capable of making after a sleepless night.

Sleep is a part of nature's plan for us, yet sometimes we are unable to enjoy it. Yang Zhen[94] was celebrated for his incorruptibility. He once

---

93 The Sanskrit term *paramitas* denotes the six necessary requirements for achieving nirvana: charity, moral conduct, patience, energy (or devotion), contemplation and knowledge.

94 Yang Zhen (A.D. ?–124) was a man of great integrity in the Late Han dynasty. He was the governor of Jingzhou at the time of the incident.

班牙人所謂siesta）時內心不免慚愧。後漢時有一位邊孝先，也是為了睡覺受他的弟子們的嘲笑，「邊孝先，腹便便，懶讀書，但欲眠。」佛說在家戒法，特別指出「貪睡眠樂」為「精進波羅密」之一障。大蓋倒頭便睡，等着太陽曬屁股，其事甚易，而掀起被衾，跳出頓煖，至少在肉體上作「頂天立地」狀，其事較難。

其實睡眠還是需要適量。我看倒是睡眠不足為害較大。「睡眠是自然的第二道菜」，亦即最豐盛的主菜之謂。多少身心的疲憊都在一陣「裝死」之中滌除淨盡。車禍的發生時常因為駕車的人在打瞌睡。衙門機構一些人員之一張鐵青的臉，傲氣凌人，也往往是由於睡眠不足，頭昏腦漲，一肚皮的怨氣無處發洩，如何能在臉上綻出人類所特有的笑容？至於在高位者，他們的睡眠更為重要，一夜失眠，不知要造成多少紕漏。

睡眠是自然的安排，而我們往往不能享受。以「天知地知我知子知」聞名的楊震，我想他睡覺沒有困難，至少不會失眠，因為他光明

told a lobbyist that the bribe the lobbyist offered him was not a secret, but rather a criminal act "known to heaven and earth as well as to you and me." I believe that he, with his honesty and integrity, would have had no difficulty in falling asleep. At least he would not have suffered from insomnia. A person, whose mind is troubled by fears, worries or desires, will toss and turn in bed. Such a person will not be able to close his eyes, whether in life or in death. Chuangtzu said, "Sages have no dreams." And, according to the *Surangama sutra*, "when vain hopes are eliminated, sleeping and waking will always be the same." Both authors affirm that a person with a peaceful mind naturally enjoys deep and peaceful sleep. Those, who toil and moil, leading a simple life and working from sunrise to sunset, are not likely to be troubled with insomnia. I have heard about many folk remedies for insomnia, which would have victims of this sleep disorder count numbers or draw human profiles in their minds. These suggestions all have the same purpose: suppress the vain desires of an insomniac and put everything out of his mind, but I wonder how well such treatments work. Insomnia creates anxiety and anxiety feeds insomnia, thus creating a vicious circle, which makes it impossible for a person to get a wink of sleep, and soon comes daybreak before he realizes.

One cannot sleep properly without a bed. The ancients sat and slept on mats spread on the floor. I had an experience of sleeping on a *tatami* floor and did not find it to my liking. The earthen or brick *kang* used as a bed by people in northern China, which is a later invention, is slightly better than a floor. Modern beds are indeed a great improvement. Beds should be large rather than small. What is called a double bed today, which is only four to five feet wide, has barely enough room for one sleeper to toss about in, let alone two passionate lovers between the sheets.

磊落。心有恐懼，心有罣礙，心有忮求，倒下去只好輾轉反側，人尚未死而已先不能瞑目。莊子所謂「至人無夢」，《楞嚴經》所謂「夢想消滅，寢寐恆一」，都是說心裏本來平安，睡時也自然塌實。勞苦分子，生活簡單，日入而息，日出而作，不容易失眠。聽說有許多治療失眠的偏方，或教人計算數目字，或教人想像中描繪人體輪廓，其用意無非是要人收斂他的顛倒妄想，忘懷一切，但不知有多少實效。愈失眠愈焦急，愈焦急愈失眠，惡性循環，只好瞪着大眼睛，不覺東方之既白。

睡眠不能無牀。古人席地而坐臥，我由「榻榻米」體驗之，覺得不是滋味。後來北方的土炕磚炕，即較勝一籌。近代之牀，實為一大進步。牀宜大，不宜小。今之所謂雙人牀，闊不過四五尺，僅足供單人翻覆，還說什麼「被底鴛鴦」？

In *Twelfth Night*, Shakespeare mentions a huge bed in a hotel in Ware, England, which was seven feet six inches high, ten feet nine inches long, ten feet nine inches wide, had exquisite carvings on it and could sleep twelve persons. The size of that bed was indeed impressive, but the twelve sleepers so accommodated would hardly find themselves in an enviable situation, as they would closely resemble canned sardines. In terms of size, however, one would have to acknowledge the pre-eminence of many antique beds in China. My old home in Beijing had such an antique bed. This bed, manufactured in Hangzhou and equipped with a mattress made of woven bamboo strips, was over nine feet long, over six feet wide and over eight feet high, including its tester. With paneled walls on three sides and two drawers side by side at the bottom, it looked like a small cabin. The most delightful feature, however, was a board shelf built across the bed, which could hold books, teacups, desk lamps, and even an assortment of fresh and preserved fruits—all very helpful when I read in bed. Sleeping on a western-style spring bed gives one the feeling of lying on a pile of cotton, which may be all right in winter but is intolerably hot in summer. What is more, the way people in the West make their beds is not comfortable. It has the sleeper placed between two sheets and the sides of the blanket tucked under the mattress. When the sleeper turns in bed, his shoulders will be exposed. When he stretches his legs, the bed cover will hold down his toes. One of the eight commandments for Buddhists is: "Thou shalt not sit on a tall and large bed." This teaching runs counter to my ideal of a bed and I long for the huge bed in my old family home to this day.

Posture varies from sleeper to sleeper and it is neither possible nor necessary for any sleeper to maintain the "bow-like" posture all the time, as recommended by Taoists. The supine posture with the belly

莎士比亞《第十二夜》提到一張大床，英國Ware地方某旅舍有大牀，七尺六寸高，十尺九寸長，十尺九寸闊，雕刻甚工，可睡十二人云。尺寸足夠大了，但是睡上一打，其去沙丁魚也幾希，並不令人羨慕。講到規模，還是要推我們上國的衣冠文物。我家在北平既藏有一舊牀，杭州製，竹蔑為繃，寬九尺餘，深六尺餘，牀架高八尺，三面隔扇，下面左右牀櫃，儼然一間小屋，最可人處是牀裏橫放架板一條，圖書，蓋碗，桌燈，四乾四鮮，均可陳列其上，助我枕上之功。洋人的彈簧牀，睡上去如落在棉花堆裏，冬日猶可，夏日燠不可當。而且洋人的那種舖被的方法，將身體放在兩層被單之間，把毯子裏在牀墊之上，一翻身肩膀透風，一伸腿腳趾戳被，並不舒服。佛家的八戒，其中之一是「不坐高廣大牀」，和我的理想正好相反，我至今還想念我老家裏的那張高廣大牀。

睡覺的姿態人各不同，亦無長久保持「睡如弓」的姿態之可能與必要。王右軍那樣的東牀坦腹，不失為瀟灑。即使佝僂著，如死蚯

exposed, made famous by the scholarly Wang Xizhi,[95] may well be the sign of a free spirit. Even if a sleeper curls up like a dead earthworm, or lies prostrate like a toad, it is nobody else's business. The people of certain areas in northern China have the habit of sleeping in their birthday suits as if practicing nudism under the blanket, winter or summer, and there is nothing immoral about it. Only thunderous snoring is a most undesirable thing to do in sleep. Zhang Ruiyi, a writer during the Song dynasty, told an amusing story in his *Gui'er Ji* (or *A Collection of Stories Heard but Unconfirmed*). One day, when Liu Chuifan called upon a Taoist priest named Kou Chao, he was told by an acolyte that the priest was taking a nap. While waiting outside the bedroom, Liu heard the priest's snoring, which was loud but pleasing to the ear. "Mr. Kou," he observed, "makes music in his sleep, and this is the music of Huaxu."[96] This so-called "music of Huaxu" was first reported in a story about Chen Tuan.[97] According to *Xianfo Qizong* (or *Strange Stories about Taoist and Buddhist Immortals*): One day, when Chen Tuan was living on Mount Hua, someone came to visit him but found him sleeping. An extraordinary person, was sitting by the bed, listening to the recluse's snoring and writing it down with a brush.

---

95 Wang Xizhi (321–379), alias Wang Yishao, is the most celebrated Chinese calligrapher. The following story is recorded in *Shishuo Sinyu* (see footnote 44): "When Xijian, the Grand Tutor to the Crown Prince, was in Jingkou, he sent a servant to Prime Minster Wang Dao with a letter in which he revealed his intention to find a prospective son-in-law. The prime minister said to the messenger, 'Go to the east wing of my house and make your own choice.' The servant returned and said to the grand tutor, 'The young men in the Wang family are all very nice. When my mission became known, they all appeared on their best behavior. The only exception was a young man who remained in his bed with his belly exposed, as if he had not heard the news.' The grand tutor said, 'This is the right one.' Upon further inquiry he learned that the young man was the prime minister's son Yishao and married his daughter to him."

96 A legendary state in ancient China.

97 See footnote 92.

蚓，匍匐着，如癩蝦蟆，也不干誰底事。北方有些地方的人士，無論嚴寒酷暑，入睡時必脫得一絲不掛，在被窩之內實行天體運動，亦無傷風化。唯有鼾聲雷鳴，最使不得。宋張端義《貴耳集》載一條奇聞：「劉垂範往見羽士寇朝，其徒告以睡。劉坐寢外聞鼻鼾之聲，雄美可聽，曰：『寇先生睡有樂，乃華胥調。』」所謂「華胥調」見陳希夷故事，據《仙佛奇踪》，「陳摶居華山，有一客過訪，適值其睡，旁

Out of curiosity, the visitor asked the person what he was doing. The person said, "I am recording the primordial music of Huaxu being played by the master." I have never visited the kingdom of Huaxu and have not had the opportunity to enjoy its music. As for snoring, the only kind of music I can more or less identify it with is the "new jazz." There might be something in it that is actually "loud but pleasing to the ear." However, I still prefer to have people not making music in their sleep.

Sleep may also provide an escape from reality. Anyone who is tired of living but will not leave this world voluntarily, may as well turn his back, walk away from all things and, like an ostrich, bury his head in a pillow or his own elbows. As he drifts off, he can temporarily block out all the unpleasant things and hateful persons. Out of sight, out of mind. Chen Jiru, a writer in the Ming dynasty, recorded the following story in *Zhenzhu Chuan*[98]: Xu Guangpu, the prime minister, was fond of airing his opinions regarding state affairs, thereby incurring the hatred of a fellow courtier named Li Min and his partisans. In later years, Xu grew reticent and often dozed off at state meetings, thus earning for himself the sobriquet of "Snoozing Prime Minister". This person, who had risen to the position of prime minister but chose to keep quiet and doze off at meetings, was indeed a smart fellow who knew how to look after his own safety. In doing so, he took one step further than circumspection in actions and humility in words. And this does not seem to be a lost art in modern-day politics.

---

98 *Zhenzhu Chuan*, or *A Ship of Pearls*, is a collection of miscellaneous stories and anecdotes.

有一異人，聽其息聲，以墨筆記之。客怪而問之，其人曰：『此先生華胥調混沌譜也。』」華胥氏之國不曾遊過，華胥調當然亦無從欣賞，若以鼾聲而論，我所能辨識出來的譜調頂多是近於「爵士新聲」，其中可能真有「雄美可聽」者。不過睡還是以不奏樂為宜。

睡也可以是一種逃避現實的手段。在這個世界活得不耐煩而又不肯自行退休的人，大可以掉頭而去，高枕而眠，或竟曲肱而枕，眼前一黑，看不慣的事和看不入眼的人都可以暫時撇在一邊，像駝鳥一般，眼不見為淨。明陳繼儒《珍珠船》記載着：「徐光溥為相，喜論事，大為李旻等所嫉，光溥後不言，每聚議，但假寐而已，時號睡相。」一個做到首相地位的人，開會不說話，一味假寐，真是懂得明哲保身之道，比危行言遜還要更進一步。這種功夫現代似乎尚未失傳。

Trash

As long as man eats grains and other foodstuffs, he will produce excrement. If no waste is discharged, the body will not enjoy good health. A home operates in a similar manner. As long as it takes in various supplies to satisfy its daily needs, it will produce trash. One look at the volume and content of the trash produced by a home is usually enough to give us a rough idea of its social standing. This will tell us whether it belongs to the old gentry or the *nouveaux riches*; whether it is the home of a well-educated man or a small merchant; whether it is a typical Chinese family or a Westernized household. What goes in as supplies determines what comes out as refuse.

Trash disposal is a problem. The most simple and convenient way is to open your front door, look around to see that the coast is clear, empty your garbage can onto the street and close the door behind you. Out of sight, out of mind. It is no concern of yours if your garbage gets blown away amid clouds of dust. Actually some people make a practice of placing burnt-out perforated coal blocks[99] squarely in the middle of the street, their rationale being that, when crushed by

---

99 These cylindrical fuel blocks, made from a mixture of coal dust and clay, are normally eight inches high and six inches in diameter, with perpendicular perforations.

垃　圾

　　人吃五穀雜糧，就要排洩。渣滓不去，清虛不來。家庭也是一樣，有了開門七件事，就要產生垃圾。看一堆垃圾的體積之大小，品質之精麤，就可以約略看出其階級門第，是縉紳人家還是暴發戶，是書香人家還是買賣人，是忠厚人家還是假洋鬼子。吞納什麼樣的東西，不免即有什麼樣的排洩物。

　　如何處理垃圾，是一個問題。最簡便的方法是把大門打開，四顧無人，把一筐垃圾往街上一丟，然後把大門關起，眼不見心不煩。垃圾在黃塵滾滾之中隨風而去，不干我事。真有人把燒過的帶窟窿的煤球平平正正的擺在路上，他的理由是等車過來就會輾碎，

passing traffic, the remains of these coal blocks will nicely fill in the potholes in the pavement. Such "public-spirited" people are to be found everywhere. In fact, every street corner and every vacant lot are being used as garbage dumps. Since many people have chosen to relieve themselves at those spots, why can't people dump garbage there? Time and again, people in the streets also contribute to the production of trash by brashly and carelessly throwing away bits of chewed sugar cane, strips of water melon rind or pieces of orange peel. While ox cart drivers are required to clean up the droppings of their animals, it is a cause for regret that no one walks behind our fruit-munching *homo sapiens* in the street to clean up his litter.

There used to be a creek, or rather a ditch, near where I live. This creek was said to be a tributary of a certain canal. The stream that ran underneath the small bridge was once clear to the bottom and fit for swimming. But, after years of neglect, the creek became increasingly choked with silt. The waterway grew more and more narrow, and a multicolored scum was often seen floating on the surface. There was no reason to assume that any family in the neighborhood had not discovered it to be a convenient garbage dump. At dawn, pajama-clad housewives would be seen emptying their chamber pots into the creek, and unkempt and barefoot housemaids would pitch in the contents of their dustpans from the bank. There was a fine-looking gentleman who would empty his wastebasket into the creek and amuse himself by watching the sheets and envelopes drifting slowly down the stream. But the most "liberal-handed" people were construction workers who would dump big loads of debris on the banks, creating waterside landfills. Sometimes a wooden clog, half a rotten grapefruit, the bloated carcass of a cat, a dog, or a pig was spotted drifting down from upstream. Thanks to the intercession of a certain person of influence, this creek was eventually converted into an underground sewer topped by an asphalt road. Since then, the creek has lost its role as a

正好填上路面的坑窪，像這樣好心腸的人到處皆有。事實上每一個牆角，每一塊空地，都有人善加利用傾倒垃圾。多少人在此隨意便溺，難道不可以丟些垃圾？行路人等有時也幫着生產垃圾，一堆堆的甘蔗渣，一條條的西瓜皮，一塊塊的橘子皮，隨手拋來，瀟灑自如。可憐老牛拉車，路上遺矢，尚有人隨後剷除，而這些路上行人食用水果反倒沒有人跟着打掃！

　　我的住處附近有一條小河，也可以說是臭水溝，據說是什麼圳的一個支流，當年小橋流水，清可見底，可以游泳其中，年久失修，漸漸壅淤，水流愈來愈窄而且表面上常漂着五彩的浮渣。這是一個大好的傾倒垃圾之處，鄰近人家焉有不知之理。於是穿着條紋睡衣的主婦清早端着便壺往河裏傾注，蓬頭跣足的下女提着畚箕往河裏倒土，還有儀表堂堂的先生往裏面倒字紙簍，多少信箋信封都緩緩的漂流而去，那位先生顧而樂之。手面最大的要算是修繕房屋的人家把大批的灰泥磚瓦向河邊倒，形成了河埔新生地。有時還從上流漂來一隻木板鞋，半個爛文旦，死貓死狗死豬漲得鼓溜溜的！不知是受了哪一位大人先生的恩典，這一條臭水溝被改為地下水道，上面鋪了柏油路，從此這條水溝不復發生承受垃圾的作用，使

garbage dump, much to the chagrin of the inhabitants of the neighborhood.

Most homes in more highly developed areas are equipped with a garbage box placed just outside the front gate. Such a grayish rectangular concrete box, taking up the place traditionally reserved for a stone lion or mounting-block, looks quite ugly. The design of the box has been carefully thought out, and it has a door and a cover. But both the door and the cover will disappear before long, and the "treasure" in the box will be fully exposed to the public eye. In such a case, those neighbors whose homes are not so equipped begin to treat the exposed box as public property and come to take advantage of it, often loading it to the point of overflowing. As a result, any home that is equipped with a garbage box will soon have a stinking dump outside its front gate. Though made of reinforced concrete, these boxes will warp, crack, break, disintegrate and collapse after being hit a few times by passing traffic.

More ingenious builders will leave an opening at the foot of an enclosing wall and fit it up with an iron door that is secured with a padlock. A garbage box will be built behind that door for the exclusive use of the family. No trespassing, please! But even this is no guarantee. Very soon the padlock will be stolen, the ring on the door will be missing, finally the door will stay open, and the place will become a public garbage dump just the same.

Scavengers are people with the greatest interest in trash. Practitioners of this trade have a hard life, which requires them to get up early and go to bed late. They have to rake and comb each heap of trash to see if there are items to be salvaged. They collect things discarded by others, which they appropriate without sacrificing their honesty. After this raking and combing operation, however, the heap will never be the same, and the garbage will be scattered all over in such a mess that

得附近居民多麼不便！

在較為高度開發的區域，家門口多置垃圾箱。在應該有兩個石獅子或上馬磴的地方站立着一個四四方方的烏灰色的水泥箱子，那樣子也夠腌臢的。這箱子有門有蓋，設想週到，可是不久就會門蓋全飛，裏面的寶藏全部公開展覽。不設垃圾箱的左右高鄰大抵也都不分彼此惠然肯來，把一個垃圾箱經常弄得腦滿腸肥。結果是誰安設垃圾箱，誰家門口臭氣四溢。箱子雖說是鋼骨水泥做的，經汽車三撞五撞，也就由酥而裂而破而碎而垮。

有人獨出心裁，在牆根上留上一寶穴，裝以鐵門，門上加鎖，牆裏面砌垃圾箱，獨家專用，謝絕來賓。但是亦不可樂觀，不久那鎖先被人取走，隨後門上的扣環也不見了，終於是門戶洞開，左右高鄰仍然是以鄰為壑。

對垃圾最感興趣的是拾爛貨的人。這一行夙興夜寐，滿辛苦的，每一堆垃圾都要加上一番爬梳的功夫，看有沒有可以搶救出來的物資。人棄我取，而且取不傷廉。但是在那一爬一梳之下，原狀

one will be horrified to look at. For all the efforts to keep everything spic-and-span behind the gate, the outdoor scene remains a sorry sight.

The world has many problems that defy solution, and trash is perhaps one of them. I have heard that certain countries have garbage incineration facilities or are using chemicals that can eat garbage away without leaving a trace. This sounds like a tale from *The Arabian Nights*. The sight of the garbage outside my house often turns my thoughts to the so-called economic takeoff and progress that have become common topics of conversation among people high and low and in and outside of the government. Nothing under the sun is perfect. Is it not good to have a minor defect like this as a presage of future takeoff and progress? At the same time, it occurs to me that this problem is not limited to the trash outside the homes and that trash exists in each and every sector of society. What can we do about it?

不可恢復，堆變成了攤，狼藉滿地，慘不忍睹。家門以內儘管保持清潔，家門以外不堪聞問。

　　世界上有許多問題永久無法解決，垃圾可能是其中之一，聞說有些國家有火化垃圾的設備，或使用化學品蝕化垃圾於無形，聽來都像是《天方夜譚》的故事。我看了門口的垃圾，常常想到朝野上下異口同聲的所謂起飛，所謂進步，天下物無全美，留下一點缺陷，以為異日起飛進步的張本不亦甚善？同時我又想，難以處理的豈只是門前的垃圾，社會上各階層的垃圾滔滔皆是，又當如何處理？

Tourism

Once a foreign professor on vacation made a stopover in Taiwan. Before setting out, he had indirectly approached an acquaintance of mine to write me a letter, asking me to give him help. Conducting guided tours is not my avocation, but such a request from a friend could not be turned down. As my experience would demonstrate, the role of a "street interpreter" is by no means an easy one because this old professor and his wife wanted me to take them to visit a street known as Hagglers Alley. I hesitated for a moment because I did not know what street had arrogated to itself the honor of this appellation. A haggler is a person who bargains. Since this couple had never been to such a place, it was only natural that they would want to see it for themselves. In the Han dynasty there was an apothecary in Chang'an named Han Kang, who offered his wares at fixed, non-negotiable prices.[100] Because of his honesty, his name has gone down in history and his story has come down to us as an example of virtue. The professor would have made me feel prouder if he had spoken to me about this legend. But, on second thought, I realized that Han Kang had been an exceptional person, and that such persons had been few and far between in our history and were even harder to find nowadays. The fact that one particular street had come to be called

---

100 For the story of Han Kang, see also the article entitled "Hagglers" in this book.

觀　光

　　一位外國教授休假旅行，道出台灣，事前輾轉託人來信要我予以照料，導遊非我副業，但情不可卻。事實證明「馬路翻譯」亦不易為，因為這一對老夫婦要我帶他們到一條名為Hagglers Alley的地方去觀光一番，我當時就躊躇起來，不知是哪一條街能有獨享這樣的一個名稱的光榮。所謂haggler，就是「討價還價的人」。他們沒有見過這種場面，想見識一下，亦人情之常。我們在漢朝就有一位韓康，賣藥長安，言不二價，名列青史，傳為美談。他若是和我談起這段故事，我當然會比較的覺得面上有光，我再一想，韓康是一位逸士，在歷史上並不多見，到如今當然更難找到。不提他也罷。一

Hagglers Alley might be sufficient proof that no haggling was practiced in any other street. This reasoning could do much toward saving our national face. All right, I would take them for a turn in the downtown area. The visitors noticed my hesitation and took out a traveler's guide from a suitcase and showed me the relevant page. To my surprise, Hagglers Alley was listed there as one of the eight major attractions in Taipei. Fortunately the booklet did not give the Chinese name of that street, nor did it say where it was located. In fact, the exciting experience of haggling could be obtained on almost every street.

Relying on the traveler's guide, the couple also wanted to see the aboriginal dance. Speaking of dancing, it dates back to ancient times in Chinese history. Regrettably, we have only a vague idea of our ancient "rainmaking dance and song" from the classics. As for such classical dances as *nishang yuyi, jianqi* and *huntuo*,[101] only their names have survived. What these tourists wanted to see was something of more ancient and primitive heritage. The cruder the better. Aborigines that "cropped their hair, tattooed their bodies, painted their arms, or buttoned their coats on the left side," appealed to them. They were greatly disappointed when I told them that they would have to travel to the mountain villages to see that kind of aboriginal dance. I knew in my heart that they must be anxious to see a scene of *chucao* (head-hunting), although they did not say so. Who does not want to witness the cannibalistic custom of the Formosans after he or she has read Swift's *A Modest Proposal*? Later, they were thrilled when they saw

---

101 *Nishang yuyi* is said to have been originally a fairy dance. According to legend, Emperor Xuanzong (685–762) visited in dream the celestial Moon Palace where he saw this dance performed by hundreds of fairy maidens dressed in colorful silk. After he woke up, he recorded from memory both the music and the dance and ordered his court musicians and dancers to perform them. On the other hand, *jianqi* and *huntuo* were originally martial dances traditionally performed by female dancers in male costumes.

條街以「討價還價」為名，足以證明其他的街道之上均不討價還價，這也還是相當體面之事。好，就帶他們到城裏去走一遭。來客看出我有一點躊躇，便從箱篋中尋出一個導遊小冊，指給我看，台北八景之一「討價還價之街」赫然在焉。幸好其中沒有說明中文街名，也沒有說明在什麼地方。在幾乎任何一條街上都可以進行討價還價之令人興奮的經驗。

按照導遊小冊，他們還要看山胞跳舞。講到跳舞，我們古已有之，可惜「舞雩歸詠」的情形只能在書卷裏依稀體會之，就是什麼霓裳羽衣劍器渾脫之類，我們也只有其名。觀光客要看的是更古老的原始的遺留！越簡陋的越好！「祝髮文身錯臂左衽」，都是有趣的。我告訴他們這種山胞跳舞需要到山地去方能看到，這使他們非常失望。（我心裏明白，雖然他們口裏沒有說出，他們也一定很想看看「出草」的盛況哩。讀過Swift的《一個低調的建議》的人，誰不想參觀一下福爾摩薩的生吃活人肉的風俗習慣？）後來他們在出賣「手工藝」的地方看到袖珍型的「國劇臉譜」，大喜過望，以為這必定是幾千年

some miniature masks on sale at a handicraft store, taking them for relics from some millennia-old customs. I tried very hard to explain to them that the masks were not like those made by natives of the African hinterlands or the South Sea Islands. These masks, I told them, only represented the various types of facial make-up in Peking opera. But they still obstinately showed a sincere joy, and the corners of their mouths revealed what we call a "serendipitous smile". They promptly opened their wallets and bought several sets of the masks as gifts for their relatives and friends at home in order to prove they had seen certain things here that were worth seeing.

A friend of mine once played host to a female tourist. After savoring our world-famous gourmet dishes, she felt a sudden impulse to return the favor. The guest insisted that she herself would prepare a dinner consisting of traditional dishes from her own country for the host family to enjoy. She also insisted on going personally to the market to do the necessary shopping. In short, she wanted to see a Chinese market for herself. The fact that our markets were fully and amply stocked indicates that we were living well. We needed no ration coupons, and every shopper could emerge from the market fully loaded, their shopping baskets overflowing with foodstuff. Poultry and fish were freshly killed before the eyes of the customers, and such shows of uncanny skills were presented without extra charge. Although the patrons jostled each other in the market, one shopper might still hold up his or her umbrella and let the rainwater drip on another shopper's head, or push a bicycle recklessly through the crowd and allow its tires to rub off their mud on someone else's clothes. Since these things were done reciprocally, people were able to take them in their stride. A lady, with facial makeup, secretly slipped an extra piece of fresh bacon into her basket, but the sharp-eyed and nimble-handed butcher quickly retrieved it. At first, the parties to this incident exchanged an angry stare, but their stares turned quickly and mysteriously into

幾萬年前的古老風俗的遺留。我雖然極力解釋這只是「國劇」的「臉譜」，不同於他們在非洲內地或南海島嶼上所看到的土人的模型，但是他們仍很固執的表示衷心喜悅，嘴角上露出了所謂a serendipic smile（如獲至寶的微笑），慷慨解囊，買了幾份，預備回國去分贈親友，表示他們看到了一些值得一看的東西。

我有一個朋友，他家裏曾經招待過一位觀光女客。她飽餐了我們的世界馳名的佳餚之後，忽然心血來潮想要投桃報李，堅持要下廚房親手做一頓她們本國的飯食，以娛主人。並且表示非親自到市場採辦不可。到我們的菜市場去觀光！我們的市場裏的物資充斥，可以表示出我們的生活的優裕，不需要配給券，人人都可以滿載而歸，個個菜筐都可以「青出於籃」，而且當場殺雞宰魚，表演精彩不另收費。市場裏雖然顧客摩肩接踵，依然可以撐着雨傘，任由雨水滴到別人的頭上，依然可以推着腳踏車在人叢中橫衝直撞，把泥水擦在別人的身上，因為彼此互惠之故，亦能相安。薄施脂粉的一位太太順手把額外的一條五花三層的肉塞進她的竹籃裏，眼明手快的屠商很迅速的就把那條肉又抽了出來，起初是兩造怒目而視，隨後

smiles. Thus, a quarrel was avoided at the right moment and no feelings were hurt. These interesting episodes at the market easily caught the eye of an observer and our guest watched each and all with shocked disbelief and secret amusement. Later, in all innocence the host asked the guest what the differences were between our markets and those in her country. She replied curtly, "There's no mud on the floor in our markets."

This same tourist was then taken as a guest to the Sun Moon Lake and put up in a VIP suite at a newly completed guesthouse. Everything went well, and she was undaunted even by the boatmen who rudely solicited customers or the photographers who dogged tourists at their heels. But around midnight she woke up the whole house with a loud scream when she spotted a big, shiny cockroach wielding its long antennae and scampering up her bedcover. When the cause became known, all sympathy seemed to go with the cockroach. In fact, the cockroach is ubiquitous in the world and has a longer history than the human race. This disgusting creature is extremely peaceful and never puts up any resistance to human efforts to destroy and exterminate it. Its only weapons are its opposition to birth control and its devotion to procreation. Foreign women are known to have fainted at the sight of a rat, so one should not be surprised when they scream at the sight of a cockroach. Dragon and lion dances may be proper entertainment for our honored guest. By comparison, a single cockroach is really nothing to get excited about.

Should we not compare a tourist who leaves Taiwan without seeing the exhibits at the Palace Museum to someone who ventures into a treasure-trove but comes out empty-handed? But I really hope that our tourists will not have to cool their heels with a long line of elementary school students who have water canteens strapped to their shoulders and bean paste buns in their hands, waiting to be admitted

不知怎的又相視而笑，適可而止，不傷和氣。市場裏的形形色色實在是大有可觀，直把我們的觀光客看得不僅目瞪口呆，而且心蕩神怡。主人很天真，事後問她我們的菜市與她們國家的菜市有何分別，她很扼要的回答說：「敝國的菜市地面上沒有泥水。」

這位觀光客又被招待到日月潭，下榻於落成不久的一座大廈中之貴賓室，一切都很順利，即使拖人的船夫和釘人的照相師都沒有使他喪膽，但是到了深更半夜一隻賊光溜亮的大型蟑螂舞動着兩根長鬚爬上被單，她便大叫一聲驚動了全樓的旅客。事情查明之後，同情似乎都在蟑螂那一方面。蟑螂遍佈全世界，它的歷史比人類的還要久遠，這種討厭的東西酷愛和平，打它殺它，永不抵抗，它唯一的武器是反對節育努力生產。外國女人看見一隻老鼠都會暈倒，見蟑螂而失聲大叫又何足奇？舞龍舞獅可以娛樂嘉賓，小小一隻蟑螂不成敬意。

來台觀光而不去看故宮古物，豈不等於是探龍頷而遺驪珠？可是我真希望觀光客不要遇到那大排長隊的背着水壺拿着豆沙麵包的小學生，否則他們會要誤會我們的小學生已經惡補收效到能欣賞周

to the Museum. Otherwise, they may get the wrong impression that our schoolchildren are being effectively crammed with knowledge of our history to the extent that they are able to admire the sacrificial vessels of the Zhou and Han dynasties. Natural landscape, however beautiful or magnificent, is "the picturesque work of God"; it has nothing to do with human efforts. As for culture, that is all man-made. Concrete evidences of Chinese culture may be found among the treasures of the Palace Museum, which houses what is arguably the most complete collection of artifacts of Chinese culture. Certainly, such an array of cultural relics has no equal in the world. The only regret is that the glories of our ancestors provide no help to their descendants who have been uprooted and displaced. And, even if we are resolved to prove ourselves worthy of our ancestry, we must not do so by trying to replicate the double-boiler designed in the reign of King Wu Ding[102] and use it to cook rice. We must still resort to our electric cooker to do the job.

---

102 Wu Ding (1324–1265 B.C.) was the twentieth emperor of the Shang dynasty.

彝漢鼎的程度了。江山無論多麼秀美壯麗，那是「天開圖畫」，與人無關。講到文化，那都是人為的。我們中國文化，在故宮古物中間可以找到實證。也可以說中國文化幾盡萃於是。這樣的文物展覽，當然傲視全球，唯一遺憾的是，祖先的光榮無助於孝子賢孫之廳蓬斷梗！而且縱然我們知道奮發，也不能再製「武丁甂」來炊飯，仍須乞靈於電鍋。

Dogs

The following entry is to be found in the "Notes on the Four Barbarian Tribes" appended to the *History of the Five Dynasties* (907–960): "In the Kingdom of Dogs, all the males have human bodies but dogs' heads. Their bodies are covered with long hair instead of clothes. They fight wild beasts with their bare hands and communicate by barking. Their wives are human and speak Chinese. All the sons born to them are canines, while all their daughters are humans. They practice intermarriage and are cave dwellers. The males eat their food raw, while the females follow human dietary habits." Since this passage forms part of our official history, we must accept the story at its face value, however incredible it may sound. I rather hope that such a kingdom really exists somewhere and that we will be allowed to visit it. Those Chinese-speaking females will be a great help to tourists. Creatures with human bodies and dogs' heads may be counted as another masterpiece of God, even if their appearance is not as awesome and exotic as that of a sphinx. We should not, therefore, hold any racial prejudice against them. Besides, persons "with head of roebuck and the eyes of the rat"[103] can be seen swaggering around in human society in great numbers. It is regrettable that the books of history are too sketchy on the subject and give us no clue about where to find them.

---

103 An expression commonly used to describe an ugly, cunning and sneaky person.

狗

　　《五代史》〈四夷附錄〉:「狗國,人身狗首,長毛不衣,手搏猛獸,語為犬嘷。其妻皆人,能漢語,生男為狗,女為人,自相婚嫁。穴居食生,而妻女人食。」語出正史,不相信也只好姑妄聽之。我倒是希望在什麼地方真有這麼一個古國,讓我們前去觀光。妻女能漢語,對觀光客便利不少。人身狗首,雖然不及人面獅身那樣的雄奇,也算另一種上帝傑作,我們不可懷有種族偏見,何況在我們人群中,獐頭鼠目而昂首上驤者也比比皆是。可惜史籍記載太欠詳盡,使人無從問津。

As our population continues to expand, the number of dogs seems also to be growing at a very quick pace. In the past, when I took my usual walk at dawn, only occasionally did I see one or two mangy dogs either curled up in front of some house or rummaging through the garbage bins, and I would stay my course without bothering them or they me. But it is different now. I often come upon big, tall German shepherds that run past me from behind, huffing and puffing, with their big tongues hanging out. I realize that their owners are training them to retrieve things. I just as often come upon dachshunds with large, floppy ears that like to sniff around my legs before waddling away. I am even more likely to see three to five dogs of native breeds scampering about in the street. I have no way of knowing whether they are playing with each other or quarreling over some female friend. On such an occasion, I can only retrace my steps or make a detour to avoid them.

Don't assume that I have an extreme dislike for dogs. Mark Twain once said, "Dogs are different from people. You take a stray home and feed it until it has grown a shiny coat of new hair, and it won't bite you after that." I believe that what we call loyal dogs are to be found both here and elsewhere, in ancient as well as modern times. *Soushen Ji*[104] tells the story of a loyal dog that saved its master's life. And there is a Ming opera entitled *The Tale of a Loyal Dog*. People who keep dogs do not always expect to be requited for their kindness. You only have to notice the way your dog quietly keeps you company to realize what a lovable creature it is. There is a common saying: "When a big tree falls, all the monkeys on it run away."[105] How can it be otherwise, since

---

104 A collection of supernatural and esoteric stories written by Gan Bao, a scholar and historian of the Eastern Jin dynasty (317–419).

105 A metaphor referring to the desertion of a great man by his followers after his fall.

　　我們的人口膨脹，狗的繁殖好像也很快。我從前在侵晨時分曳
杖街頭，偶然看見一兩隻癩狗在人家門前蜷臥，或是在垃圾箱裏從
事發掘，我走我的路，各不相擾。如今則不然，常常遇見又高又大
的狼犬，有時氣咻咻的伸着大舌頭從我背後趕來，原來是狗主人在
訓練他檢取東西。也常常遇到大耳披頭的小獵犬，到小腿邊嗅一下
搖頭幌腦而去。更常看到三五隻土狗在街心亂竄，是相撲為戲，還
是爭風動武，我也無從知道，遇到這樣的場面我只好退避三舍繞道
而行。

　　不要以為我極不喜歡狗。馬克吐溫說過：「狗與人不同。一隻喪
家犬，你把他迎到家裏，餵他，餵得他生出一層亮晶晶的新毛，他
以後不會咬你。」我相信，所謂義犬，古今中外皆有之。《搜神記》記
載着一椿義犬救主的故事；明人戲曲也有過一篇《義犬記》。養狗不
一定望報，單看他默默的廝守着你的樣子，就覺得他的是可人。樹

monkeys, like human beings, are primates? Dogs are different; they do not despise poor families and they love their old homes. Incidents of dogs biting their masters are not unknown, yet those were rabid dogs. A rabid dog will bite its master as well as complete strangers, but it should not be held responsible for this, just as a son who kills his own father in a moment of "insanity" will be found not guilty of the crime. (The difference is that the life of a rabid dog is never spared and, guilty or not guilty, it is not allowed to remain in this world to live out its natural life.) One of the rules for *Trithikas* (literally, "outsiders", i.e., non-Buddhists or heretics) in India was the so-called "dog-rule", which required the devotees to live like dogs and actually eat human feces. The *Sastra* (or *Commentary on the Prajna-paramita Sutra*) criticizes it, saying that "rules such as this are condemned by the wise, and such sufferings will not be rewarded with good." In fact, dogs have their fortes, many of which deserve our emulation. But scatophagy is definitely not one of them, even though it is mentioned in one of the twenty-four stories exemplifying filial piety.[106]

Dogs have a long history of association with the human race. The royal dog-keeper of the Zhou dynasty (1122–255 B.C.) and the kennel warden of the Han dynasty (206 B.C.–A.D. 189) were palace officials close to the emperors. From this it may be inferred that dogs have long occupied an important position in our favorite pastimes involving "dogs, horses, music and women". The dog is listed as one of the six domestic animals.[107] Mencius said, "If chickens, pigs, dogs and swine are raised without missing their proper seasons, there will be meat for septuagenarians." In his times, only people in old age had

---

106 One of the stories tells about Yu Qianlou, a district magistrate in the Southern Qi dynasty (479–502), who tasted his father's feces in order to help the physician diagnose the cause of the old man's illness.

107 The six animals are: the horse, the ox, the goat, the chicken, the dog and the pig.

倒猢猻散，猢猻與人同屬於靈長類，樹倒焉有不散之理；狗則不嫌家貧，他知道戀舊。不過狗咬主人的事也不是沒有發生過。那是狗患了恐水病，他咬了別人，也咬了主人，他自己是不負責任的，猶之乎一個「心神喪失」的兒子殺死爸爸也會被判為無罪一樣。(不過瘋犬本身必無生理，無論有罪無罪，都不能再俛仰天地之間而克享天年。)印度外道戒，有一種狗戒，要人過狗一般的生活，真個的吃人糞便，《大智度論》批評說「如是等戒，智所不讚，痛苦無善報。」其實狗也有他的長處，大有值得我們人效法者在，吃糞是大可不必的，縱然二十四孝裏也列為一項孝行。

　　狗與人類打交道，由來已久。周有犬人，漢有狗監，都是帝王近侍，可見在犬馬聲色之娛中間老早就佔了重要的地位。犬為六畜之一，孟子說「雞豚狗彘之畜，無失其時，七十者可以食肉矣。」老

the right to eat dogs. Nie Zheng[108] became a dog butcher to support his mother, and nobody criticized him for that. A lot of people do not eat dog meat; they cannot possibly enjoy this delicacy as long as they remember some of the things dogs feed on. I do not believe in the benefit of eating certain things as tonics in the right seasons, even though people with congenital deficiencies or acquired disorders fully deserve our sympathy. However, one is quite surprised to hear the argument that eating dog meat constitutes cruelty to animals and a barbaric act. Recently there has been a revival of popular interest in the *Three-Character Classic*,[109] which contains the following lines: "Horses, cattle and goats, / chickens, dogs and pigs,/ are six animals / which people raise." Why do people raise them? Traditions permitted the substitution of dogs for larger domestic animals (i.e., cattle, sheep or pigs) as offerings at local, small-scale sacrificial rites. Why is the slaughter of dogs alone called barbaric? The French eat snails without bringing discredit to their culture. Once I saw chow dogs on sale at a market in Guangzhou. They all looked fat and plump and were kept in a row of cages. Even though they had not been raised on canned chow, one could assume that they hardly ever fed on human excrement, and the sanitary conditions did not appear to be a problem.

The steady growth of the dog population may be a good thing. "Dogs that bark in deep alleys and cocks that crow atop mulberry trees." are celebrated in verse. These are indispensable features of rural life. But urban dogs create a different atmosphere. The verses: "Cocks crow in the sky; / Dogs bark amid the clouds." are to be understood literally. These urban animals occupy an entirely different social

---

108 Nie Zheng was a native of the state of Han during the period of the Warring States (475–211 B.C.). He was befriended by a nobleman named Yan Sui, who sought to have his political rival removed. Nie promised to assassinate Yan's rival, but he waited until after his mother's death to carry out the plot.

109 Formerly a traditional primer for young pupils.

人有吃狗肉的權利，聶政屠狗養親，沒有人說他的不是。許多人不吃香肉，想想狗所吃的東西便很難欣賞狗肉之甘脆。我不相信及時進補之說，雖然那些先天不足後天虧損的人是很值得同情的。但是有人說吃狗肉是虐待動物，是野蠻行為，這種說法就很令人驚異。《三字經》是近來有人提倡讀的，裏面就說「馬牛羊，雞犬豕，此六畜，人所飼」，人飼了牠是為了什麼？歷來許多地方小規模的祭祀，不用太牢，便用狗。何以單單殺狗便是野蠻？法國人吃大蝸牛，無害於他們的文明。我看見過廣州菜市場上的菜狗，胖胖嘟嘟的，一籠一籠的，雖然不是餵罐頭長大的，想來決不會經常服用「人中黃」，清潔又好像不成問題。

　　狗的數目日增，也許是一件好事。「狗吠深巷中，雞鳴桑樹顛」，雞犬之聲相聞，是農村不可或缺的一種點綴。都市裏的狗又是一番氣象，真是「雞鳴天上，犬吠雲中」，身價不同。我清晨散步時

position. The dogs I meet during my promenades at dawn are mostly pedigreed and have been given a new kind of "liberal education," which teaches them to dash about recklessly and do as they please. Telephone poles are natural and logical places for posters, and certainly dogs will not pass up any opportunity to leave their marks on them. Some of the dogs wear tags around their necks to show that they have paid tax, and taxpayers certainly have the right to use the streets and alleys, including perhaps the freedom to relieve themselves anywhere they wish. I have been told by some dog-keepers that one of the purposes of walking their dogs in the morning is to let their dogs relieve themselves outside their homes. How can we blame our canine friends for doing this when we know that human beings are often seen "facing a wall and holding their legs apart" to do the same? To be honest, there are a few old-fashioned people among the dog-owners who consider it necessary to muzzle their dogs while walking them, thus curbing the desire of their canine friends to choose human legs for breakfast, or to exercise remote control by means of a leash. This, however, is the exception rather than the rule. Most dog-owners will give their dogs absolute freedom, allowing them to run around as if in a no-man's-land.

The "Beware of the Dog" sign is now seldom seen on the doors of houses and may eventually be replaced by another sign that reads: "No Dog on Premises." One reason for this decline is that the need for such a warning no longer exists. German shepherds with black muzzles, or bulldogs with loose skins that form wrinkles over their faces, or spitzes with pointed snouts and white coats often show part of their faces under the doors, and that is already a sufficient deterrent. Elegant mansions and humble abodes keep different kinds of dogs that match their respective social standings. As long as the dogs are kept in their homes, they are no concern of other people, and the owners are free to raise them, feed them, love them and dote on them. However,

所遇見的狗,大部分都是系出名門,而且所受的都是新式的自由的教育,橫衝直撞,為所欲為。電線桿子本來天生的宜於貼標語,狗當然不肯放過在這上面做標識的機會。有些狗脖子上掛着牌子,表示他已納過稅,納過稅當然就有使用大街小巷的權利,也許其中還包涵隨地便溺的自由。我聽一些犬人狗監一類的人士說,早晨放狗,目的之一便是讓牠在自己家門之外排洩。想想我們人類也頗常有「腳向牆頭八字開」的時候,於狗又何尤?說實在話,狗主人也偶爾有幾個思想頑固的,居然給狗戴上口罩,使得他雖欲「在人腿上吃飯」而不可得,或是繫上一根皮帶加以遙遠控制。不過這種反常的情形是很少有的,通常是放狗自由,如入無人之境。

門上「內有惡犬」的警告牌示已少見。將來代之而興的可能是「內無惡犬」。警告牌少見的原故之一是其必需性業已消失。黑鼻尖黑嘴圈的狼狗,臉上七稜八瓣的牛頭狗,尖嘴白毛的獅狸狗,都常在門底下露出一部分嘴臉,那已經發生狗多的嚇阻力量。朱門蓬戶,都各有其身分相當的狗居住其間。如果狗都關在門內,主人豢之飼之

the owners should never allow their dogs to leave their homes without taking some precautionary measures. If their dogs bite somebody, the incident may be considered only a minor infraction, but the dogs themselves may end up in the pots of an eatery that specializes in canine stew. It would be a pity if a dog with a noble pedigree should become a seasonal tonic. But then the responsibility for this mishap should not fall on the restaurant.

愛之寵之，與人無涉；如果放牠出門，而沒有任何防範，則一旦咬人固是小事一端，他自己卻也有在香肉店尋得歸宿的可能。屠宰名犬進補，實在煞風景。可是這責任不該由香肉店負。

Old Age

Time marches with measured steps, never quickening nor slackening its pace. You hardly know when it was that you began to be surrounded by a crowd who insist on placing you at the seat of honor at every banquet, and naturally it dawns on you that soon enough you will be in the company of your ancestors. There is always somebody around to grab your arm and support you when you are going up or coming down a flight of steps. This is to remind you that you have already reached the venerable age of a sexagenarian or septuagenarian and there is the danger that you might take a false step and break a few bones in the fall. Babies seem to have grown much taller in a flash and begin to toddle and stumble in front of you, calling you grandpa or grandma. This obviously makes you age more rapidly.

In fact, an aging person needs no reminder. You need only to look in a mirror to see how much you have changed. What has happened to your once glossy and luxuriant hair? It has turned from black to brown, from brown to gray and from gray to white. It has grown thin, become sparse and finally disappeared without a trace, making you look very much like a bald crane. What has happened to your neat, pearly teeth? They have either turned brown as if from smoking, or developed crevices between them, or revealed yawning gaps left by lost teeth. Your face is now covered in bumps and wrinkles and

老　年

時間走得很停勻，説快不快，説慢不慢。不知從什麼時候起在宴會中總是有人簇擁着你登上座，你自然明白這是離入祠堂之日已不太遠。上下台階的時候有人在你肘腋處狠狠的攙扶一把，這是提醒你，你已到達了杖鄉杖國的高齡，怕你一跤跌下去，摔成好幾截。黃口小兒一幌的功夫就竄高好多，在你眼前趷趷跼跼的跑來跑去，喊着阿公阿婆，這顯然是在催你老。

其實人之老也，不需人家提示。自己照照鏡子，也就應該心裏有數。烏溜溜毛氄氄的頭髮哪裏去了？由黑而黃，而灰，而斑，而毿毿然，而稀稀落落，而牛山濯濯，活像一隻禿鷲。瓠犀一般的牙齒哪裏去了？不是薰得焦黃，就是裂着罅隙，再不就是露出七零八落的豁口。臉上的肉七稜八瓣，而且還平添無數雀斑，有時排列有

sometimes marred by countless freckles, some of which seem to be arranged in stellar configurations resembling Ursa Major, Scorpio, etc. The flaccid fold under your chin has become an empty sack, and if you give it a tug, it will take quite a while for the two loose layers of skin to return to their original shape. In the space between your thick brows has appeared a growth of fine hairs that resemble wheat awns or a rabbit's whiskers. Tears emerge from your eyes without a cause, and sometimes the corners of your eyes exude a gummy substance that hardens into a deposit of tiny little beads there. In short, old age is inseparable from ugliness. According to *Erya*,[110] "brown hair, the loss of teeth, a dolphin-like back and a dust-color complexion are all signs of longevity." Longevity it may be, but ugliness *is* ugliness.

Old age has many other symptoms. Your memory fails even before you drink the waters of Lethe. What you read in a book goes quickly out of your mind before your back is turned. It would be like looking for a needle in a haystack if you tried to find it again. You come across old friends you have not seen for a few years. They look familiar to you, but you cannot remember their names. Suppose you have more than three things to do when you leave home, you must tie as many knots on a rope, but there is still the risk that you may forget what each knot stands for. If you have written them down in a notebook, you may still forget where you have put it. Perhaps your brain has been in service too long and has inevitably suffered wear and tear, so your memories have naturally blurred. Your eyesight has also dimmed and you spend the whole day repeatedly putting on and taking off your glasses. Your ears have gone bad and can no longer hear the sounds of music, although you don't mind that too much. The most embarrassing experience is that, in a conversation, you talk about one

---

110 An ancient book of uncertain date and authorship containing commentaries on
      the classics.

序如星座，這個像大熊，那個像天蠍。下巴頦兒底下的垂肉變成了空口袋，捏着一揪，兩層鬆皮久久不能恢復原狀。兩道濃眉之間有毫毛秀出，像是麥芒，又像是兔鬚。眼睛無端淌淚，有時眼角上還會分泌出一堆堆的桃膠凝聚在那裏。總之，老與醜是不可分的。《爾雅》：「黃髮、齯齒、鮐背、耈老、壽也。」壽自管壽，醜還是醜。

老的徵象還多的是。還沒有喝忘川水，就先善忘。文字過目不旋踵就飛到九霄雲外，再翻尋有如海底撈針。老友幾年不見，覿面說不出他的姓名，只覺得他好生面善。要辦事超過三件以上，需要結繩，又怕忘了哪一個結代表哪一樁事，如果筆之於書，又可能忘記備忘錄放在何處。大概是腦髓用得太久，難免漫漶，印象當然模糊。目視茫茫，眼鏡整天價戴上又摘下，摘下又戴上。兩耳聾聵，無以與乎鐘鼓之聲，倒也罷了，最難堪是人家說東你說西。齒牙動

thing while the other person or people talk about another thing. Your teeth have become loose; when you eat, you look like a ruminant chewing the cud and sometimes you even need a bib. Your legs fail you when you climb. Your back aches after a long sitting. After spending the night in bed, all your joints feel stiff, yet you have not slept a wink; instead, you have waited for dawn with open eyes. And these are not all.

One need not get sentimental about growing old or try to hide it. Flowers bloom and fade. Trees flourish and wither. Huan Wen[111] was choked with emotion when he saw that the trunks of the willows he had planted had grown to ten spans in circumference, and he said feelingly, "As are trees, so are human beings, only worse." With tears in his eyes, he touched a branch and held on to a twig. Perhaps the general, a man of untrammeled spirit, should not have appeared so mawkish. A person should consider himself lucky if, after going through so many violent storms and tempests in life, he has managed to survive and reach a ripe old age and can still keep his body and soul together and be a part of this world. Rong Qiqi[112] said, "There are stillborn babies and children who die in infancy." For that reason, a nonagenarian like him should regard longevity as a blessing in life. It is useless to complain about growing old, so one may as well act happy about it. Birth, age, sickness and death are part and parcel of life. Some people do not like to be called old and, when calculating their age, always insist on following the Western rather than the Chinese

111 Huan Wen (321–373) was a famous general and kingmaker of the Jin dynasty.
112 A recluse and contemporary of Confucius. According to the book entitled *Liezi*: On a trip to Mount Tai, Confucius came across Rong Qiqi, who was playing a harp and singing merrily. Confucius asked the recluse what made him so happy. Rong said that he was happy because the God of Heaven had made him a human being and a male person at that and had allowed him to live to the age of ninty.

搖，咀嚼的時候像反芻，而且有時候還需要戴圍嘴。至於登高腿
頓，久坐腰痠，睡一夜渾身關節滯澀，而且睜着大眼睛等天亮，種
種現象不一而足。

老不必嘆，更不必諱。花有開有謝，樹有榮有枯。桓溫看到他
「種柳皆已十圍，慨然曰：『木猶如此，人何以堪！』攀枝執條，泫然
流淚。」桓公是一個豪邁的人，似乎不該如此。人吃到老，活到老，
經過多少狂風暴雨驚濤駭浪，還能雙肩承一喙，俛仰天地間，應該
算是幸事。榮啟期說：「人生有不見日月不免襁褓者。」所以他行年
九十，認為是人生一樂。嘆也無用，樂也無妨，生、老、病、死，
原是一回事。有人諱言老，算起歲數來斷斷計較按外國算法還是按
中國算法，好像從中可以討到一年便宜。更有人老不歇心，怕以皤

way of computing as if, by doing so, they could win back one lost year.[113] Some people cannot stop worrying and, afraid to let others see their white hair, have taken pains to have it dyed black. Middle-aged ladies, who have lost their youthful looks, have sought the help of cosmetic surgeons or makeup artists for rhinoplasty or liposuction or the extravagant use of the eyebrow pencil and cosmetics, making their heavily shadowed eyes look like two dark holes. There is a common saying: "Old things turn into demons; old people turn into monsters." It is bad enough to be old; why go to all the trouble of turning oneself into a monster?

Old people should act their age. Indeed, an elderly person behaving like a youngster is like winter with spring weather, a bad omen. Cicero said, "A person, however old he may be, always thinks he can live one more year." Yet this cannot be regarded as an extravagant wish. There are many kinds of debts to repay or collect, and this might just give one enough time to settle them. A wise person sets his mind on important business, while a fool sets his mind on small matters. Each uses his own method of reckoning and has his own important decisions to make. At the very least, one should not get oneself into trouble, or get in somebody else's way, or become a nuisance to others. Someone asked Sophocles whether he had fallen in love again in his old age. He replied aptly, "Heaven forbid! I had as much difficulty fleeing from that kind of thing as fleeing from a wicked master." It means that an elderly person no longer yearns for a romantic tryst in a garden under the moon. But that does not mean that elderly people, like withered trees and dead ashes, are destined to spend their days in loneliness. Life is like a trip to the mountains. Young men and women climb the slopes hand in hand. They enjoy many delightful things they see on

---

113 Chinese people count a person's age from the time of his conception and consider a baby to be one year old at birth.

皤華首見人，偏要染成黑頭。半老徐娘，駐顏無術，乃乞靈於整容郎中化裝師，隆鼻隼，抽脂肪，掃青黛眉，眼眶塗成兩個黑窟窿，「物老為妖，人老成精。」人老也就罷了，何苦成精？

　　老年人該做老年事，冬行春令實是不祥。西塞羅說：「人無論怎樣老，總是以為自己還可以再活一年。」是的，這願望不算太奢。種種方面的人欠欠人，正好及時做個了結。賢者識其大，不賢者識其小，各有各的算盤，大主意自己拿。最低限度，別自尋煩惱，別礙人事，別討人嫌。有人問莎孚克利斯，年老之後還有沒有戀愛的事，他回答得好：「上天不准！我好容易逃開了那種事，如逃開兇惡的主人一般。」這是說，老年人不再追求那花前月下的綺旎風光，並不是說老年人就一定如槁木死灰一般的枯寂。人生如遊山。年輕的男男女女攜着手兒陟彼高岡，沿途有無限的賞心樂事，興會淋漓，

the way, and yet they may experience some frustrations, or hesitate at crossroads. When dusk comes and they begin to go downhill with each other's support, what they experience is another kind of joy. Bai Juyi[114] described his sleep in a poem: "An old sleeper often wakes up in the small hours; / His strength is sapped by illness before his years. / Gone are his five desires and all his ambitions, / For no worldly thing will he shed his tears." The poem may sound philosophical, but not without a tinge of sadness. The five desires relate to wealth, beauty, fame, diet and sleep. It is not easy to rid oneself of all the five desires. There are always things a person is reluctant to forego in life. Is it not true that, after all the tears he had shed in resignation, the poet still could not give up poetry and wine?

---

114 See footnote 65.

也可能遇到一些挫沮，歧路徬徨，不過等到日云暮矣，互相扶持着走下山岡，卻正別有一番情趣。白居易《睡覺詩》：「老眠早覺常殘夜，病力先衰不待年，五欲已銷諸念息，世間無境可勾牽。」話是很灑脫，未免淒涼一些。五欲指財、色、名、飲食、睡眠。五欲全銷，並非易事，人生總還有可留戀的在。江州司馬淚溼青衫之後，不是也還未能忘情於詩酒麼？

Deafness

Recently, whenever I was engaged in a conversation with friends, I would notice that some of them keep lowering their voices, as if they were about to let me into some important secrets and were speaking under their breath for fear of being overheard. I never liked people who speak at the top of their lungs in a voice as shrill as a cock's crow or as unpleasant as the sound of cracked cymbals, because they made me nervous. Dirge-singers may feel free to raise their voices so that their songs will reach the clouds or be echoed among the trees, but the voice of a participant in an ordinary conversation should not exceed the decibel level necessary for him to be heard. But I also got nervous if my friends seemed to be whispering to me all the time, so that I could only see their lips move without hearing the sounds, especially when they seemed to turn down their volume extra low for all the nouns and verbs in a sentence. It seemed very strange that more and more people were talking to me this way. I said to myself, "No wonder it is stated in the book on physiognomy that a person with a sonorous voice is destined for high office, and persons so destined are few and far between." My solution to this problem was, first of all, to move my chair closer until our knees almost touched, then stretch my non-rubber neck, prick up my ears, tilt my head, and finally cup my ears with both hands for better reception. Despite all these devices, I could only pick up a string of conjunctions, adjectives

聾

　　近來和朋友們晤談，覺得有幾位說話的聲音越來越小，好像是隨時要和我談論什麼機密大事，喁喁噥噥，生怕隔牆有耳。我不喜歡聽扯着公雞嗓、破鑼嗓、嘩啦嘩啦叫的人說話，他們使我緊張。撫節悲歌的時候，不妨聲振林木，響遏行雲，普通談話應以使對方聽到為度。可是朋友們若是經常和我吱吱喳喳的私語，只見其囁嚅，不聞其聲響，尤其是說到一句話裏的名詞動詞一律把調門特別壓低，我也着急。很奇怪，這樣對我談話的人漸漸多起來了。我心想，怪不得相書上說，聲若洪鐘，主貴，而貴人本是不多見的。我應付的方法首先是把座席移近，近到促膝的地步，然後是把並非橡皮製的脖子伸長，揪起耳朵，欹耳而聽，最後是舉起雙手附在耳後擴大耳輪的收聽效果。饒是這樣，我有時還只是斷斷續續的聽清楚

and articles from what my friends were saying. It took me quite a while to realize that my friends were not lowering their voices and that the real problem was that I was experiencing hearing loss.

I am well over sixty and certainly can no longer claim (with Confucius) to be able "to hear anything said and perceive at once its abstruse meaning". Deafness is, however, a natural phenomenon among people who have reached my age. According to *Huainan zi*,[115] "King Yu of the Xia dynasty[116] had three orifices in each ear." Only a universally recognized great sage like him who is endowed with great wisdom and sagacity may have such ears. Common people like us, with our ordinary human bodies, are only slightly better than deaf worms and dare not wish to possess such an exceptionally developed organ. Each year, starting from the season called "Frost's Descent", [117] the leaves on the trees begin to turn yellow, then red, and will wither and fall. All these we have taken for granted. Why then should we make a fuss when we see the first signs of aging in a human body which is made of flesh and blood and has for several decades weathered many storms of life? No tree in the world can stay green for ten-thousand years and deciduous trees such as the willow will shed their leaves at the first sign of autumn. The difference is only a matter of time. With this in mind, I calmly accepted the verdict when I found out myself that I was going deaf. I knew that there were so many good people, both ancient and modern, to keep me company in this misery. Beethoven began to have hearing problems due to otitis media at the age of twenty-seven, and his condition grew steadily worse until he became completely deaf at forty-nine. From then on, people could communicate with him only by writing rather than speech. But his

---

115 See footnote 34.

116 See footnote 35.

117 One of the twenty-four seasonal periods on the lunar calendar.

了對方所説的一些聯接詞形容詞和冠詞而已。久之，我明白了，不是別人囁口，是我自己重聽。

　　耳順之年早過，當然不能再「耳聞其言，而知微旨」。聾瞶毋寧説是人生到此的正常現象之一。《淮南子》説「禹耳三漏」，那是天下之大聖，聰明睿知，一個耳朵才能有三個穴，我們凡夫俗子修得人身，已比聾蟲略勝一籌，不敢希望再有什麼畸形發展。霜降以後，一棵樹的葉子由黃而紅，由枯萎而搖落，我們不以為異。為什麼血肉之軀幾十年風吹雨打之後，剛剛有一點老態龍鍾，就要大驚小怪？世界上沒有萬年常青的樹，蒲柳之姿望秋先落，也不過是在時間上有遲早先後之別而已。所以我發現自己日益聾蔽，夷然處之。我知道古往今來，有多少好人在和我作伴。貝多芬二十七歲起就在聽覺上有了礙障，患中耳炎，然後愈來愈嚴重，到了四十九歲完全

deafness did not prevent him from composing music. At the age of fifty-six, Du Fu[118] wrote a poem on his deafness, which includes the following lines: "I became deaf two months ago. / When will I lose my eyesight, too?" And, thanks to his deafness, he was now spared "the mournful wails of monkeys in autumn / and the noisy twitters of sparrows at dusk." He only regretted that he had not gone blind, as if he would not be satisfied till he lost his eyesight as well. Yet, for several years after that, the poet continued to be very productive.

Needless to say, deafness creates certain inconveniences. When I am home by myself, I cannot hear the doorbell. I still hear nothing when the visitor keeps banging on my door with his fist until he loses his patience and climbs over the wall to get into the house. Then I can only apologize and shrug and force a smile. Sometimes, when I am sitting with someone in a room and engaged in a conversation with him, he will talk about one thing while I will talk about something else. We have as much communication as that between a donkey and a horse, and his questions are met with my irrelevant answers. It often takes me quite a while to realize what the real subject is. If he has a sense of humor, he will just smile at the misunderstanding. If he lacks patience, he will stamp his foot and shake his head and I will feel embarrassed. When a person crosses a street, he must keep his eyes wide open and his ears pricked in order not to get hit by those cars or motorcycles that are operated by reckless drivers or riders. Pedestrians with poor eyesight and bad ears are particularly exposed to this danger. Fortunately, I have long since confined my promenades to a prescribed area and shunned the general area west of such-and-such road and north of such-and-such street.

But there are occasions when a deaf person has certain advantages. When someone raises a question that you do not want to answer or

118 See footnote 81.

聾了，人家對他談話只能以紙筆代喉舌，可是聾沒有妨礙他作曲。杜工部五十六歲作「耳聾」詩，「眼復幾時暗？耳從前月聾！」好像「猿鳴秋淚缺，雀噪晚愁空」皆叨耳聾之賜，獨恨眼尚未暗！一定要耳不聰目不明才算滿意！可是此後三數年他的詩作仍然不少。

耳聾當然有不便處。獨坐齋中，有人按鈴，我聽不見，用拳頭擂門，我還是聽不見，急得那人翻牆跳了進來。我道歉一番聳聳肩作鴛鴦笑。有時候和人晤言一室之內，你道東來我道西，驢唇不對馬嘴，所答非所問，持續很久才能弄清話題，幽默者莞爾而笑，性急者就要頓足太息，我也覺得窘。鬧市中穿道路，需要眼觀四路耳聽八方，要提防市虎和呼嘯而來的騎摩托車的拚命三郎，耳不聰目不明的人都容易吃虧，好在我早已為我自己畫地為牢，某一條路以西，某一條路以北，那一帶我視為禁區。

聾子也有因禍得福的時候。凡是不願或不便回答的問題一概可以不動聲色的置之不理，顧盼自若，面部無表情，大模大樣的作大

find it inconvenient to answer, you can ignore it by looking deadpan, or look about with perfect composure and a face devoid of emotion or even swagger around like an important person. Nobody will suspect that you are pretending to be deaf. If he keeps pressing the question, you can keep turning a deaf ear to it, and the question will eventually be dropped without getting an answer. The world is too full of sounds, such as the chirps of insects, the croaks of frogs, the shrieks of cicadas, the twitters of birds, the rustle of leaves in the wind, and the sounds of raindrops falling on plantain leaves. I can tolerate all these sounds of nature, but the sounds issuing from the human larynx and the noises produced by machines operated by people are often unbearable. These would often happen when I had the greatest need for peace. I would hear the sonic boom of a jumbo jet flying over my roof, or the noise of some neighbors hailing cabs and shouting goodbye to each other after a night's game of mahjong, or the frantic honking of motorists who used their horns rather than pressed doorbells. Lately I have ceased to complain about such noises, because I can hardly hear them, even though they are deafening to others. But the benefit of deafness does not stop here. In this world, detractors far outnumber eulogists. At least, people are often begrudged the praise they deserve until after their death. Bai Juyi[119] celebrated the completion of his cottage on Censer Peak[120] with a poem, which contains the following lines:"From now on I will have peace around me, / And be spared the sounds of whispering backbiters." If he had gone deaf, he would not have had

119 See footnote 65.
120 A peak in the Lu Mountains in northern Jiangxi province.

人物狀，沒有人疑到你是裝聾。他一再的叮問，你一再的充耳不聞，事情往往不了了之。人世間的聲音太多了，蟲啾、蛙鳴、蟬噪、鳥囀、風吹落葉，雨打芭蕉，這一切自然的聲音都是可以容忍的，惟獨從人的喉嚨裏發出來的音波和人手操作的機械發出來的聲響，往往令人不耐。在最需要安靜的時候，時常有一架特大的飛機唏哩嘩啦的從頭上飛過，或是芳鄰牌局初散在門口呼車道別，再不就是汽車司機狂撳喇叭代替按門鈴，對於這一切我近來就不大抱怨，因為「五音令人耳聾」，我聽不大見。耳聾之益尚不止此。世上說壞話的人多，說好話的人少，至少好話常留在人死後再說。白居易香爐峰下草堂初成，高吟「從茲耳界應清淨，免見啾啾毀譽聲。」

to build a cottage on a mountain top in order to have peace. It is said that a dying person will gradually lose all his faculties except hearing, so that after he has breathed his last, he can still be upset by the sobs of his family gathered around him. I am afraid that he will be equally upset by the absence of such sobbing. Indeed, he would be better off if he had gone deaf.

Editor's Note: The annexed article on Beethoven's ears that included in the original Chinese text is omitted due to copyright matters.

如果他耳聾，他自然耳根清淨，無需誅茅到高峰之上了。有人説，
人到最後關頭，官感失靈，最後才是聽覺，所以易簀之際，有人哭
他，他心煩，沒有人哭他，怕也不是滋味，不如乾脆耳聾。

編者按：中文原著載有關於貝多芬耳聾的附記，囿於版權問題予以刪除。

Retirement

The system of retirement has existed in China since ancient times. According to the *Book of Rites*[121] (in the chapter entitled *"Qu Li"* or "Explanation of Rites"), "government officials must relinquish their duties at the age of seventy." To relinquish one's duties means to resign one's office; that is to say, to hand over one's official functions to the king by reason of age. And this is what we call retirement today. Rules must be observed, yet there are people who consider themselves above rules. "Rules are not made for people like us," they declare. In particular, a septuagenarian can follow his own inclinations without breaking any rule,[122] as if he could do as he pleased. In general, people who have reached the age of seventy begin to show some signs of decrepitude and confusion. But there are luckier and exceptionally endowed people, who remain hale and hearty at such an advanced age and beyond and are still capable of attending meetings and cutting ribbons. Any attempt to force them into retirement will run counter to our noble tradition of showing respect for meritorious service and age.

---

121 See footnote 70.

122 Words used by Confucius to describe himself. "At the age of fifteen I decided to devote myself to learning; at thirty I became established; at forty I was no longer in doubt; at fifty I became acquainted with the mandate of Heaven; at sixty, nothing I heard could upset me; at seventy I followed my own inclinations without breaking any rule." (*Analects of Confucius*)

退　休

　　退休的制度，我們古已有之。《禮記·曲禮》：「大夫七十而致事。」致事就是致仕，言致其所掌之事於君而告老，也就是我們如今所謂的退休。禮，應該遵守，不過也有人覺得未嘗不可不遵守。「禮豈為我輩設哉？」尤其是七十的人，隨心所欲不踰矩，好像是大可為所欲為。普通七十的人，多少總有些昏聵，不過也有不少得天獨厚的幸運兒，耄耋之年依然矍鑠，猶能開會剪綵，必欲令其退休，

"Be patient, young fellows," they say. "Sooner or later we are going to pass the baton. So don't complain that, because we are still here, you are being denied your opportunity for advancement."

The reluctance to step down after reaching the age of retirement also appears to be a centuries-old Chinese tradition. There is a poem entitled "Refusal to Retire", written by Bai Juyi,[123] which reads as follows:

> Retirement at the age of seventy
> Is clearly stipulated by law.
> Why are they turning a deaf ear?
> Because they're addicted to power.
> 'Tis a pity that octo- and nonagenarians,
> Though toothless and dim-sighted,
> Still hanker after fame and wealth
> And worry about their families day and night,
> Reluctant to give up their caps with blue tassels
> Or their carriages with vermilion wheels.
> Too weak to carry their seals of office,
> With a constant stoop they show up at court.
> Who doesn't love wealth and power?
> Who will not cling to royal favors?
> But they, so advanced in years, should retire
> And, having achieved fame, step down.
> What they used to sneer at when young
> Is what makes them tarry when they are old.
> How wise were the Shus of Han!
> Why were they so different from us all?
> The road out of the capital lies deserted
> And none follows their footsteps into retirement.

---

123 See footnote 58.

未免有違篤念勳耆之至意。年輕的一輩，勸你們少安勿躁，棒子早晚會交出來，不要抱怨「我在，久壓公等」也。

　　該退休而不退休。這種風氣好像我們也是古已有之。白居易有一首詩〈不致仕〉：

> 七十而致仕，禮法有明文。
> 何乃貪榮者，斯言如不聞？
> 可憐八九十，齒墮雙眸昏。
> 朝露貪名利，夕陽憂子孫。
> 掛冠顧翠綏，懸車惜朱輪。
> 金章腰不勝，傴僂入君門。
> 誰不愛富貴？誰不戀君恩？
> 年高須告老，名遂合退身。
> 少時共嗤誚，晚歲多因循。
> 賢哉漢二疏，彼獨是何人？
> 寂寞東門路，無人繼去塵！

The allusion is to Shu Guang and his nephew Shu Shou, who retired on the same day from their respective positions as Grand Tutor and Assistant Tutor to the Crown Prince. On that occasion, a farewell party was held outside the gate of the eastern capital. Members of the nobility, high officials of state, friends and followers arrived in hundreds of carriages to see them off. Even people in the street who witnessed the scene all joined in singing their praises. Some even bemoaned their departure and shed a few tears. The great stir created by the retirement of two elderly officials indicated that voluntary retirement was then something uncommon. What people commonly saw were officials who showed up at court with a constant stoop, still hankering after wealth and power and clinging to royal favors. The poet's regret that "none follows their footsteps into retirement" also indicated that the story of the Shus had remained unrepeated to his day.

In the past, an educated man, who devoted a decade of his life to the rigorous study of the classics, had only one dream: to do well in the civil service examinations and eventually be appointed to a government position. When that dream came true, he would display unconcealed pride and satisfaction. Despite the fatigue from work or the burden of old age and infirmities, he would cling to his post and be reluctant to relinquish his official dignities. Very few such superannuated office-holders still had great aspirations. Most of them stayed on only because they were unwilling to give up the rewards that came with their posts, great or small. It is a universal truth that a person is light of heart after he is released from official duties. But a light heart comes with a light purse and the many inconveniences it entails. Moreover, as soon as a person relinquishes his post and becomes unemployed, his influence and power as a boss with a large troop of subordinates at his beck and call are gone forever. How miserable he will be when he loses even his chauffeured car and

　　漢朝的疏廣及其兄子疏受位至太子太傅少傅，同時致仕，當時的「公卿大夫故人邑子，設祖道供張東都門外，送者車數百兩。辭決而去。道路觀者皆曰：『賢哉二大夫！』或嘆息為之下泣。」這就是白居易所謂的「漢二疏」。乞骸骨居然造成這樣的轟動，可見這不是常見的事，常見的是「傴僂入君門」的「愛富貴」「戀君恩」的人。白居易「無人繼去塵」之嘆，也說明了二疏的故事以後沒有重演過。

　　從前讀書人十載寒窗，所指望的就是有一朝能春風得意，紆青拖紫，那時節躊躇滿志，縱然案牘勞形，以至於龍鍾老朽，仍難免有戀棧之情，誰捨得隨隨便便的就掛冠懸車？真正老驥伏櫪志在千里的人是少而又少的，大部分還不是捨不得放棄那五斗米，千鍾祿，萬石食？無官一身輕的道理是人人知道的，但是身輕之後，囊橐也跟著要輕，那就諸多不便了。何況一旦投閒置散，一呼百諾的烜赫的聲勢固然不可復得，甚至於進入了「出無車」的狀態，變成了

becomes a lowly pedestrian who sneaks about or walks hurriedly in the street, keeping his head low to avoid recognition. How unbearable will be his situation when the supply of white charcoal for his braziers in winter, potted flowers and bonsai for each season of the year and such miscellaneous items as toilet paper, heretofore provided automatically by his staff in the general services department, is suddenly cut off. One should therefore think thrice before deciding to retire and, after thinking thrice, one is likely to stay put rather than make a move.

Nowadays, the system of retirement is no longer limited to public service. Teachers, too, must retire when their respiratory systems have become almost completely clogged with chalk dust—not necessarily for fear that they might suddenly be asphyxiated and collapse in the classroom, but rather to make way for others who would like to enter the teaching profession. It is generally believed that teachers should have no qualms about retiring, because they are held in little respect and always live from hand to mouth. Yet, when it becomes known that a teacher has submitted his application for retirement, his relatives and friends will come to him in flocks, all looking worried, sad and nearly in tears, trying to dissuade him from making the move. "Why retire?" they will ask him. "Your hair is not completely white. Your back is not stooped. Your hands are not shaking and your legs can still carry you." And so on. They seem to imply that one should wait until all his hair has turned silver, or his body is bent like a question mark, or he is stricken with Parkinson's disease and walks with a shuffling gait, to apply for permission to retire. Indeed, certain people had waited until they were on their deathbeds and their friends had to rush through their applications for retirement and worry that they might breathe their last while their applications were still going through the red tape, thus losing their retirement benefits. Some close and far-sighted friends will chime in with their eloquent advice: "You must not think of retiring under any circumstances. Life in retirement

匹夫徒步之士，在街頭巷尾低着頭逡巡疾走不敢見人，那情形有多麼慘。一向由庶務人員自動供應的冬季炭盆所需的白炭，四時陳設的花卉盆景，乃至於瑣屑如衛生紙，不消說都要突告來源斷絕，那又情何以堪？所以一個人要想致仕，不能不三思，三思之後恐怕還是一動不如一靜了。

如今退休制度不限於仕宦一途，坐擁皋比的人到了粉筆屑快要塞滿他的氣管的時候也要引退。不一定是怕他春風風人之際忽然一口氣上不來，是要他騰出位子給別人嚐嚐人之患的滋味。在一般人心目中，冷板凳本來沒有什麼可留戀的，平凡吃不飽餓不死，但是申請退休的人一旦公開表明要撤絳帳，他的親戚朋友又會一窩蜂的皇皇然，戚戚然，幾乎要垂泣而道的勸告說他：「何必退休？你的頭髮還沒有白多少，你的脊背還沒有彎，你的兩手也不哆嗦，你的兩腳也還能走路……」。言外之意好像是等到你頭髮全部雪白，腰彎得像是「？」一樣，患上了柏金孫症，走路就地擦，那時候再申請退休也還不遲。是的，是有人到了易簀之際，朋友們才急急忙忙的為他趕辦退休手續，生怕公文尚在旅行而他老先生沉不住氣，弄到無休可退，那就只好鼎惠懇辭了。更有一些知心的抱有遠見的朋友們，會慷慨陳辭：「千萬不可退休，退休之後的生活是一片空虛，那時候

is a complete void. You would then have nothing to do and time would hang heavy on your hands. You would be bored to death. All day long you would feel lost and lonesome and depressed." And so forth. They will paint such a dreary picture of life in retirement—and not without reason because what they do in their offices consists mainly of signing in, drinking tea, chatting with each other and reading newspapers. When they cannot go back to those places to sign in, drink tea, chat and read newspapers, they will feel extremely bored.

The ideal life in retirement means living in genuine retirement, complete release from the work one used to do for a living and freedom to do something that one really enjoys. There were people who took up painting at eighty and those who started writing fiction at fifty. They all went on to achieve remarkable success. "Dogs are never too old to learn new tricks." Why can't people be as good as dogs? Retirement does not necessarily mean moving to some remote area far away from noisy cities, or living like a recluse in an urban environment. Naturally, a person will have fewer visitors after he really retires and closing the door to visitors. A retiree will suffer if he is occasionally thought to have some residual value.

閒居無聊，悶得發慌，終日徬徨，悒悒寡歡……」。把退休後生活形容得如此淒涼，不是沒有原因的，因為平夙上班是以「喝喝茶，簽簽到，聊聊天，看看報」為主，一旦失去喝茶簽到聊天看報的場所，那是會要感覺無比的枯寂的。

理想的退休生活就是真正的退休，完全擺脫賴以餬口的職務，作自己衷心所願意作的事。有人八十歲才開始學畫，也有人五十歲才開始寫小說，都有驚人的成就。「狗永遠不會老得到了不能學新把戲的地步。」何以人而不如狗乎？退休不一定要遠離塵囂，遯跡山林，也無需大隱藏人海，杜門謝客──一個人真正的退休之後，門前自然車馬稀。如果已經退休的人而還偶然被認為有賸餘價值，那就苦了。

Anger

A person looks his ugliest when angry. In anger, a face that is normally as beautiful as a lotus blossom will turn livid and pale, even ashen. This, plus the contorted muscles on his face, his staring eyes and bristling hair, will indeed make a person's countenance more than repulsive. As the saying goes, "When anger rises in the heart, evil intent is bound to start." Anger brings about a change that is both psychological and physiological. Very few people can control their tempers when their purposes are crossed. Young people are prone to anger and one cross word is enough to start a quarrel. However, many elderly people are just as irascible and touchy. I had an older relative by marriage who was over eighty and hemiplegic. He had the habit of reading newspapers in the morning. Each day he would put on his glasses and lay out the newspapers before him. Moments later, he would be pounding the table, fuming with rage and letting loose a torrent of abuse. He did not like what he read in the newspapers. He could not do without the newspapers, but they only made him angry. At such an hour, everyone in his family would stay out of his sight, and nobody wanted to be caught by his rage which, like a thunderstorm, would go as quickly as it had come.

怒

　　一個人在發怒的時候，最難看。縱然他平夙面似蓮花，一旦怒而變青變白，甚至面色如土，再加上滿臉的筋肉扭曲，眥裂髮指，那副面目實在不僅是可憎而已。俗語說：「怒從心上起，惡向膽邊生」，怒是心理的也是生理的一種變化。人逢不如意事，很少不勃然變色的。年少氣盛，一言不合，怒氣相加，但是許多年事已長的人，往往一樣的火發暴躁。我有一位姻長，已到杖朝之年，並且半身癱瘓，每晨必閱報紙，戴上老花鏡，打開報紙，不久就要把桌子拍得山響，吹鬍瞪眼，破口大罵。報上的記載，他看不順眼。不看不行，看了嘔氣。這時候大家躲他遠遠的，誰也不願逢彼之怒。過一陣雨過天晴，他的怒氣消了。

According to the *Book of Poems*,[124] "When the ruler shows his anger, the rebellion of his subjects will quickly stop; when the ruler creates public well-being, the rebellion of his subjects will quickly end." This means that, in a fit of anger, a person in power can crush a rebellion and cause things to return to normal. For ordinary people, however, it will be better if they keep their temper under control and avoid getting into trouble. A person in a fury loses countless blood cells in his body and causes a sharp rise in his blood pressure. In short, anger is bad for a person's health. Worse still, when his blood boils with rage, his mind becomes muddled, and he is likely to speak or act out of line, causing injury to himself as well as others. "Count the number of days in which you did not get angry," says Epictetus, the Greek philosopher. "In the past, I used to get angry every day; sometimes I got angry every other day; later on, I got angry once every three or four days. If you have not been angry for thirty days at a stretch, you should make offerings to the gods to express your gratitude." A decrease in the number of such outbreaks is a result of self-discipline. The method of self-discipline is very hard to explain. "When you are angry at someone else's shamelessness," says Marcus Aurelius of Rome, another stoic philosopher, "you should ask yourself, 'Can that shameless person not exist in this world?' That is impossible. Do not demand what is impossible." This does not mean that we need not impose sanctions on a bad person; it only means that we need not get angry. If anger cannot be avoided, it should at least be controlled so as not to become excessive. The Buddhists list *Krodha* (anger) as one of the three poisons.[125] They believe that "a heart full of anger causes greater destruction than a conflagration" and that controlling anger is one of the basic requirements of self-cultivation. According to

---

124 Chinese title *Shi Jing*. It is the first anthology of Chinese poetry and was compiled by Confucius.

125 The other two poisons are *raga* (cupidity) and *moha* (ignorance).

　　詩云：「君子如怒，亂庶遄沮；君子如祉，亂庶遄已。」這是說有地位的人，赫然震怒，就可以收撥亂反正之效。一般人還是以少發脾氣少惹麻煩為上。盛怒之下，體內血球不知道要傷損多少，血壓不知道要昇高幾許，總之是不衛生。而且血氣沸騰之際，理智不大清醒，言行容易踰分，於人於己都不相宜。希臘哲學家哀皮克蒂特斯說：「計算一下你有多少天不曾生氣。在從前，我每天生氣；有時每隔一天生氣一次；後來每隔三四天生氣一次；如果你一連三十天沒有生氣，就應該向上帝獻祭表示感謝。」減少生氣的次數便是修養的結果。修養的方法，說起來好難。另一位同屬於斯多亞派的哲學家羅馬的瑪可斯·奧瑞利阿斯這樣說：「你因為一個人的無恥而憤怒的時候，要這樣的問你自己：『那個無恥的人能不在這世界存在麼？』那是不能的。不可能的事不必要求。」壞人不是不需要制裁，只是我們不必憤怒。如果非憤怒不可，也要控制那憤怒，使發而中節。佛家把「瞋」列為三毒之一，「瞋心甚於猛火」，克服瞋恚是修持

the *Book of Yandan Zi*,[126] "the face of a blood-brave person turns red in anger; the face of a vein-brave person turns purple in anger; the face of a bone-brave person turns pale in anger; the face of a mind-brave person does not change color in anger." I think that a person can become "mind-brave" only through extreme austerity and self-cultivation. A person born with a face that will betray no emotions is, indeed, exceptionally endowed.

In the early years of the Qing dynasty, a writer named Li Fu published a collection of his essays under the general title of *Mutang Leigao*. In one of the essays, entitled "The Story of the House without Anger", he said, "Though I am over forty, I have not yet learned to control my emotions, nor have I succeeded in changing my temperament. I made mistakes due to anger and, despite my repentance, I soon became angry again. For fear that I will remain an irascible person to the end, I have named my home the 'House without Anger'." It is an excellent essay and, true to his character as a scholar, it clearly expresses the author's fear of and vigilance against anger.

---

126 This book, whose authorship is unknown, contains stories about Prince Dan of the state of Yan who lived in the third century B.C. during the period of the Warring States.

的基本功夫之一。《燕丹子》説：「血勇之人，怒而面赤；脈勇之人，怒而面青；骨勇之人，怒而面白；神勇之人，怒而色不變。」我想那神勇是從苦行修練中得來的。生而喜怒不形於色，那天賦實在太厚了。

清朝初葉有一位李紱，著《穆堂類稿》，内有一篇〈無怒軒記〉，他説：「吾年逾四十，無涵養性情之學，無變化氣質之功，因怒得過，旋悔旋犯，懼終於忿戾而已，因以『無怒』名軒。」是一篇好文章，而其戒謹恐懼之情溢於言表，不失讀書人的本色。

Taciturnity

One of my friends was a man of few words. One day he came to see me with a hint of a smile at the corners of his mouth, and I knew that was his way of greeting friends. I showed him into the living room and he gladly took a seat. Determined to test his equanimity and see how long he could remain silent, I broke my habit and kept my mouth shut. We sat facing each other without exchanging a single word, while the clock on the wall seemed to tick more loudly than usual. Growing impatient, I opened a tin of cigarettes and offered it to him. He began to smoke one cigarette after another, making an audible sound with each long pull. I gave him a cup of tea and he started to sip it repeatedly, while looking around him with perfect composure. After he had finished the third cup of tea and consumed half a tin of cigarettes, though I did not yawn or stretch, he rose to take his leave, without having said a word from beginning to end. This friend of mine is now dead, but I can never forget that wordless visit he paid to me. It is a surprise to me that the manners of the people of the Six Dynasties (A.D. 222–589), who "came because of what they have heard and left after seeing what they have seen",[127] can still be seen in our times.

---

127 The following episode was recorded in *Shishuo Xinyu*: Zhong Hui, a man of great talent and ability of the Jin dynasty, did not know Ji Kang, an accomplished

沉　默

　　我有一位沉默寡言的朋友。有一回他來看我，嘴邊綻出微笑，我知道那就是相見禮，我肅客入座，他欣然就席。我有意要考驗他的定力，看他能沉默多久，於是我也打破我的習慣，我也守口如瓶。二人默對，不交一語，壁上的時鐘的答的答的聲音特別響。我忍耐不住，打開一聽香煙遞過去，他便一枝接一枝的抽了起來，巴答巴答之聲可聞。我獻上一杯茶，他便一口一口的翕呷，左右顧盼，意態蕭然。等到茶盡三碗，煙罄半聽，主人並未欠伸，客人興起告辭，自始至終沒有一句話。這位朋友，現在已歸道山，這一回無言造訪，我至今不忘。想不到「聞所聞而來，見所見而去」的那種六朝人的風度，於今之世，尚得見之。

The following story is recorded in a book written by Zhang Dingsi of the Ming dynasty and entitled *Langye Dai Zui Bian*: "Liu Qizhi, a royal counselor, had the habit of maintaining his silence when he received his visitors. Such a visit often lasted a whole day without a word passed between the host and the guest. When a visitor got very tired and rose to take his leave, the host would not hear of it and would repeatedly press him to stay. When asked why he had acted that way, Liu replied that, out of a hundred people, only one or two can sit in silence from morning till dusk without yawning, stretching or leaning, and those who can are destined for greatness. His prediction was repeatedly tested and invariably proved to be correct." This story shows that there has been no lack of precedents for such a silent reception between host and guest. But the remark about taciturnity as a "mark of greatness" is food for thought. A so-called great person is supposed to appear lofty and out of reach. Even if he is not remote and inaccessible, he should at least give the impression of being profound and unfathomable. For this reason, most people in high places have the peculiar trait of fixing their eyes on the ceiling and keeping their faces deadpan. When you ask a question, the person will play deaf without saying yes or no. How can such a person not be destined for greatness? A profound exterior is a good cover for an internal void. Such a person is most suited to take a place in the council of state (or a temple). It is recorded in *Kongzi Jiayu*[128] that Confucius "visited the

---

scholar and musician. He went with a group of eminent persons to see Ji. They found him doing the work of a blacksmith, while his friend Xiang Xiu was working the blast furnace. Ji continued to work with his sledgehammer, appearing to pay no attention to the visitors and, for a while, without exchanging a word with them. When Zhong rose to leave, Ji asked him, "What have you heard that causes you to come? What have you seen that causes you to leave?" Zhong replied, "I came because of what I had heard, and I am leaving after seeing what I have seen."

128 Or *The Family Records of Confucius*, a fragmentary book of uncertain date and authorship.

　　明張鼎思《瑯琊代醉編》有一段記載：「劉器之待制對客多默坐，
往往不交一談，至於終日。客意甚倦，或謂去，輒不聽，至留之再
三。有問之者，曰：『人能終日危坐，而不欠伸欹側，蓋百無一二，
其能之者必貴人也。』以其言試之，人皆驗。」可見對客默坐之事，
過去亦不乏其例。不過所謂「主貴」之說，倒頗耐人尋味。所謂貴，
一定要有一副高不可攀的神情，縱然不拒人千里之外，至少也要令
人生莫測高深之感，所以處大居貴之士多半有一種特殊的本領，兩
眼望天，面部無表情，縱然你問他一句話，他也能聽若無聞，不置
可否。這樣的人，如何能不貴？因為深沉的外貌，正好掩飾內部的
空虛，這樣的人最宜於擺在廟堂之上。《孔子家語》明明的寫着，孔

temple of his remote ancestor named Hou Ji, at the right entrance of which was a bronze statue whose mouth was tightly closed and whose back bore the inscription: 'An ancient who was careful with his words.'" Surely, that statue was not intended as a model for the man in the street.

A royal counselor must speak his mind, just as someone who has a bone lodged in his throat cannot rest until he has spat it out. In fact, it is his responsibility to advise and admonish and, when he speaks, it is not for the mere pleasure of speaking. Cocks crow and dogs bark, each performing a useful function. If an adviser to the government keeps his mouth shut or his tongue tied, can he stand comparison with a cock or a dog? As for the good and just people in general, they are either disgruntled with the affairs of the world or worried by the dangers of the time. Most of them remain silent, but there are a few who "would rather speak out and die than keep quiet and live." Such outspoken critics may win the praises and laments of the world, but they do this at the risk of their good names and even their lives. They can only look to history for the vindication they deserve. Where one has the "freedom to remain silent," to relinquish this freedom is also an exercise of personal freedom. In the present age, silence is the last freedom remaining.

A person of learning and virtue, who has long banished all mundane problems and worries from his mind, is naturally in a better position to appreciate the world of silence. This kind of silence does not imply swallowing words that come to one's lips but the total absence of such words. There is a saying: "He who knows speaks not; he who speaks knows not." When the Buddha held up a flower to show to his followers at a gathering on the Spiritual Peak, the audience was silent. Only Kasyapa revealed a smile. That knowing smile spoke volumes. Lianchi, an eminent Buddhist monk, once wisely observed: "Regarding the vinegar

子「入太祖后稷之廟，廟堂右階之前有金人焉，三緘其口，而銘其背曰：『古之慎言人也。』」這廟堂右階的金人，不是為市井細民作榜樣的。

謇諤之臣，骨骾在喉，一吐為快，其實他是根本負有諍諫之責，並不是圖一時之快。雞鳴犬吠，各有所司，若有言官而箝口結舌，寧不有愧於雞犬？至於一般的仁人君子，沒有不憤世憂時的，其中大部分憫默無言，但有間或也有「寧鳴而死，不默而生」的人，這樣的人可使當世的人為之感喟，為之擊節，他不能全名養壽，他只能在將來歷史上享受他應得的清譽罷了。在有「不發言的自由」的時候而甘願放棄這一項自由，這也是個人的自由。在如今這個時代，沉默是最後的一項自由。

有道之士，對於塵勞煩惱早已不放在心上，自然更能欣賞沉默的境界。這種沉默，不是話到嘴邊再咽下去，是根本沒話可說，所謂「知者不言，言者不知。」世尊在靈山會上，拈華示眾，眾皆寂然，惟迦葉破顏微笑，這會心微笑勝似千言萬語。蓮池大師說得好：「世間釀醯醇醴，藏之彌久而彌美者，皆繇封錮牢密不泄氣故。

and wine in the world, the longer they age, the better they become, because they are kept in air-tight and hermetically sealed containers. As the ancients said, if you keep your mouth shut without saying a word for twenty years, even the Buddha cannot find fault with you in the end. How right they were!" If you keep your mouth shut for twenty years, you may develop bad breath. But, when the faculty of speech is held in check, the mind becomes lucid like water and the heart, like a pearl, will rise to the surface. And there will be no need for words. The Carthusian Order of the Catholic Church also enjoins silence on its members in their daily lives as a form of self-discipline. Normally they are not allowed to converse with each other. "There is absolute truth in this, but I have already forgotten my words, even if I wish to explain it."

"Where am I to find a person who has forgotten his words so that I may speak with him?" asked Zhuangzi.[129] Nowadays, it is just as difficult to find a friend who really knows the value of taciturnity.

---

129 Or Chuang-tzu (?369–295 B.C.), born Zhuang Zhou, a Chinese mystic and philosopher. His work (also called *Zhuangzi*), together with Laozi's *Daode Jing*, forms the basis of Taoism.

古人云：『二十年不開口說話，向後佛也奈何你不得。』旨哉言乎！」二十年不開口說話，也許要把口悶臭，但是語言道斷之後，性水澄清，心珠自現，沒有饒舌的必要。基督教Carthusian教派也是以沉默靜居為修行法門，經常彼此不許說話。「此中有真意，欲辯已忘言。」

　　莊子說：「吾安得夫忘言之人，而與之言哉？」現在想找真正懂得沉默的朋友，也不容易了。

View from a Window

A window is like a picture frame, although with a lattice added to it. Every time you look out of a window, you see a picture. The picture you see may be beautiful or ugly, elegant or vulgar, quiet or noisy with activities, but that is entirely dependent on luck. I am currently an expatriate, occupying a room on the second floor of a white house. I have a desk by the window, at which I spend my days writing, resting and meditating. Only when I raise my head and look out the window do I see an endless succession of pictures like a film. I am going to write down what I have seen from my window—perhaps in the manner of a peepshow that used to be operated by a fellow with a big gold tooth at the Tianqiao Plaza in Beijing.

This white house is a building literally covered with white paint, although it does not have a white thatched roof nor any exposed timber. This may sound like the white house in a blind alley described in *Hanshi Waizhuan*,[130] but the house is actually a colonial one with its typical angular and boxy exterior. When I draw the curtain, the first thing I see is a tremendous expanse of sky. Since the sky is the roof and the earth is the floor of our universe, you would say, "Doesn't

---

130 A collection of miscellaneous writings on poetry by Han Ying, a writer of the
   second century B.C.

窗　外

　　窗子就是一個畫框，只是中間加些櫺子，從窗子望出去，就可以看見一幅圖畫。那幅圖畫是妍是媸，是雅是俗，是鬧是靜，那就只好隨緣。我今寄居海外，樓身於「白屋」樓上一角，臨窗設几，作息於是，沉思於是，只有在抬頭見窗的時候看到一幅幅的西洋景。現在寫出窗外所見，大概是近似北平天橋之大金牙的拉大篇吧？

　　「白屋」是地地道道的一座刷了白顏色油漆的房屋，既沒有白茅覆蓋，也沒有外露本材，說起來好像是《韓詩外傳》裏所謂的「窮巷白屋」，其實只是一座方方正正的見棱見角的美國初期形式的建築物。我拉開窗帘，首先看見的是一塊好大好大的天。天為蓋，地為輿，

everybody see the sky?" But it is not so. I used to live in a city that ranks first in the world in population density. There, all I could see was a small piece of the sky, as if I were sitting in a well and looking up. There were high-rises before me, behind me, to my left and to my right. Atop those buildings were either water tanks or TV antennas or multicolored wash hung out to dry. A frog sitting on the bottom of a well might have seen just as much of it. The white house is located in a remote, out-of-the-way area, and there is nothing around it to block my view, especially because, on the eastern side across the street, there is the playground of an elementary school. The ground is carpeted by grass and, from time to time, children are to be seen gamboling and frolicking there. On the northern side is a large vacant lot overrun by weeds which, until recently, sported a myriad of starry yellow flowers but now look withered and seared. In the midst of these weeds rise several tall trees, a mixture of firs and maples, all standing ramrod and firm. On the southern side across the street stand two neighboring houses and on the western side a third. One afternoon, after the rain had stopped, I suddenly saw a rainbow, a clear and unbroken 180-degree arc, like a multicolored sash spanning the sky. The ancient belief that rainbows were dragons that drank water from rivers and lakes must have been inspired by sights like this. Countless times I had seen a rainbow appearing in the sky after a storm, but I have never seen one so spectacular and awe-inspiring, neither before nor since. The world outside my window is so empty and vast that sometimes on a rainy day, the raindrops seem invisible and soundless. I see only people holding their umbrellas and water coursing down the sloping road like a running stream.

There is a constant shuttle of traffic but few pedestrians on the road. At dawn every day, an elderly couple with gray hair are to be seen jogging around the playground, huffing and puffing, but never stopping until they have completed a certain number of laps. One of

誰沒看見過天？但是，不，以前住在人煙稠密天下第一的都市裏，我看見的天僅是小小的一塊，像是坐井觀天，迎面是樓，左面是樓，右面是樓，後面還是樓，樓上不是水塔，就是天線，再不然就是五色繽紛的曬洗衣裳。井底蛙所見的天只有那麼一點點。「白屋」地勢荒僻，眼前沒有遮攔，尤其是東邊隔街是一個小學操場，綠草如茵，偶然有些孩子在那裏蹦蹦跳跳；北邊是一大塊空地，長滿了荒草，前些天還綻出一片星星點點的黃花，這些天都枯黃了，枯草裏有幾株參天的大樹，有樅有楓，都直挺挺的穩穩的矗立着；南邊隔街有兩家鄰居；西邊也有一家。有一天午後，小雨方住，驀然看見天空一道彩虹，是一百八十度完完整整的清清楚楚的一條彩帶，所謂虹飲江皋，大概就是這個樣子。虹銷雨霽的景致，不知看過多少次，卻沒看過這樣規模壯闊的虹。窗外太空曠了，有時候零雨濛濛，竟不見雨腳，不聞雨聲，只見有人撐着傘，坡路上的水流成了渠。

路上的汽車往來如梭，而行人絕少。清晨有兩個頭髮頒白的老者繞着操場跑步，跑得氣咻咻的，不跑完幾個圈不止，其中有一個

them is accompanied by a huge black dog which, in addition to doing this exercise, seldom passes a power pole without stopping to leave a mark or forgets to choose a spot on the lush turf on which to apply a little organic fertilizer. On fine days, I often see girls in their late teens and blue jeans walking barefoot by the roadside. Their fair-skinned feet are completely bare and their soles are coated with dirt. I don't know what will happen to them if there happen to be such things as thumbtacks or broken glass on the road. The Japanese writer Saneatsu Musakoji told the following story: "Tradition has it that a certain man named Kume became an immortal fairy after he had fled human passions and gone through the tremendous hardships of self-cultivation in the mountains. One day, while sailing on a cloud over a certain place, he caught sight of a young washerwoman with very white legs which dazzled and entranced him, and the desires of the flesh were suddenly revived in him. Thereupon he found himself tumbling down from the cloud." (quoted from a note to "A Poem without a Title" by Zhou Mengdie) I am in no danger of falling out of my window, as I do not feel dazzled or entranced by the sight. I only wonder if walking barefoot is one of the ways members of the younger generation express their revolt against conventions and cultures. I am afraid that in the future some people may prefer to walk on all fours or even upside down on their hands. Won't that be more radical and avant-garde? As for men with long hair and full beards, they are now ubiquitous, and this fad has caught on even among the Chinese people (including some students and waiters). How defenseless are human beings against fads and customs!

Garbage collection on Thursday mornings is another interesting scene. In our area, garbage disposal is an operation performed not by a government agency, but by a private company. Each house stores its trash in a couple of lidded tin cans. Every Thursday the tenants move their garbage cans to the front of their houses to be picked up.

還有一條大黑狗作伴。黑狗除了運動健身之外，當然不會輕易放過一根電線桿子而不留下一點記號，更不會不選一塊芳草鮮美的地方施上一點肥料。天氣晴和的時候常有十八九歲的大姑娘穿着斜紋布藍工褲，光着腳在路邊走，白皙的兩隻腳光光溜溜的，腳底板踩得髒兮兮，路上萬一有個圖釘或玻璃碴之類的東西，不知如何是好？日本的武者小路實篤曾經說起：「傳有久米仙人者，因逃情，入山苦修成道。一日騰雲遊經某地，見一浣紗女，足脛甚白，目眩神馳，凡念頓生，飄忽之間已自雲頭跌下。」(見周夢蝶詩〈無題〉附記) 我不會從窗頭跌下，因為我沒有目眩神馳。我只是想：裸足走路也算是年輕一代之反傳統反文明的表現之一，以後恐怕還許有人要手腳着地爬着走，或索興倒豎蜻蜓用兩隻手走路，豈不更為徹底更為前進？至於長頭髮大鬍子的男子現在已經到處皆是，甚至我們中國人也有沾染這種習氣的(包括一些學生與餐館侍者)，習俗移人，一至於此！

　　星期四早晨清除垃圾，也算是一景。這地方清除垃圾的工作不由官辦，而是民營。各家的垃圾貯藏在幾個鉛鐵桶裏，上面有蓋，到了這一天則自動送到門前待取。垃圾車來，並沒有八音琴樂，也

The sanitation truck comes unheralded by jingling notes produced from a music box or human cries and calls. The only sounds heard on the occasion are the clangs and bangs made by the metal cans. The truck has a two-man crew, both tall and husky, one carrying the cans and emptying them into the truck and the other also helping out when not driving. All the time, they are on the double, never slackening their pace for a moment. After the garbage is emptied into the truck, the crusher is switched on, and the trash is pulverized in no time, and it will no longer be possible to sort out bottles and cans and place them in baskets or hang them on the outside of the truck. Each house pays a monthly fee of $2.70, but the contracting company complains and asks each family to move its garbage cans to the curbside in order to save labor, or else pay an extra dollar.

My window looks out on a bus stop. There are no grim-faced conductors on board. It is the driver who opens and closes the door, collects fares and gives out transfer tickets. Fortunately there are few passengers, so the driver has the leisure and good mood to bid each one "Good morning!" as he gets on. There is a bus about every twenty minutes. This is, of course, a losing operation, but it has to be maintained despite the financial loss. Each bus, with its meager load of three to five passengers, looks rather dismal and dreary. Many of the passengers are senior citizens with poor eyesight, shaky limbs, hearing loss and slow response, and these buses are their only means of transportation. There are some younger passengers who take these buses to and from work, perhaps because they cannot find a place in the city to park their cars. One passenger appears to be a blue-collar worker. He shows up below my window at exactly the same time every morning, takes his time to open his lunch box, take out a thermos and drink a cup of coffee before boarding the bus.

I have not seen a rat scampering across the road, let alone the

沒有叱咤吆喝之聲，只聞唏哩嘩啦的鐵桶響。車上一共兩個人，一律是彪形黑大漢，一個人搬鐵桶往車裏摜，另一個司機也不閒着，車一停他也下來幫着搬，而且兩個人都用跑步，一點也不從容。垃圾摜進車裏，機關開動，立即壓絞成為碎碴，要想從垃圾裏撿出什麼瓶瓶罐罐的分門別類的放在竹籃裏掛在車廂上，殆無可能。每家月納清潔費二元七角錢，包商叫苦，要求各家把鐵桶送到路邊，節省一些勞力，否則要加價一元。

公共汽車的一個招呼站就在我的窗外。車裏沒有車掌，當然也就沒有晚娘面孔。所有開門，關門，收錢，掣給轉站票，全由司機一人兼理。幸虧坐車的人不多，司機還有閒情逸致和乘客說聲早安。二十分鐘左右過一班車，當然是虧本生意，但是貼本也要維持。每一班車都是疏疏落落的三五個客人，淒淒清清慘慘。許多乘客是老年人，目視昏花，手腳失靈，耳聽聾聵，反應遲緩，公共汽車是他們唯一交通工具。也有按時上班的年輕人搭乘，大概是怕城裏沒處停放汽車。有一位工人模樣的候車人，經常準時在我窗下出現，從容打開食盒，取出熱水瓶，喝一杯咖啡，然後登車而去。

我沒有看見過一隻過街鼠，更沒看見過老鼠肝腦塗地的陳屍街

crumpled body of a rat crushed by passing traffic. There are many feral cats around, nearly always fat and rotund, with sleek and glossy fur. Jars and cans of cat food line the shelves of supermarkets. All department stores carry brushes, outfits, collars and cleaning stuffs for cats. Almost every day I can see a gang of cats, some white and some black, playing in the vacant lot on the northern side. Now they chase each other, now they cuddle together, now they roll on the ground. The most interesting things to watch are squirrels, which arch their bodies, dart around in leaps and bounds and scamper up the fir trees at the sound of coming traffic. Outside my window I keep a plateful of birdseed, a mix of corn and other things, which attracts sparrows in flocks, but not robin redbreasts; the latter will take a look at it and fly away. They are carnivorous and feed on dead slugs and live earthworms.

This is about all I have seen out of my window. In his "Ode Written on the Tower over the City Gate", Wang Can[131] wrote, "Alas, this city, though beautiful, is not my home, and I have no desire to tarry." And he went on to say, "In times of yore, while as an expatriate in the state of Chen, Confucius pined for his home. When Zhong Yi was a prisoner in the state of Jin, he refused to play anything except the music of his native state of Chu. Even though Zhuang Xi was a high-ranking official in the state of Chu, he sang nothing but songs of the state of Yue.[132] It is human nature to be emotionally attached to one's homeland. Can adversity or prosperity cause a change of heart?" As I write this article, I am homesick.

Seattle, September 22, 1972.

The Mid-autumn Festival.

---

131 Wang Can (177–217), alias Wang Zhongxuan, was a poet of the state of Wei.
    This ode was written when he was displaced by war and took refuge in Jingzhou.
132 All the persons mentioned in this part of the ode lived during the Spring and
    Autumn period (722–481 B.C.).

心。狸貓多得很，幾乎個個是肥頭胖腦的，毛也澤潤。貓有貓食，成瓶成罐的在超級食場的貨架上擺着。貓刷子，貓衣服，貓項鍊，貓清潔劑，百貨店裏都有。我幾乎每天看見黑貓白貓在北邊荒草地裏時而追逐，時而親暱，時而打滾。最有趣的是松鼠，弓着身子一竄一竄的到處亂跑，一聽到車響，倉卒的爬上樅枝。窗下放着一盤鳥食，黍米之類，麻雀群來果腹，紅襟鳥則望望然去之，他茹葷，他要吃死的蛞蝓活的蚯蚓。

窗外所見的約略如是。王粲登樓，一則曰：「雖信美而非吾土兮，曾何足以少留！」再則曰：「昔尼父之在陳兮，有歸歟之嘆音。鍾儀幽而楚奏兮，莊舄顯而越吟。人情同於懷土兮，豈窮達而異心？」臨楮悽愴，吾懷吾土。

　　　　　　　　　六一、九、廿二、壬子中秋於西雅圖

The Story of a Cat

Cats are cute little things that like to cuddle up to you; sometimes they also like to rub their bodies against your legs or sniff at your feet. But the caterwauling of alley cats upon the return of spring after a long winter greatly offends the ear. It begins with a staccato purring then suddenly breaks out into a ruckus of wails and biting sounds, making a terrible racket that seems to rock the whole world and raise hell. On such an occasion you cannot hope to enjoy a moment's sleep. Because of that, some people feel compelled to get out of bed in the middle of the night and use long bamboo poles to chase them away. According to tradition, a certain Buddhist monk wrote the following poem: "Caterwauling, O caterwauling! / Each note rises above another. / This old monk, too, feels the season's calling, / But dare not tell it to any other." The monk felt deeply for the cats, and presumably he would not have chased them with a long bamboo pole.

My old home in Beijing was located in a long, narrow alley. In the dead of one winter night, after the peddlers of such midnight snacks as water radish and stiff dough dumplings had finished their rounds, all was quiet except for the sounds of the watchman's clappers in the distance. Suddenly the silence was shattered by the wails of cats on the roof, which sounded at times like grumbles and complaints and at

貓 的 故 事

　　貓很乖，喜歡偎傍着人；有時候又愛蹭人的腿，聞人的腳。唯有冬盡春來的時候，貓叫春的聲音頗不悅耳。嗚嗚的一聲一聲的吼，然後突然的哇咬之聲大作，唏哩嘩喇的，鏗天地而動神祇。這時候你休想安睡。所以有人不惜昏夜起床持大竹竿而追逐之。相傳有一位和尚作過這樣的一首詩：「貓叫春來貓叫春，聽他愈叫愈精神，老僧亦有貓兒意，不敢人前叫一聲。」這位師父富同情心，想來不至於掄大竹竿子去趕貓。

　　我的家在北平的一個深巷裏。有一天，冬夜荒寒，賣水蘿蔔的，賣硬麵餑餑的，都過去了，除了值更的梆子遙遠的響聲可以說是萬籟俱寂。這時候屋瓦上嗥的一聲貓叫了起來，時而如怨如訴，

other times like shouts and curses. Then came a burst of noises made by the cats jumping from one roof to another and back, causing great disturbances to my whole family. This hubbub continued for several nights in a row.

The windows of the houses in Beijing were covered with paper instead of glass panes, and the openings in the lattice were just wide enough for a cat to get through. It had only to make a hole with one stroke of its paw to gain free passage. One night in late spring, while I was asleep, I seemed to hear some noise coming from the paper window of my study across the small courtyard. In the morning a hole was discovered on the lattice, apparently caused by the intrusion of some stray cat, which was probably driven by hunger to hunt for a rat in the room. After I had papered up the hole, I was surprised to find the next morning that the cat had returned, entering and exiting by the same route. I felt a little upset by this incident and said to myself, "Once is a misdemeanor; twice is an unpardonable offense." On the third night the intruder not only invited itself into the room again but also messed up the things on the desk and the bookcases and left countless quadrifid footprints on the desk. I could no longer control my rage. Our cook was a resourceful person who, in addition to his culinary skill, was adroit in many little tricks. He had long harbored a grudge against cats because they had often spirited away cuts of meat from the kitchen cupboard and dragged them to the bottom of the stove, or climbed to the top of a wall with fish in their mouths. So he had put his mind to work and devised a simple but effective way to trap cats. His method was to secure one end of an iron wire to a nail fixed on the window lattice where cats usually passed through and make a noose at the other end of the wire. The noose took the shape of a round loop, which he adjusted properly and placed on the lattice. When all was done, he would calmly wait to catch the intruder alive. When a cat tried to get into the room, its front legs would come in first, followed

時而如訴如罟，然後一陣跳踉，竄到另外一間房上去了，往返跳躍，攪得一家不安。如是者數日。

　　北平的窗子是糊紙的，窗櫺不寬不窄正好容一隻貓兒出入，只消他用爪一劃即可通往無阻。在春暖時節，有一夜，我在睡夢中好像聽到小院書房的窗紙響，第二天發現窗櫺上果然撕破了一個洞，顯然的是有野貓鑽了進去。大概是餓極了，進去捉老鼠。我把窗紙補好。不料第二天貓又來，仍從原處出入，這就使我有些不耐煩，一之已甚豈可再乎？第三天又發生同樣情形，而且把書桌書架都弄得凌亂不堪，書桌上印了無數的梅花印，我按捺不住了。我家的廚師是一個足智多謀的人，除了調和鼎鼐之外還貫通不少的左道旁門，他因為廚房裏的肉常常被貓拖拉到竈下，魚常被貓叼着上了牆頭，懷恨於心，於是殫智竭力，發明了一個簡單而有效的捕貓方法。法用鐵絲一根，在窗櫺上貓經常出入之處釘一個鐵釘，鐵絲一端繫牢在鐵釘之上，另一端在鐵絲上做一活扣，使鐵絲作圓箍形，把圓箍伸縮到適度放在窗櫺上，便諸事完備，靜待活捉。貓竄進屋的時候前腿伸入之後身軀勢必觸到鐵絲圓箍，於是正好套在身上，

by its body, which would inevitably touch the wire loop. The noose would trap it and dangle it in the air. The more it struggled, the tighter the noose would get. When he found out that I was greatly distressed by a cat without knowing what to do, he volunteered to set up such a device on the window of the study for me. At first I had no faith in his contraption but saw no harm in trying. That night I did hear some noise. When I got up the next morning and went over to investigate, I saw to my consternation a skinny cat hanging there, more dead than alive.

To all the cats he had caught, the cook had administered stern justice without any mercy. But when I saw the skinny cat, I was moved by its pitiable look and interceded with the cook for clemency. As a result, it was decided to commute its sentence and set it free. But the cook insisted on giving it a little punishment by attaching an empty tin can to the loose end of the wire that was still tied around its body, and then he opened the front door and let it go. We saw the cat run away like a streak, with the can trailing behind it and making a lot of noise, like a car that leaves the church, carrying a newly-wedded couple away on their honeymoon. The faster it ran, the louder was the noise made by the can. In a panic the cat ran faster and faster and was soon pursued by a pack of stray dogs that had been drawn to it by the clangor. Together they kicked up a cloud of dust and, after emerging from the alley, they veered and sped north. I had no way of knowing what happened to the cat afterward, and I thought that, after going through this bitter experience, it would definitely stay away from my study. The window was papered anew, and I looked forward to a night of peaceful sleep.

That night I was awakened by the sound of a tin can. At first it made loud clanks on the brick pavement in the backyard. Then it appeared that something was climbing up the jujube tree and dragging

活生生懸在半空，愈掙扎則圓箍愈緊。廚師看我為貓所苦無計可施，遂自告奮勇為我在書房窗上裝置了這麼一個機關。我對他起初並無信心，姑妄從之。但是當天夜裏居然有了動靜，早晨起來一看，一隻瘦貓奄奄一息的赫然掛在那裏！

廚師對於捉到的貓向來執法如山，不稍寬假，我看了貓的那副可憐相直為她緩頰。結果是從輕發落予以開釋，但是廚師堅持不能不稍予膺懲，即在貓身上原來的鐵絲繫上一隻空罐頭，開啟街門放她一條生路。只見貓一溜煙似的唏哩嘩喇的拖着罐頭絕塵而去，像是新婚夫婦的汽車之離教堂去度蜜月。跑得愈快，罐頭響聲愈大，貓受驚乃跑得更快，驚動了好幾條野狗跟在後面追趕，黃塵滾滾，一瞬間出了巷口往北而去。她以後的遭遇如何我不知道，我心想她吃了這個苦頭以後絕對不會再光顧我的書房。窗戶紙從新糊好，我準備高枕而眠。

當天夜裏，聽見鐵罐響，起初是在後院磚地上嘩啷嘩啷的響，隨後像是有東西提着鐵罐猱升胯院的棗樹，終乃在我的屋瓦上作

the can along. Soon the clangor moved to the roof, which had parallel ridges of tiles with troughs in between them. When the tin can was dragged across the ridges, it produced a series of clear, distinct clinks and clanks. The sound made me shiver. Could it be the ghost of the cat? Or the same cat that had spent the whole day running with the can trailing behind, then went into hiding somewhere and finally returned to my house for another visit? What was there in my house that it was so irresistibly attracted to?

Then the can fell to the ground with a loud crash; obviously the wire had broken. Almost simultaneously I heard the cat climbing down by the lilac tree in front of my bedroom window and jumping to the ground with a plop. It gave a low groan that sounded like a sigh of relief when a burden was suddenly removed. Then the paper on the window of my study was ripped again—history had repeated itself.

This time I made up my mind to mete out a heavy penalty rather than just tying a tin can to the culprit—if I could recapture it alive. I went straight to the study to conduct an investigation of the scene and noticed something unusual. On the floor lay several books that had fallen from the top shelf of a large bookcase, which almost reached the ceiling. I pricked up my ears and heard snores coming from the shelf. Why had the cat picked such a place to sleep in? I brought a stepladder and climbed up for a look. I was flabbergasted to see the skinny cat cuddling and giving suck to four kittens.

The four black-and-white kittens wriggled and snuggled up to their mother. It seemed that they had not yet opened their eyes and were obviously newly born. When a woman gives birth to a child on board a train or ship, it is traditionally regarded as a happy event and both the mother and the child will thereafter be entitled to all sorts of preferential treatment. Now that such a happy event had taken place in my study and the mother had given birth to not just one baby, but

響。屋瓦是一壠一壠的，中有小溝，所以鐵罐越過瓦壠的聲音是格登格登的清晰可辨。我打了一個冷戰，難道是那隻貓的陰魂不散？她拖着鐵罐子跑了一天，藏躲在什麼地方，終於黃夜又復光臨寒舍？我家究竟有什麼東西值得使她這樣的念念不忘？

　　嘩啷一聲，鐵罐墜地，顯然的是鐵絲斷了。幾乎同時，噗的一聲，貓順着我窗前的丁香樹也落了地。她低聲的呻吟了一聲，好像是初釋重負後的一聲嘆息。隨後我的書房窗紙又撕破了——歷史重演。

　　這一回我下了決心，我如果再度把她活捉，要用重典，不是繫一個鐵罐就能了事。我先到書房裏去查看現場，情況有一些異樣，大書架接近頂棚最高的一格有幾本書灑落在地上。傾耳細聽，書架上有呼嚕呼嚕的聲音。怎麼貓找到了這個地方來酣睡？我搬了高凳爬上去窺視，嚇我一大跳，原來是那隻瘦貓擁着四隻小貓在餵奶！

　　四隻小貓是黑白花的，咕咕容容的在貓的懷裏亂擠，好像眼睛還沒有睜開，顯然是出生不久。在車船上遇到有婦人生產，照例被視為喜事，母子好像都可以享受好多的優待。我的書房裏如今喜事臨門，而且一胎四個，原來的一腔怒火消去了不少。天地之大德曰

a litter of four, the fury I had felt a moment before quickly dissipated. Birth is the greatest gift in the world, and this should apply to all sentient beings. Because of the kittens, the cat had risked all sorts of dangers to come back in order to suckle them. Indeed, no mother can show greater love for her children.

After I had discovered her secret, the cat must have felt that their safety was threatened and overnight managed to move all the kittens out of the study to an unknown place.

生，這道理本該普及於一切有情。貓為了她的四隻小貓，不顧一切的冒着危險回來餵奶，偉大的母愛實在是無以復加！

　　貓的秘密被我發現，感覺安全受了威脅，一夜的功夫她把四隻小貓都叼離書房，不知運到什麼地方去了。

Huagan

A long time ago while I was in college, I had a course on John Milton. One day, when we came to *Paradise Lost*, Book III, ll. 437–439, which read:

> ...on the barren plains
> Of Sericana, where Chineses drive
> With sails and wind their cany waggons light...

The professor raised his head and swept his eyes over the class. Seeing that I was the only student with black hair and a yellow complexion, he asked me, "Are there really wagons with sails in your country?" I told him that China was a vast country where local customs varied, that I had been to only a limited number of places there and that I had neither seen nor heard of wagons with sails. He concluded that it was nevertheless a very good idea to put sails on wagons.

Only decades later did I learn that there were indeed wagons with sails in southwestern China. Movies produced in Taiwan have also shown scenes shot on location of vehicles with sails scooting on a beach. I have no excuse for the paucity of my knowledge. It is quite natural that Milton, with his extensive knowledge and erudition, should have great admiration for a country with an ancient civilization such as China. Yet he did not see our *huagan*.

滑　竿

　　從前在學校讀英國詩人米爾頓的《失樂園》，讀到卷三第四三
七行：

　　　……在中國的荒原上
　　　中國人駕駛着
　　　掛帆的輕便的藤車……

教授抬起頭來往下面掃視，看見只有一個人是黑頭髮黃面孔的，便
問道：「你們貴國是真有這樣張帆的車子麼？」我告訴他說，敝國地
方很大，各地風俗不同，我到過的地方有限，沒有看見過也沒有聽
說過車上掛帆。教授的結論是，無論如何，車上掛帆是一個很好的
辦法。

　　過了好幾十年我才有機會聽人講起我們西南一帶確有帆車。台
灣的電影上也有帆車在海灘上飛馳的外景。自己的見聞之譾陋實在
是無話可說，米爾頓博學多識，對於我們文明古國當然不勝其景仰
了。可是他還沒有看見過我們的滑竿。

A *huagan* is a kind of sedan chair borne by two bearers, but it is a sedan chair in the simplest and lightest possible form. Two long bamboo poles borne on the shoulders of two bearers form a means of transportation. It has been pointed out that the Chinese pictograph for bearer in "sedan chair bearer" shows a person carrying two poles on his shoulders. A *huagan* consists of a square of burlap strung between the two poles to form a net, in the fashion of a canvas hammock. The passenger has the feeling of lying snugly on a soft pouch. Lest his feet be left dangling, a bamboo crosspiece is nicely placed in front and attached by ropes to the poles to serve as a footrest. This vehicle has no parts so that maintenance is never a problem. When hailed by a customer, the bearers have only to pick up the poles and put them on their shoulders; when not in service, one of them can put the poles together and tuck them under his arm in order to go anywhere. Need a place to park? That is not a problem at all; the thing can be propped against a wall without taking up any space.

When I was a child, my mother took me to Hangzhou to visit my grandmother. She told me on the way that, when we got off the train, we would ride in a sedan chair, and that I should sit still in it, otherwise the sedan chair might capsize. But I could not imagine how a sedan chair carried by eight bearers could be in danger of capsizing. It was only after we had arrived in Hangzhou that I realized how ugly the thing they called a sedan chair there was. It looked like a black wicker basket, tall and slender and top-heavy, borne by only two bearers, one in front and the other in rear, and it seemed to sway and totter even when nobody was riding in it. By comparison, a *huagan* provides a much safer ride, as the passenger would have great difficulty getting out of the soft pouch in which he was seated, even if he tried .The passenger on a *huagan* must, however, adopt a reclining posture and remain rigid and stiff all the time he is being carried. He will cut a rather poor figure, because the way he is carried around makes him

滑竿是兩人抬的一種轎子，其簡單輕便到了無以復加的程度。兩根長長的竹竿，往兩個人的肩膀上一架，就是交通工具。有人說抬轎的人之所以稱為轎夫，是因為那「夫」字是象形的，象一個人肩膀上放兩根竿。兩竿之間吊起一塊麻布，自成一個輭兜，活像外國的帆布吊床，乘客往上一躺，輭糊糊的一點也不硌得慌，怕兩隻腳沒交代，前面有繫着的一根竹篾，正好把腳放上去，天造地設。根本沒有零件，所以永遠沒有修理的問題。有客來，往肩上一搭；沒有生意，一個人把兩根竹竿並在一起，往腋下一夾就可以走路。停放的地方麼？那更簡便了，豎着在牆邊一靠，不佔空間。

小時候到杭州外婆家去，母親囑咐我，下了火車要坐轎子，千萬不可以動彈，否則有翻落之虞。我心想八人大轎抬着焉有翻落之理。到了杭州，才知道所謂轎子竟是那樣寒傖的東西，像是一個黑油簍，細細高高，頭重腳輕，前後一共只有兩個人抬，沒有人坐進去也好像是搖搖欲墜。滑竿比較穩當多了，坐在輭兜裏想掙脫出來都不大容易。只是坐滑竿必須用半臥的姿式，直挺挺的抬着招搖過市，縱不似舁屍行殯，也像是傷患病殘，樣子不大雅觀。從前皇帝出行，「乘肩輦，具威儀」，必定不是躺着的。可是滑竿在上山下山

look like a sick or wounded person, if not a corpse, on a stretcher. In the past, when an emperor traveled, he was invariably described as "riding in a sedan chair, looking awesome and dignified." He could not have looked that way lying down. But a *huagan* is well suited for travels up and down a mountain. On an ascent the passenger may feel a little upside down, but not to the extent that the food in his stomach might be regurgitated. On a descent he will not be thrown headlong into the valley. A *huagan* can negotiate all the circuitous turns and zigzags on a mountain path exactly as one wishes and in a breeze. In contrast, a big sedan chair borne by eight persons would prove cumbersome and slow.

Life is too hard on *huagan* bearers, though. Some people consider it inhuman even to ride in a rickshaw. But a rickshaw has wheels, and a vehicle on wheels is a machine. The invention of the wheel was an important milestone in the history of civilization. The *huagan* also operates on the lever principle and is not considered too primitive, although it is much simpler by comparison. The weight of the passenger is borne by four shoulders, and the crux of the matter is how much the passenger weighs. A commotion will occur among the *huagan* bearers when they are approached by a group of customers, including one that appears to weigh a quarter of a ton. Each team will try to pick up a lighter load, and the hapless pair on whom the heavy burden falls will grumble all the way. And no one can blame them if he takes a look at their legs, which are no thicker than a pair of sorghum stalks but have to sustain so heavy a burden for such a long journey. The passenger, seated in an elevated position, will not fail to hear the heavy breathing of the *huagan* bearers and their resounding footfalls on the flagstone pavement. Neither will he fail to notice the varicose veins that spread like webs over their legs or the thick calluses that have formed on their shoulders as a result of constant chafing.

的時候就非常方便，例如登好漢坡，坐在滑竿上可能微有倒懸之感，腹內的東西決不至於岔了出來，下來的時候也不會一頭栽了下去。而峯迴路轉，左彎右旋，無不夷猶如意。登山喝道的八人大轎反倒覺得笨重難行了。

滑竿夫太苦。有人坐人力車猶嫌其不人道。車下究竟有輪，輪子就是機械，那是人類文明史上的一大里程碑。滑竿也利用上了槓桿原理，並不算是太原始，不過簡單得多。一個人的重量由四個肩膀承之，問題在那一個人的重量究竟有多少。三五個人雇乘滑竿，其中若有一位是「五百斤油」，那幾個滑竿夫要發生一陣騷亂，誰都想避重就輕，不幸的那一對一路上要呶呶不休。這也怪不得他們，看看他們的腳桿，細得像是秫稭，任重而道遠。坐滑竿的人是「人上人」，不會聽不到滑竿夫的咻咻的喘息，以及腳後跟走在石板上通通的響，不會看不到他們腿上網狀的靜脈瘤，以及肩膀上摩擦出來的厚厚的繭。

There is not a single *huagan* bearer that does not look gaunt and emaciated. Standing in a row in front of a wall, they look as if they had all been air-dried, or rather like those "stiffs" left at the roadside by some fabled necromancers of Chengzhou when they put up at an inn for the night.[133] Each *huagan* bearer is clad in a blue cotton long gown and wears an indispensable turban. Most of them have a glib tongue and the gift of the gab. A short smoking pipe is tucked under a long cloth band worn around their waists, to which a tobacco pouch is attached. There are, of course, other things besides tobacco that are more refreshing and more capable of giving them a lift and that they enjoy talking about when they are in high spirits. Once I rode in a *huagan* on a trip to Mount Jinyun near Beipei, a small town in Sichuan province. On the way I heard the *huagan* bearers chanting their vulgar ditty in alternate parts:

> A: Close up tight in front!
>
> B: Open up behind.
>
> A: Smooth and shiny!
>
> B: Curved and wavy.
>
> A: Very slippery!
>
> B: Walk steadily.
>
> A: A flower seen from afar.
>
> B: A girl we see so near!
>
> A: Let my son call her mummy dear.

---

133 Necromancers of Chengzhou, a district in Hunan province, were commissioned by the surviving families of people who had died recently in far away places to bring back with them the bodies of the deceased by using magic to make the corpses walk like zombies all the way home. When a necromancer put up at a roadside inn, he left his charge propped against a wall for the night.

滑竿夫沒有不是鳩形鵠面的，他們一排靠在牆根上站着，像是風乾了的人，像是傳說中辰州趕屍的人夜晚宿店時所遺棄在路邊的貨色！可是他們每人一襲藍布長衫，還少不了一頂布纏頭。多半是伶牙利齒，能言善道。腰間橫繫着一根褡布，斜插着一根短煙管，掛着一隻煙荷包。除了煙草之外，當然還有更能提神解乏的東西，精神興奮的時候，議論風生。有一回我到四川北碚的縉雲山，一路上聽滑竿夫邊走邊説一些唱和的俚語：

> 甲：「前面靠得緊！」
> 乙：「後面擺得開。」
> 甲：「亮光光！」
> 乙：「水波浪。」
> 甲：「滑得很！」
> 乙：「踩得穩。」
> 甲：「遠看一枝花。」
> 乙：「走近看是她！」
> 甲：「教我的兒喊她媽。」

Thereupon, the "flower" by the roadside blushed from ear to ear and spat at them. The *huagan* bearers burst into triumphant laughter and, with newly found strength in their legs, braced themselves and quickened their steps uphill.

唱到這裏，路邊的那「一枝花」紅頭漲臉的啐他一口。滑竿夫們勝利的笑了起來，腳底下格外有力，精神抖擻，飛步上山。

Books

In olden times people liked to boast about their good birth. It might not be absolutely necessary for one to be of noble or aristocratic descent, but at least he must have been born into a house redolent of "book aroma" in order for him to be considered a truly respectable person. The term "book aroma" calls for an explanation. In former days, books were printed on several kinds of bamboo paper, such as *maobian* and *lianshi*. After such books had been kept in a poorly ventilated room for a long time, the paper and the pine-soot ink used in book printing would naturally combine to produce a smell that was close, but not identical, to the scent of sandalwood. It could not be likened to the fragrance of laurel blossoms or orchids, nor was it refreshing or particularly pungent. In the absence of a better name, it was referred to as "book aroma". A private library would keep its door and windows tightly closed at all time, and this aroma would seem particularly strong the moment one stepped into the room, but one would get used to it by and by. Modern books that are printed and bound in the Western style use a different kind of paper and ink, which seem to produce a kerosene-like odor that may in no way be called an aroma.

Aroma or no aroma, one can always benefit from reading books. That is why there are so many bibliophiles in the world to ensure that

書

從前的人喜歡誇耀門第，縱不必家世貴顯，至少也要是書香人家才能算是相當的門望。書而曰香，蓋亦有說。從前的書，所用紙張不外毛邊連史之類，加上松煙油墨，天長日久密不通風自然生出一股氣味，似沉檀非沉檀，更不是桂馥蘭薰，並不沁人脾胃，亦不特別觸鼻，無以名之名之曰書香。書齋門窗緊閉，乍一進去，書香特別濃，以後也就不大覺得。現代的西裝書，紙墨不同，好像有一股煤油味，不好說是書香了。

不管香不香，開卷總是有益。所以世界上有那麼多有書癖的人，讀書種子是不會斷絕的。買書就是一樂，舊日北平琉璃廠隆福

the genes of book lovers will pass on without interruption. Buying books is one of the greatest pleasures in life. In former times, the bookstores on Fulong Temple Street in the Liulichang district of Beijing held a very strong attraction for readers. Once you stepped into a bookstore, you had only to give a nod to the clerk behind the counter before heading straight to the inner quarters. The manager would come out of his office to greet you and usher you into the parlor, where the two of you would sit down and take your time discussing business. Never underestimate this manager. He was likely to be more knowledgeable than you were in bibliography and textual research. After he had found out who you were, he could act on your behalf in the search for the books you wanted. As soon as he had found them, he would dispatch a messenger together with a sample volume to your home. If you liked it, you could keep it for a trial. If you did not, the messenger would take it back. All this was done in a most polite and amicable manner. As to the price, you could talk about it at a more convenient time after the holiday. Under such circumstances, it would be very difficult for an educated person not to become a "book addict". Eventually, he would be surrounded by books in his library and would hardly be able to find a place to sit down. He would then look around with enormous pride and say to himself in a pedantic voice, "When a man has ten thousand books in his possession, why should he want to be a king who rules over a hundred cities?" Nowadays, it is relatively easy to find the books we want to buy, but the pleasure of book hunting and the joy felt on the occasion of a successful search are proportionately reduced. When you go browsing in a crowded bookstore, you expect to do so in the fashion of a grazing cow, in a leisurely and unhurried manner. However, if a store clerk keeps his eyes on you and suspects you of being a "thief with a refined taste", you cannot feel completely at ease. In that case, the sooner you get out of that hostile environment, the better. Worse still, some of

寺街的書肆最是誘人，你邁進門去向櫃台上的夥計點點頭便趨後堂，掌櫃的出門迎客，分賓主落座，慢慢的談生意。不要小覷那位書賈，關於目錄版本之學他可能比你精。蒐訪圖書的任務，他代你負擔，只要他摸清楚了你的路數，一有所獲立刻專人把樣函送到府上，合意留下翻看，不合意他拿走，和和氣氣。書價麼，過節再說。在這樣情形之下，一個讀書人很難不染上「書淫」的毛病，等到四面卷軸盈滿，連坐的地方都不容易勻讓出來，那時候便可以顧盼自雄，酸溜溜的自嘆「丈夫擁書萬卷，何假南面百城？」現代我們買書比較方便，但是蒐訪的樂趣，蒐訪而偶有所獲的快感，都相當的減少了。擠在書肆裏瀏覽圖書，本來應該是像牛吃嫩草，不慌不忙的，可是若有店夥眼睛緊釘着你，生怕你是一名雅賊，你也就不會

the books on display are unopened—an outright rejection of any attempt at browsing.

"On the seventh day of the seventh month, Hao Long went outdoors and lay supine in the sun. When someone asked him what he was doing, he said, 'I am sunning my books.'" (See *Shishuo Xinyu*[134]) Mr. Hao had all his books stored in his "belly",[135] so he could sun himself and his books at the same time. He had been able to commit all his books to memory, perhaps because the number of books available in those days was relatively small. Sima Guang[136] was another ardent lover of books. In a piece of advice to his sons, he said, "Each year, on some fine days between the start of the dog days and the Double-Ninth Festival,[137] I would clean up some desks and tables and move them out into the sunshine. On top of them I would line up my books with their "brains" exposed to the sun. As a result, my books have remained in a perfect condition in spite of their age." The "brain" of a book is its inner edge that holds the binding, whereas the outer edge of a book is called the "mouth". He also developed fastidious reading habits, which he described in detail: "As to reading a book, I will first clean the desk and spread a cloth on it to cushion the book before sitting down to read. If I prefer to walk and read at the same time, I will carry the volume on a rectangular board, never daring to hold it with bare hands for fear that the dirt on my hands might rub off on the book and that I might disturb its brain. When I have finished reading a page, I will place my right thumb sideways to the edge of that page and, with the help of the index finger, turn it over lightly in order not to rub or

---

134 See footnote 51.

135 The belly of a person was traditionally thought to be the seat of memory.

136 Sima Guang (1016–1086) was an outstanding scholar and statesman of the Song dynasty.

137 See footnote 57.

怎樣的從容，還是早些離開這是非之地好些。更有些書不裁毛邊，乾脆拒絕翻閱。

「郝隆七月七日，出日中仰臥，人問其故，曰：『我曬書』。」（見《世說新語》）郝先生滿腹詩書，曬書和日光浴不妨同時舉行。恐怕那時候的書在數量上也比較少，可以裝進肚裏去。司馬溫公也是很愛惜書的，他告誡兒子說：「吾每歲以上伏及重陽間視天氣晴明日，即淨几案於當日所，側群書其上以曬其腦。所以年月雖深，從不損動。」書腦即是書的裝訂之處，翻葉之處則曰書口。司馬溫公看書也有考究，他說：「至於啟卷，必先几案潔淨，藉以茵褥，然後端坐看之。或欲行看，即承以方版，未曾敢空手捧之，非惟手污漬及，亦慮觸動其腦。每至看竟一版，即側右手大指面襯其沿，隨覆以次指

crumple it. I am greatly displeased to see that most of you use your fingers to pinch and pull up a page." (See *Songbei Leichao* or *A Collection of Anecdotes of the Song Dynasty*.) Today, books are not as expensive and hard to get as they used to be, and modern books, due to their improved binding techniques, wear far better than those produced in the Song dynasty that used the "butterfly binding" method.[138] But, generally speaking, an educated person still cherishes his books. When he receives a new book, he will wrap it in a jacket. He will also give it the necessary sunning, dusting and safekeeping. I have seen veritable collectors who love their books to the point of totally refraining from reading them. Their Chinese books are kept in *de luxe* protective casings complete with ivory pins used as bolts. Those in foreign languages are leather bound with gold lettering. All are neatly arranged on glazed bookcases that turn the whole room into an endless display of treasure. Such a place bears a close resemblance to the fabled "Blessed Land of Langhuan".[139] The books they have collected have become bric-a-brac or curios.

It has been said: "He who lends books is a fool; he who returns them is also a fool." This adage has a more elaborate version: "He who lends books is a fool; he who treasures them is a second fool; he who demands their return is a third fool; and he who returns them is a fourth fool." Both versions clearly reflect the bitter truth that people who borrow books seldom return them. Books should be kept in a secret and secure place; they should not be left unguarded so as to invite thieves. It is a most aggravating experience to see a complete set of books rendered incomplete when one volume has been out on

---

138 A binding method in which each sheet in a book is folded once and then bound up with the other sheets by threads in such a way that it could open completely like the wings of a butterfly.

139 Name of the library of the Jade Emperor, King of Heaven.

面，撚而夾過，故得不至揉熟其紙。每見汝輩多以指爪撮起，甚非吾意。」(見《宋稗類鈔》) 我們如今的圖書不這樣名貴，並且裝釘技術進步，不像宋朝的「蝴蝶裝」那樣的嬌嫩，但是讀書人通常還是愛惜他的書，新書到手先裹上一個包皮，要曬，要揩，要保管。我也看見過名副其實的收藏家，愛書愛到根本不去讀它的程度，中國書則錦函牙籤，外國書則皮面金字，庋置櫃櫥，滿室琳瑯，真好像是嫏嬛福地，書變成了陳設，古董。

有人說「借書一癡，還書一癡。」有人分得更細：「借書一癡，惜書二癡，索書三癡，還書四癡。」大概都是有感於書之有借無還。書也應該深藏若虛，不可慢藏誨盜。最可惱的是全書一套借去一本，

loan for a long time and never returned. Xie Zhaozhi, a writer in the Ming dynasty, was the editor of *Wu Zazu* (or *Five Categories of Miscellaneous Writings*). The book contains the story of an "imperial counselor by the name of Yu who keeps the tens of thousands of books he has collected in a library located in the middle of a pond and accessible only by a single-plank bridge which is removed at night. A sign on the door reads: 'The library admits no visitors. The books permit no borrowers.'" That is a very good arrangement, but few people can afford it.

Reading affords pleasure, and that is why there are people who can be so absorbed in a book as to neglect sleep and food. But there are other people who start to yawn at the sight a book. For them, reading is the best cure for insomnia. "A person who does not read," said Huang Tingjian,[140] "allows worldliness and vulgarity to permeate his entire being. When he looks at himself in the mirror, he sees an abominable face. When he converses with other people, his words are insipid." But that depends on what kind of books he reads. If he reads nothing but obscene and frivolous books, how can he expect ever to achieve the refined taste of an educated person? Indeed, one will find it hard to listen to the "Admonition to Study" given by Emperor Zhenzong of the Song dynasty without disgust: "A rich family needs no fertile farms; the books will provide grains in abundance. A person need not build his own house; the books will provide a golden mansion. If he hates to travel unattended, the books will provide a carriage and a team of horses. He needs no matchmaker to find a wife; the books will provide him with a beautiful bride. A man with an ambition to fulfill must diligently study the six classics." Books are treated here merely as a stepping stone for a person to realize his worldly

---

140 Huang Tingjian (1045–1109) was a famous poet and calligrapher of the Song dynasty.

久假不歸，全書成了殘本。明人謝肇淛編《五雜俎》，記載一位「虞參政藏書數萬卷，貯之一樓，在池中央，小木為杓，夜則去之。榜其門曰：『樓不延客，書不借人。』」這倒是好辦法，可惜一般人難得有此設備。

　　讀書樂，所以有人一卷在手往往廢寢忘食。但是也有人一看見書就哈欠連連，以看書為最好的治療失眠的方法。黃庭堅說：「人不讀書，則塵俗生其間，照鏡則面目可憎，對人則語言無味。」這也要看所讀的是些什麼書。如果讀的盡是一些猥屑的東西，其人如何對有書卷氣之可言？宋真宗皇帝的〈勸學文〉，實在令人難以入耳：「富家不用買良田，書中自有千鍾粟，安居不用架高堂，書中自有黃金屋，出門莫恨無人隨，書中車馬多如簇，娶妻莫恨無良媒，書中自有顏如玉，男兒欲遂平生志，六經勤向窗前讀。」不過是把書當做敲

ambitions, and he was advised to spend his days boning up on the six classics for no other purpose than to do well in the civil service examinations. A person who spent ten years studying for those examinations suffered the worst kind of hardships, and yet all the hardships might not necessarily guarantee a better life. By contrast, in the first lecture in *Sesame and Lilies*, John Ruskin urged people to establish a kinship with the ancients by reading their works. Such advice can only have come from someone with a refined taste and profound thoughts. All year round, ancient saints and sages and a troop of world-renowned authors line up on bookshelves, waiting for your call. You can summon or dismiss them with a wave of your hand. Qu Yuan,[141] who used to stroll and sing by the lakeside, will promptly answer your call. Li Bai and Du Fu,[142] frequent visitors to the Rice Grain Mountain, will arrive together. If you like foreign-language plays, you can have the best repertory pieces of the Globe Theater staged in your home whenever you wish. Aristotle can repeat his peripatetic discourses to you. And that is the real pleasure of reading.

People in certain parts of China are particularly fond of gambling. To them the Chinese word for "book" is taboo because it sounds just like the Chinese word for "lose" (*shu*). Among them, reading a *shu* (book) becomes reading a *sheng* (to win). For the same reason, gamblers in many parts of China make it a rule not to allow anybody to sit reading a book behind them. Life is a gamble. A person may devote every bit of his mind and energy to it but still come out a loser. If he becomes addicted to books, he is bound to become dull-witted and end up a pedant. How can such a person not suffer disastrous defeats and losses

---

141 See footnote 55.

142 Li Bai (or Li Po) and Du Fu (or Tu Fu) are the two most celebrated Chinese poets. The Rice Grain Mountain was located in a suburb of the capital city Chang'an.

門磚以遂平生之志，勤讀六經，考場求售而已。十載寒窗，其中只是苦，而且吃盡苦中苦，未必就能進入佳境。倒是英國十九世紀的羅斯金，在他的《芝麻與白百合》第一講裏，勤人讀書尚友古人，那一番道理不失雅人深致。古聖先賢，成群的名世的作家，一年四季的排起隊來立在書架上面等候你來點喚，呼之即來揮之即去。行吟澤畔的屈大夫，一邀就到；飯顆山頭的李白杜甫也會連袂而來；想看外國戲，環球劇院的拿手好戲都隨時承接堂會；亞里士多德可以把他逍遙廊下的講詞對你重述一遍。這真是讀書樂。

我們國內某一處的人最好賭博，所以諱言「書」，因為「書」與「輸」同音，讀書曰讀勝。基於同一理由，許多地方的賭桌旁邊忌人在身後讀書。人生如博弈，全副精神去應付，還未必能操勝算。如果沾染上書癖，勢必呆頭呆腦，變成書獸，這樣的人在人生的戰場

on life's battlefield? For that reason, we may burrow into the secret world of books, but we must also burrow out of it. Zhu Hui'an[143] wrote: "When will it end if you bury your head among books? You had better thrown them away and find the joys of youth." That is an absolute truth and truism.

---

143 Literary name of Zhu Xi (or Chu Hsi, 1130–1200), the most famous neo-Confucian philosopher.

之上怎能不大敗虧輸？所以我們要鑽書窟，也還要從書窟裏鑽出來。朱晦庵有句「書冊埋頭何日了，不如拋卻去尋春」是見道語，也是老實話。

Cruelty to Animals

In 1824 the British established a "Society for the Prevention of Cruelty to Animals". A similar society (A.S.P.C.A.) was established in the United States forty-two years later. It now has about six hundred local chapters throughout the country. Similar bodies also exist in other parts of the world. All these groups are dedicated to the purpose of preventing people from deliberately causing unnecessary sufferings to animals. The benevolence of a kind-hearted person extends even to birds and beasts. The law of Hong Kong prohibits poultry vendors from tying chickens or ducks together by their legs and hanging them upside down on the handlebars of a bicycle, or holding too many of them in one tiny cage. Its purpose is to allow these feathered creatures a little more comfort before their throats are cut, and no one can say that this is not a display of godlike mercy. I once saw a fishmonger at a market in Guangzhou point to a live fish about two feet long swimming in a tank and ask a customer which part of it he would like to buy. The customer said that he wanted the part on its back. Thereupon, the fishmonger whipped out a boning knife, cut down a piece from the back and returned the blood-soaked, half-backed fish to the water tank, where it would remain until it was sold off to other customers piece by piece. Fishmongers in many parts of the country would scale fish alive before cutting open their bellies. One would see loose scales flying in all directions while the fish flapped and thrashed about in

虐　待　動　物

　　1824年英國人成立了一個「防止虐待動物協會」。四十二年後美國也成立了這樣的一個協會，目前美國約有六百個這樣的組織。全世界現在都有類似的會社。其宗旨是防止有意的把不必要的痛苦加在動物身上。藹然仁者之所用心，澤及禽獸。香港禁止雞鴨販子把幾隻雞鴨繫在一起倒掛在腳踏車的把手上，或是把過多的雞鴨塞在小小的籠子裏，那意思是要那些扁毛畜牲在那最後血光之災以前能活得舒適一點，不能不說是菩薩心腸。我看見過廣州的菜市裏的魚販，指着盆裏二尺來長的一條活魚問你要買哪一塊，你說要背上那一塊，他便颼的抽出一把牛耳尖刀，在魚背上血淋淋的切下一塊給你，那條缺了半個背的魚依舊放還到水盆裏去，等到別的主顧來再零刀碎剮。許多地方的市場裏，賣魚的都是不先開膛就生批逆鱗，只見鱗片亂飛，魚不住的打挺。賣田雞的更絕，唰的一下子把整張

pain. But a frog vendor performs a feat that is even more mind-boggling. Swish! He tears off the entire skin of a live frog and leaves that white, skinless creature to hop and skip about madly, creating a horrid scene for the bystanders.

When I was a boy, my family had two carriages, one of which was put in the charge of Little Zhang, the driver, whose responsibility included buying forage and other provisions for the mule. Taking a lesson from the corrupt government officials of the time, he would pocket thirty per cent of the allowance and cut back on the forage. Being underfed, the mule was very skinny and too weak to run and became a really jaded beast. On reaching a thoroughfare, the mule was expected to quicken its gait into a trot. At that moment, Little Zhang would take out an awl he had hidden in his sleeve and apply a quick jab to the animal's haunch. In a panic the mule would dash forward, while blood came streaming down its thigh. This was discovered soon enough and Little Zhang was sent away to look for another job. Since my childhood I have always wondered why a human being can be so terribly hard-hearted, but at that time I was convinced that Little Zhang was the only person in the world capable of such cruelty.

Although one should not deliberately cause "unnecessary" pain to animals, it is assumed that "necessary" pain is exempted from this rule. Peking duck is a gourmet dish of universal renown and requires a unique skill of preparation that is most adroitly practiced by the poultry farmers of Tongzhou, a city located by the Canal. First, they roll a specially prepared feed into sticks that are slightly thicker and longer than weenies. Then they hold a duck's bill wide open, force a feed stick down its throat and give its neck a quick, downward rub. These steps form a quick sequence that is repeated seven or eight times in a row till the duck is gasping for breath, too weak to utter a sound. Even then the duck is not allowed to waddle back to the river, but is

的皮活剝下來，剝出白生生的田雞亂蹦亂跳。站在旁邊看着都心驚膽戰。

我小時候，家裏有兩輛轎車，其中一輛交由小張駕御，騾子的草料及一應給養都由他包辦。小張深諳官場習慣，經手三分肥，剋扣草料。騾子吃不飽，就跑不動，瘦骨嶙峋的，真正的是駑塞之乘，但是到了通衢大道之上又非驕驤一陣不可，小張就從袖裏取出一把錐子，仿照蘇秦引錐刺股的故事，在騾子的臀部上猛攮一下，騾子一驚，飛馳而前，鮮血順着大腿滴流而下。這事不久就被發現，小張當然也立即另尋高就去了。我從小就很詫異一個人心腸何以硬得這樣可怕，但是當時以為世界上僅有小張一個人是這樣的狠。

一個人不可以有意的把「不必要的」痛苦加在動物身上，想來「必要的」痛苦則不在此限。北平烤鴨是中外馳名的美味，它的製法特殊——這是瀕臨運河的通州人的拿手，用特備的拌好的食糧搓成一根根的橛子，比香腸還要粗長一些，劈開鴨子的嘴巴硬往裏塞，然後用手順着鴨脖往下一攞，再塞一根，再攞一下。接連七八根塞下去，鴨子連叫喚的力氣都沒有了，只賸下奄奄一息。這時候不能放

thrown into a specially constructed small pen that holds about eighty to a hundred ducks so closely packed that there is absolutely no room for any movement. There they are given only water to drink and allowed to spend their time in ease and sloth and to fatten gradually. Given two square meals a day in this fashion, the ducks will be ready for the market in a month or two. Then they are slaughtered and hung up by the neck to roast in a closed oven, and they come out delicious, juicy, crisp and tender. This process, known as "force-feeding", is rather painful, but necessary, because it would not be possible to please a gourmand's palate otherwise. On looking back, I can see that even the stabs given by Little Zhang to the hip of the mule might not have been entirely unnecessary, since, without them, he would not have been able to cut back on the forage and at the same time pretend to be discharging his duty. To cause sufferings to others in order to indulge one's own selfish pleasures merely shows the darker side of human nature. Alas! It has come to be called a "necessity".

There is no greater act of cruelty than killing. Thus the saying: "A benevolent person will not kill." Why don't people become vegetarian and obtain proteins from plants if they really want to spare animals the unnecessary pain? Half a century ago I visited the slaughterhouse in Chicago, where thousands of cattle, pigs and sheep were slaughtered at a time, either by applying a captive bolt stunner to their heads or by sticking a knife into their chests. The whole process of depilating, skinning, boning and splitting was completed in a relatively short time. Today, even more advanced techniques have been adopted. It was really a mind-blowing experience to witness the destruction of so many lives in an instant. What is most difficult for me to understand is that, despite the advances of civilization, there are still people who call themselves gentlemen but prefer to return to an age of hunters and fishermen. Rabbits, foxes, deers, wild ducks and geese, boars, fish and turtles pose no danger to the human race. As described by the

它回到河裏去，要丟到特建的一間小屋裏，百八十隻擠在裏面絕對沒有動彈的餘地，只准喝水，只准養尊處優的在裏面安息，慢慢的蹲膘。每天這樣飽餐兩次，過個把月便可出而問世，在悶爐裏一吊，香，肥，脆，嫩，此之謂「填鴨」。這過程頗為痛苦，可是有此必要，否則饕餮之士便無法大快朵頤。現在回想起來，小張椎攘髀臀，也不是沒有必要，因為不如此他無法一面剋扣糧草一面交代差事。為了自私的享受而不惜製造痛苦，這只是顯示人性之惡的一面，「必要」云乎哉！

最殘酷的事莫過於屠殺。所以說：「仁者不殺。」真要使動物不受不必要的痛苦，則人曷不蔬食，在植物方面尋求蛋白質。半世紀前我參觀過芝加哥的屠宰場，千百頭的牛豬羊，不是頭上槌一釘，便是胸口挨一刀，不大功夫而拔毛剝皮去骨切塊之事畢，如今技術當更進步。那麼多的生命毀於一旦，實在驚心動魄。我最不能了解的是：人類文明演進，何以如今還有人自命紳士而返回到漁獵時

eminent Buddhist monk Lianchi, "Traps are set in mountains. Nets are spread in seas. Countless methods are used to ensnare. Metal is bent to make hooks and straightened to make arrows. A hundred ways are found to hunt and catch." It is absurd that people murder wild animals with guns, kill fish with electric shocks and turn scientific inventions into weapons for the massacre of living creatures. They rely on their power to bully the weak and gloat over their exploits. Wild animals kept in a zoo are no better off than prisoners serving a life sentence, which in its severity ranks just below the death penalty. Some zoologists tell us that animals in captivity are not to be compared to people in prison and that actually such animals have quite a sense of security, as they know that the visitors outside their cages will not be able to harass them. When I see a huge bear pacing up and down in its cage, I can tell that it still wants out. I have also been told that hunting is necessary because, with no family planning, the populations of wildlife grow simply too fast, and that, since there is a shortage of food supply, they face the danger of death by starvation. Supposing that your neighbor has many mouths to feed and cannot support his family, do you also have the right to kill two or three of his children in order to reduce his burden?

The word "animal" has a very broad connotation, which should properly include the human race. When we talk about prevention of cruelty to animals, why don't we learn to love our families and neighbors and begin with the prevention of cruelty to our fellow men? Sometimes people resort to acts of extreme cruelty in dealing with others. Our ancient penal code abounds with rules whereby people were subjected to unnecessary torture. The chapter entitled "Qiu Guan" (literally, "offices of autumn") in *Zhou Li* (or *Rites of the Zhou Dynasty*) mentions the five severe forms of corporal punishment together with their annual quotas. "Tattooing of the face: five hundred; cutting off the nose: five hundred; castration: five hundred; cutting off the feet:

代？兔、狐、鹿、鳧雁、野豬、魚鱉，無害於人，而如蓮池大師所謂「網於山，罟於淵，多方掩取，曲而鉤，直而矢，百計蒐羅」？可笑的是：槍殺禽獸，電斃鱗魚，挾科學利器屠害生靈，恃強凌弱，而得意揚揚。禽獸放在動物園裏，等於是無期徒刑，比死刑稍次一等。有些動物學家說，不要以為檻裏的動物如處囹圄，實際是它在欄後饒有安全之感，覺得你在欄外不會騷擾到它。我看見過巨熊在檻裏幌來幌去，它還是想出來。又有人說，狩獵是必需的，因為動物沒有家庭計劃，繁殖得太快，食物供給不足，將有餓死之虞。假使你的鄰人一家食指浩繁，無以為生，你是不是也可以走過去殺掉他的三男兩女以減少他的負擔？

動物涵意甚廣，應該把人類也包括進去。防止虐待動物，曷不親親而仁仁，先從防止虐待人類始？有時候人虐待人，無所不用其極。我們古時刑法就有許多是不必要的令人痛苦。《周禮秋官》，五刑之法，「墨罪五百，劓罪五百，宮罪五百，刖罪五百，殺罪五

five hundred; death by execution: five hundred." Yet, these were penalties specified by the law, unlike the punishment called *paoluo* devised by King Zhou of the Shang dynasty as a combination of torture and amusement.[144] After the corpulent Dong Zhuo[145] was assassinated, the soldiers who were guarding his body stuck a wick into his navel, lit it and keep the human lamp burning for several days. He was lucky because this was done after his death. Had he been captured alive, he would have been subjected to more cruel treatment. People of other countries have displayed no less capacity for cruelty. Fort William in Calcutta had a lock-up that measured eighteen feet wide and fourteen feet long, with only two small windows. Of the one hundred and forty-six defenders of the East India Company who were imprisoned there, all but twenty-three died of thirst and heat overnight. This cause célèbre, which occurred in June 1756, has gone down in history as the "Black Hole" incident.

Nothing is more cruel and unnecessary than war, yet there are many people who love wars and will resort to warfare whenever they are thwarted in their ambitions. Because of this, even peace-loving people are compelled to fight in self-defense. Samuel Johnson wrote an article (printed in No. 22 of *The Rambler*) in which he described, through a dialogue between two vultures, the stupidity of the human race. Human beings, he said, are the only species that engages in mutual killing on a large scale, yet they will not eat the flesh of their victims, but leave it on the battlefield for the vultures to feed on, without knowing for what they are killing one another. Efforts are being made to prevent human cruelty to animals, but not to prevent

---

144 The king and his favorite consort named Daji amused themselves by watching this form of torture, in which a prisoner was forced to climb a heated copper column covered with grease.

145 Dong Zhuo (A.D. ?–192) was a powerful general of the Eastern Han dynasty.

百。」究竟還是明文規定的法則，像紂所作的炮烙之刑，是以酷刑兼為取樂之資。肥胖的董卓死後，守屍的人在他肚臍裏插上燈撚，點燃起來，光照數日，幸而這是死後，生前若是落在人手裏必定有更難堪的處置。外國人的殘虐，也不讓人。加爾加答的威廉堡有一間小室，十八呎寬，十四呎長，僅有兩個小窗，東印度公司的守軍一百四十六人被叛軍禁閉在裏面，一夜之間渴熱難當，僅有二十三人幸免於死，時在1756年6月，是歷史上有名的所謂「黑洞」事件。

沒有什麼事情比戰爭更殘酷更不必要，偏偏有那麼許多人好戰，所求不遂，便揮動干戈，使得愛和平的也不能不起來自衛。約翰孫博士有一篇文章（《閒遊者》第二十二期）藉兀鷹的對話寫人類的愚蠢，人類是唯一的一種動物大規模的互相殘殺而並不把對方的肉吃下去，只是拋在戰場上白白的餵兀鷹，不知那是所為何來。防止

human beings from killing each other. I wonder why we should favor the one over the other.

虐待動物，而不防止人類的互相廝殺，不曉得為什麼要這樣的厚於
彼而薄於此！

New Year Festivities in Beijing

One must spend the New Year holidays[146] at home in order really to enjoy them. A person who lives away from home tends to feel miserable due to loneliness and, being totally incapable of sharing the festive mood at the approach of the New Year, can only express his feelings in sighs. However, what is called a home must have at least two generations living under the same roof. If there are neither parents nor children around, or if a married couple are the only tenants of the house, they can only face each other eyeball to eyeball and treat each other with cold civility. What can such a household do to bring in the atmosphere of the New Year? Beijing seems far, far away; I can return to it only in dreams. But I still recall some of the New Year festivities I witnessed there as a child.

When people finished offering sacrifices to the kitchen god, the old year would be fast approaching its end. Each family immediately set itself to work. All sorts of tinware, such as incense burners, candlesticks, fruit trays and saucers, were taken out from dust-covered boxes and subjected to the annual ritual of washing and polishing. Palace lanterns, gauze lanterns and ox-horn lanterns were all taken

---

146 The New Year and all the other dates referred to in this article are those on the lunar calendar.

北平年景

　　過年須要在家鄉裏才有味道。羈旅淒涼，到了年下只有長吁短嘆的分兒，還能有半點歡樂的心情？而所謂家，至少要有老小二代，若是上無雙親，下無兒女，只剩下伉儷一對，大眼瞪小眼，相敬如賓，還能製造什麼過年的氣氛？北平遠在天邊，徒縈夢想，童時過年風景，尚可回憶一二。

　　祭灶過後，年關在邇。家家忙着把錫香爐，錫蠟籤，錫果盤，錫茶托，從蛛網塵封的箱子裏取出來，作一年一度的大擦洗。宮燈，紗燈，牛角燈，一齊出籠。年貨也是要及早備辦的，這包括廚

out of storage. The necessary supplies for the New Year holidays had to be stocked up and stored in time. Among them were dried foods and nuts for the kitchen, apples and dried fruits to be used as sacrifices to the gods and ancestors, potted peonies and narcissi to be placed in the rooms, and mixed tidbits of all sizes for children to nibble on. Honeyed breadsticks, a standard offering ordered far in advance from White Clouds Temple were delivered to the house in bowls neatly packed in large wicker-and-paper baskets. Members of the household, both young and old, would keep running into and out of the house in a frenzy. Needless to say, the housewife had to do the extra work of making new clothes, new shoes and new socks for everyone in the family. All the shoes, socks and gowns had to be brand new, even if they were made merely of homespun cloth.

Ancestral worship was one of the highlights of the New Year holidays. Photographs of ancestors on a wall of the center hall tended to show their subjects at an advanced age. Some curled their lips in a smile, others stared fiercely like the gods painted on a temple door, but all were ready to enjoy the sacrifices being offered them amidst the curling smoke of incense. In the course of the rite, their surviving descendants repeatedly and mechanically kowtowed without actually knowing why they were doing so. One could not deny that this was a form of mourning the dead and remembering one's roots. But the whole process, which consisted of offering sacrifices, burning incense, lighting candles, performing kowtows and, immediately after that, removing the sacrifices from the altar and settling down around the dining table for the New Year's Eve feast, was carried out in such a hurry that there was simply no time left for mourning or remembrance.

Eating was a major activity of the New Year holidays, but the so-called New Year dishes were stereotyped fare served in every household. A large family would order a whole hog, including its

房裏用的乾貨，拜神祭祖用的蘋菓乾菓等等，屋裏供養的牡丹水仙，孩子們吃的粗細雜拌兒。蜜供是早就在白雲觀訂製好了的，到時候用紙糊的大筐簍一碗一碗的裝着送上門來。家中大小，出出進進，如中風魔。主婦當然更有額外負擔，要給大家製備新衣新鞋新襪，儘管是布鞋布襪布大衫，總要上下一新。

祭祖先是過年的高潮之一。祖先的影像懸掛在廳堂之上，都是七老八十的，有的撇嘴微笑，有的金剛怒目，在香煙繚繞之中，享用蒸禋，這時節孝子賢孫叩頭如搗蒜，其實亦不知所為何來，慎終追遠的意思不能說沒有，不過大家忙的是上供，拈香，點燭，磕頭，緊接着是撤供，圍桌吃年夜飯，來不及慎終追遠。

吃是過年的主要節目。年菜是標準化了的，家家一律。人口旺的人家要進全豬，連下水帶豬頭，分別處理下嚥。一鍋燉肉，加上

head and entrails, which were processed separately to make them edible. A pot of stewed meat could be used to make three different dishes: one with mushrooms, another with bean vermicelli, and a third with Chinese yam. And there were huge bowls of mustard stew, jellied fish and pork skin chili sauce as well as jars of salted celery cabbage, rutabaga, etc., enough to feed the whole family. These dishes had to be cooked in advance and kept in supply, because no one would be allowed to touch a kitchen knife on New Year's Day and because markets would remain closed until after the fifth day of the new year. As a result, the New Year dishes were actually leftovers, which were served repeatedly until one's stomach turned at the sight of them.

There was a saying among country folk: "No food is more delicious than dumplings and no posture is more comfortable than lying down." Dumplings were commonly called *zhubobo* ("boiled pasta") by the people of Beijing and were regarded as a delicacy even by the townspeople. Not only were they an indispensable midnight snack on New Year's Eve, but they would reappear at every meal from the first to at least the third day of the New Year until one was sick and tired of them. This method of wearing one out by repetitive fillings was not without merit; it had the effect of suppressing one's craving for dumplings for a long time until one had forgotten this experience by the start of another New Year holiday season. Regarding the midnight snack on New Year's Eve, there was one thing that called for careful planning. A silver coin had to be placed inside one of the dumplings, as it was believed that the person who happened to eat that dumpling and find the coin would have good luck. Year after year this good luck always fell on the grandmother, if there was one in the family. Everybody else was aware of this trick and knew how it was played.

Children had rules to obey and etiquette to observe, or else they would turn into urchins. Only during the New Year holidays were the

蘑菇是一碗，加上粉絲又是一碗，加上山藥又是一碗，大盆的芥末墩兒、魚凍兒、肉皮辣醬，成缸的大醃白菜、芥菜疙瘩——管夠，初一不動刀，初五以前不開市，年菜非囤集不可，結果是年菜等於膳菜，吃倒了胃口而後已。

「好吃不過餃子，舒服不過倒着」，這是鄉下人說的話，北平人稱餃子為「煮餑餑」。城裏人也把煮餑餑當做好東西，除了除夕消夜不可少的一頓之外，從初一至少到初三，頓頓煮餑餑，直把人吃得頭昏腦漲。這種疲勞填充的方法頗有道理，可以使你長期的不敢再對煮餑餑妄動食指，直等到你淡忘之後明年再說。除夕宵夜的那一頓，還有考究，其中一隻要放進一塊銀幣，誰吃到那一隻主交好運。家裏有老祖母的，年年是她老人家幸運的一口咬到。誰都知道其中作了手腳，誰都心裏有數。

孩子們須要循規蹈矩，否則便成了野孩子，唯有到了過年時節可以沐恩解禁，任意的作孩子狀。除夕之夜，院裏灑滿了芝麻稭

rules and etiquette graciously suspended and the children were allowed to act their age. On New Year's Eve the courtyard was littered with dried sesame stalks and children would step on them to make a crackling noise. This was known as "trampling on the year". After tiring themselves out with such merrymaking, they said goodnight to their elders and went to bed. This was called "bidding farewell to the year". On that occasion, each older person would take something from his or her pocket and hand it to a child as a gift, a custom known as "ushering out the year".

As New Year's Day marked the beginning of a year, a person was not allowed to say anything that was inauspicious; instead, he should wish everybody he met a Happy New Year. A horizontal poster up on a crossbeam in the house would say: "Whoever sees this will be rich." A vertical one pasted to a pillar would say: "With the arrival of the New Year, everything will turn out just as one wishes." A square poster placed on the awning over a doorway would say: "A propitious cloud is coming from the east." On the jambs of the front door would appear a couplet expressing one's gratitude for "a gracious monarch, a happy family, / a long life and a plentiful year." If there were ugly stains on the walls, they could easily be covered up by means of a few New Year posters bearing the picture of "the God of Fortune" or that of "a fat pig guarding a house". One could write down or draw out his heart's desire on a piece of paper and put it up on the wall. In doing so, it might seem as if his dream had come true in the twinkling of an eye.

Gambling was not allowed in decent families. People who wanted to play mahjong had to go to the whorehouses in the red-light district, each equipped with sets of mahjong tiles of the best quality, hardwood gambling tables and a bevy of pretty girls to dance attendance on the customers. But this ban was waived during the New Year holidays

兒，孩子們踐踏得咯吱咯吱響，是為「踩歲」。鬧得精疲力竭，睡前給大人請安，是為「辭歲」。大人摸出點什麼作為賞賚，是為「壓歲」。

新正是一年復始，不准說喪氣話，見面要道一聲「新禧」。房樑上有「對我生財」的橫披，柱子上有「一入新春萬事如意」的直條，天棚上有「紫氣東來」的斗方，大門上有「國恩家慶人壽年豐」的對聯。牆上本來不大乾淨的，還可以貼上幾張年畫，什麼「招財進寶」，「肥豬拱門」，都可以收補壁之效。自己心中想要獲得的，寫出來畫出來貼在牆上，俛仰之間彷彿如意算盤業已實現了！

好好的人家沒有賭博的。打麻將應該到八大胡同去，在那裏有上好的骨牌，硬木的牌桌，還有佳麗環列。但是過年則幾乎家家開

and Chinese dominoes, *zhuangyuan hong*[147] and other dice games were played in almost every home with participation of both adults and children. The waiving of this ban might last fifteen days until the Lantern Festival, and these games were the only recreation for the family. Children never got tired of playing with firecrackers and would stare in wide-eyed wonderment at the huge colorful boxes containing long strings of firecrackers produced by Jiulongzhai, each coiled up to form seven to nine layers and in ever-changing designs. Firecrackers with different names, such as "missiles", "double-kicks", "flowers of peace", "seven-bang fliers", "the shelling of Xiangyang" and, lastly, "banner fire", which we proudly thought to be comparable to rockets, could be seen and heard from dusk to dawn on New Year's Eve.

Nearly all the shops on both sides of the streets would put up the shutters. The only exceptions would be the "salt and oils" stores, and even these would conduct business only through a small opening in the front door. Now and then the sounds of drums and gongs would come out from behind the shutters in wild and violent bursts that were totally devoid of rhythm or measure. This was said to be the only way employees could give vent to the steam that had been building up in them all year long. Big girls and young wives wearing all sorts of makeup would turn out to throng the streets, and housemaids who traditionally hailed from the nearby Sanhe County were distinguishable by the quivering red velvet flower each of them sported in her hair. Wherever these big girls and young wives appeared, they were mobbed by young lads who turned out in far greater numbers and rudely pushed and jostled them. The Liulichang Street area would be jam-packed. Aside from the few open-air teahouses that were deserted by all but a few small children with runny noses, there was nothing much to see at the plaza of the Temple of the Dragon King. At the entrance, however,

---

147 A game played with six dice.

賭，推牌九、狀元紅、呼么喝六，老少咸宜。賭禁的開放可以延長
到元宵，這是唯一的家庭娛樂。孩子們玩花炮是沒有膩的。九隆齋
的大花盒，七層的九層的，花樣翻新，直把孩子看得瞪眼咋舌。冲
天炮、二踢腳、太平花、飛天七響、砲打襄陽，還有我們自以為值
得驕傲的可與火箭媲美的「旗火」，從除夕到天亮徹夜不絕。

　　街上除了油鹽店門上留個小窟窿外，商店都上板，裏面常是鑼
鼓齊鳴，狂攂亂敲，無板無眼，據説是夥計們在那裏發洩積攢一年
的怨氣。大姑娘小媳婦擦脂抹粉的全出動了，三河縣的老媽兒都在
頭上插一朶顫巍巍的紅絨花。凡是有大姑娘小媳婦出動的地方就有
更多的毛頭小夥子亂鑽亂擠。於是廠甸擠得水洩不通，海王邨裏除
了幾個露天茶座坐着幾個直流鼻涕的小孩之外並沒有什麼可看，但

one could be crushed to death by the big crowd that tried to get into and out of the temple. The curio and jewelry stands inside the Temple of the God of Fire and the bookstalls and picture galleries inside the Temple of the Village God drew large crowds but few buyers. On a day after a snowstorm, the streets were covered in slush and mud, which quickly turned to ice when the wind rose. People stumbled along over the ice and snow but seemed to take the ordeal in stride. The popular activities of "sipping sour bean milk, eating salted cabbage, blowing a glass bugle and flying a big kite" (as described in a nursery rhyme) still had considerable appeal for everybody. Other attractions, such as the Temple of the God of Fortune, White Clouds Temple and Yonghe Palace Temple also drew big, jostling crowds of people, who went there to see and to be seen, only to have their noses and ears turn completely red from frostbite during each outing.

The New Year carnival would last until the fifteenth. But I remember that in one particular year it was shortened by several days. And that was the first year of the Republic (1911). On the twelfth day of the lunar New Year, at a time when the whole country was still in a mood of universal jubilation, government troops stationed at Lumicang (a suburban area within the third military district of the Northern Army under the command of General Cao Kun) mutinied and plundered the commercial establishments and civilian residences in Beijing and Tianjin for two days. They did so at the instigation of Yuan Shikai, the first president of the Republic of China.[148] As the incident took place during the first New Year holidays after the founding of the Republic, I have been unable to delete it from my mind ever since.

---

148 The mutiny and riot were staged to give the new president a pretext for staying in Beijing, supposedly to restore peace, instead of assuming his duties in Nanjing, the capital of the new Republic.

是入門處能擠死人！火神廟裏的古玩玉器攤，土地祠裏的書攤畫棚，看熱鬧的多，買東西的少。趕着天晴雪霽，滿街泥濘，涼風一吹，又滴水成冰，人們在冰雪中打滾，甘之如飴。「喝豆汁兒，就鹹菜兒，琉璃喇叭大沙雁兒」，對於大家還是有足夠的誘惑。此外如財神廟、白雲觀、雍和宮，都是人擠人、人看人的局面，去一趟把鼻子耳朵凍得通紅。

新年狂歡拖到十五。但是我記得有一年提前結束了幾天，那便是民國元年，陰曆的正月十二日，在普天同慶聲中，中華民國第一任大總統袁世凱先生嗾使北軍第三鎮曹錕駐祿米倉部隊譁變掠劫平津商民兩天。這開國後第一個驚人的年景使我到如今不能忘懷。

A Chronology of Liang Shih-chiu

Ta-tsun Chen

The practice of annexing a chronology to an author's literary work or works is an old tradition in China that goes back more than a thousand years. It is a platitude to say that there is an intimate relation between a person's life and his writings. The following chronology is no substitution for a good biography of the author, but by showing the evolution of his career, it may hold the key to a better understanding of his works, including the present volume. It is also hoped that the information provided hereunder will stimulate academic interest and lead to further study and research.

1903
Born on January 6 (the 8th day of the 12th month on the lunar calendar then in use in China) into a well-to-do family in Beijing 北京, the fourth among eleven children. His father was an official at the Beijing Police Department. His mother, a native of Hangzhou 杭州, was a homemaker, whose strong emotional tie to and influence on the author was well borne out in his writings.

1910
Began his formal education at a private elementary school named Daboge Shi taoshi xuetang 大鵓鴿市陶氏學堂 in Beijing.

1912

Riots by mutinous troops in Beijing at the instigation of the president of the newly established Republic, resulting in great financial losses to the Liang family.

1913

Transferred to a public elementary school named Xinxian hutong gongli disan xiaoxue 新鮮胡同公立第三小學.

1915

Graduated from primary school at the top of his class and, after passing a series of competitive entrance examinations with the best results, was admitted to Tsing Hua College 清華學校 in Beijing 北京, which offered an eight-year program designed to prepare students for further study in the United States.

1916

Joined a small group of classmates in forming Ximo she 戲墨社 [Calligraphy club] and started practicing Chinese calligraphy every day for two years.

1921

Joined a group of fellow students in founding Xiaoshuo yanjiu she 小說研究社 [Club for the study of fiction], which was soon enlarged and renamed Tsing Hua wenxue she 清華文學社 [Tsing Hua literary club]. Began his multifaceted literary activities, including his trials in modern Chinese poetry.

Met for the first time his future wife, Cheng Jishu 程季淑, who had graduated recently from a teachers' college and was working as a teacher at a vocational school in Beijing.

1922

Became the literary editor of *Tsing Hua zhoukan* 清華週刊 [The Tsing Hua weekly].

Published jointly with Wen Yiduo 聞一多 a booklet entitled *Dongye cao'er pinglun* 《冬夜》《草兒》評論 [Critical reviews of *A Winter Night* and *Grass*], two recently published collections of poems). It constituted a manifesto of the authors on modern Chinese poetry.

Joined Wen Yiduo 聞一多 on a plan to launch a monthly literary magazine to be named *Honghe* 紅荷 [Red lotus].

Continued his experiment in modern Chinese poetry. Most of the poems he wrote during this year and the next appeared in *Tsing Hua zhoukan* 清華週刊 [The Tsing Hua weekly] and *Chuangzao jikan* 創造季刊 [The creation quarterly]. They have been collected and published in a small volume entitled *Yashe xiaoshuo he shi* 雅舍小說和詩 [A selection from Liang Shih-chiu's early writings] published in Taipei by ChiuKo chubanshe 九歌出版社 in 1996.

1923

Graduated from Tsing Hua College in June. Played the heroine in a stage play called *John Zhang* 張約翰 as part of the commencement activities.

Published in July two critical reviews in *Chuangzao zhoubao* 創造周報 [The creation weekly].

In August, embarked with all his classmates and a number of students from other schools on the *President Jackson* in Shanghai 上海 on their trip to the United States. During the two-week journey, some of the students wrote poems and articles and posted them on the bulletin board. These works were later collected and published as a special issue of *Xiaoshuo yuebao* 小說月報 [The fiction monthly] in Shanghai under the general title of Haixiao 海嘯 [Tidal wave], from the title of a poem by Liang.

Arrived in Colorado Springs and was admitted to the English Department of Colorado College, Colorado Springs.

1924

Graduated from Colorado College in the summer and, thanks to the strong recommendation of Dean Hershey, was accepted by Harvard University for graduate studies.

Stopped over at Chicago on his way to Boston and joined a group of some twenty former classmates in founding Dajiang hui 大江會 [The great river society], an organization aimed at fostering nationalism in China. Became editor of *Dajiang jikan* 大江季刊 [The great river quarterly], which began its publication in Shanghai 上海 during this year.

Enrolled at Harvard in September and began to study, *inter alia*, Shakespeare under George Lyman Kittredge and literary criticism under Irving Babbitt. The influence of Babbitt's new humanism and conservative criticism remained undiminished throughout his life.

1925

Transferred to Columbia University in September to continue his graduate studies in English.

Tsing Hua College was restructured and renamed Tsing Hua University 清華大學.

1926

Essay: "Xiandai Zhongguo wenxue zhi langman de qushi" 現代中國文學之浪漫的趨勢 [The romantic trends in contemporary Chinese literature] was published on February 15 in *Chenbao fukan* 晨報副刊 [Literary Supplement of *The Morning News*].

Essay: "Bailun yu langman zhuyi" 拜倫與浪漫主義 [Lord Byron and romanticism] appeared in *Chuangzao yuekan* 創造月刊 [The creation monthly], Vol. I, Nos. 3 (May) and 4 (June).

Gave up the last two years of his scholarship in order to fulfill his promise to his fiancée and left the United States for China in July.

Appointed professor of English by Southeastern University 東南大學 in Nanjing 南京 upon his return to China and began his long teaching career in late August.

1927

Married his financée on February 11 in Beijing and returned with his wife to Nanjing.

Moved with his wife to Shanghai to escape civil war. Was appointed editor of *Qingguang* 青光, which was the literary supplement of *Shishi xinbao* 時事新報 [The new current affairs journal] in Shanghai, and co-editor of a magazine named *Kucha* 苦茶 [Bitter tea].

Joined Hu Shih 胡適, Xu Zhimo 徐志摩, Wen Yiduo 聞一多, Pan Guangdan 潘光旦 and Rao Zili 饒子離 in establishing Xinyue shudian 新月書店 [Crescent moon bookstore] in Shanghai and served as its editor-in-chief.

Essay: "Langman de yu gudian de" 浪漫的與古典的 [The romantic and the classical] was published by Xinyue shudian 新月書店 in June. It contained a number of critical essays on classical writers and contemporary trends.

Appointed professor of English by Jinan University 濟南大學 in September. For the next three years, he also gave lectures on

English literature at several other colleges and universities in or near Shanghai.

Attacked by Lu Xun 魯迅 in a number of articles published toward the end of the year, which set off a "war of words" that lasted for nearly three years. For the essays involved in this controversy, see ed. Bi Hua 壁華, *Lu Xun yu Liang Shih-chiu lunzhan wenxuan* 魯迅與梁實秋論戰文選 [Selected writings relating to the polemic dispute between Lu Xun and Liang Shih-chiu], published in Hong Kong by Xianggang tiandi tushu youxian gongsi 香港天地圖書有限公司 in 1979.

Collected essays: *Maren de yishu* 罵人的藝術 [The art of reviling] was published by Xinyue shudian 新月書店 in October. It was a collection of short essays that had previously appeared under one of his many pseudonyms in the literary supplement he edited. The 4th edition appeared in 1930.

Birth of daughter Wenqian 文茜 in December.

1928

Essay: "Wenxue de jilü" 文學的紀律 [Literary discipline] was published by Xinyue shudian 新月書店 in March.

The launching of *Xinyue yuekan* 新月月刊 [The crescent moon monthly journal] in October. Served on its editorial board.

Translations: *Xingfu de weishanzhe* 幸福的偽善者 (*The Happy Hypocrite* by Max Beerbolm) was published in July; *Abola yu Ailüyisi de qingshu* 阿伯拉與哀綠綺思的情書 (*The Love Letters of Abelard and Héloïse*) in November.

Birth of daughter Eryuan 二元.

1929

Translation: *Pan Bide* 潘彼得 (*Peter Pan* by James M. Barrie) was published in October.

Edited *Baibide yu renwen zhuyi* 白璧德與人文主義 [Irving Babbitt and humanism], which contained selected writings of Babbitt in Chinese translation.

1930

Essay: "Renquan lunji" 人權論集 [Essays on human rights], with Hu Shih 胡適 and Luo Longji 羅隆基, was published in January.

Translation: *Jiehun ji* 結婚集 (*Married* by Johan August Strindberg) was published in January.

Birth of son Wenqi 文騏 in April.

Appointed chairman of Foreign Languages Department and head librarian at Qingdao University 青島大學 and relocated with his family to Qingdao 青島.

A five-year project for the translation of the complete works of Shakespeare was proposed by Hu Shih 胡適. Of the five scholars entrusted with this project, only Liang took up the challenge.

1931

Essay: "Xinshi de gediao ji qita" 新詩的格調及其他 [The rhythm and other elements of modern poetry] appeared in the January issue of *Shikan* 詩刊 [Journal on poetry], a publication of Xinyue shudian 新月書店.

Translation: *Xisailuo wenlu* 西塞羅文錄 [Selected writings of Cicero] was published in April.

Essay: "Suowei 'wenyi zhengce' zhe" 所謂「文藝政策」者 [On the

so-called policies concerning literature and arts] and "Wenxue de yanzhongxing" 文學的嚴重性 [The seriousness of literature] appeared in *Xinyue yuekan* 新月月刊 [The crescent moon monthly journal], Vol. III, Nos. 3 and 4, toward the end of the year.

Death of close friend Xu Zhimo 徐志摩 in a plane crash on 19 November. He was thirty-six.

1932

Helped a newspaper named Tianjin yishi bao 天津益世報 launch a weekly section devoted to literature and arts and served as the editor.

Translation: *Zhigong Manan zhuan* 織工馬南傳 (*Silas Marner* by George Eliot) was published in January.

Made frequent contributions to a number of periodicals, including *Tushu pinglun* 圖書評論 [Book review], *Xinyue yuekan* 新月月刊 [The crescent moon monthly journal] and *Wenyi zhoukan* 文藝周刊 [Literature and arts weekly journal].

1933

Birth of daughter Wenchiang 文薔 in February.

Death of daughter Eryuan 二元 at the age of four.

Xinyue yuekan 新月月刊 [The crescent moon monthly journal] ceased publication after Vol. IV, No.7 (June).

1934

Essay: "Yuehansun" 約翰孫 [Samuel Johnson] was published in January.

Essay: "Wenxue pipinglun" 文學批評論 [Theories of literary criticism] was published in March.

Essay: "Pianjian ji" 偏見集 [A collections of prejudices] was published in July.

Left Qingdao for Beijing in July to accept an appointment as research professor and chairman of English Department, Peking University 北京大學.

1935

Launched in autumn a weekly magazine named *Ziyou pinglun* 自由評論 [Free review], whose publication lasted for more than one year.

1936

His translations of Shakespeare's *Hamlet, Macbeth, King Lear, Othello, The Merchant of Venice, As You Like It, The Tempest* and *The Twelfth Night* began to be published by the Shangwu yinshu guan 商務印書館 [The Commercial Press] in Shanghai.

1937

Japanese incursion began with the "Lugou Bridge Incident" 蘆溝橋事變 on July 7 and Beijing fell to the Japanese invaders three weeks later.

Fled alone to Nanjing and then to Changsha 長沙, in Hunan Province 湖南省.

1938

Was elected to the Guomin canzheng hui 國民參政會 [National Council] and attended its first meeting in Hankou 漢口.

Relocated with other members of Guomin canzheng hui 國民參政會 [National Council] to Chongqing 重慶 in September. Was placed in charge of a project, whose mission was to produce a new series of textbooks for primary and secondary schools.

Appointed editor of the literary supplement of *Zhongyang Ribao* 中央日報 [*The central daily news*] called *Pingming* 平明 [Dawn].

An English translation of the title article in 《罵人的藝術》 appeared as *The Fine Art of Reviling*, by William. B. Pettus, College of Chinese Studies, California College in China, Beijing, China.

1939
Relocated with the project to Beipei 北碚, a rural area near Chongqing, to escape frequent and massive bombing raids by the Japanese. Shared a small cottage built on a hillside with another family and named the cottage Yashe 雅舍. For details of the cottage, see the first article in the present volume.

1940
Joined an inspection group from the Guomin canzheng hui 國民參政會 [National Council], which visited several military regions in the north from January to March but, due to the objection of Mao Zedong 毛澤東, was unable to make the scheduled top at Yan'an 延安.

Began to write informal essays for *Xingqi pinglun* 星期評論 [The weekly review] in Chongqing at the invitation of its editor. These articles appeared in a special column under the general title of "Yashe xiaopin" 雅舍小品 [A cottager's sketchbook].

1942
Almost died of acute appendicitis in spring.

Was branded as a champion for bourgeois literature and art by Mao Zedong 毛澤東 at a symposium held in Yan'an in May.

Essay: "Guanyu wenhua zhengce" 關於文化政策 [On cultural policy] appeared in *Wenhua xianfeng* 文化先鋒 [The cultural vanguard], Vol. I, No.8 (May).

Translation: *Paoxiao shanzhuang* 咆哮山莊 (*Wuthering Heights* by Emily Brontë) was published in May.

1943

Was appointed professor of English at the College of Social Education (part-time) and lectured on history of Western drama.

1944

Reunited with his wife and children, who had arrived from Beijing in summer.

1945

Unconditional surrender announced by Japan on August 10.

Translation: *Ji'erfei xiansheng de qingshi* 吉爾菲先生的情史 (*Mr. Gilfil's Love Story* by George Eliot) was published in Chongqing.

1946

His close friend Wen Yiduo 聞一多 was assassinated in Kunming 昆明 on July 15.

Returned to Beijing in summer; was appointed professor of English by Beijing Normal University 北京師範大學 in August.

Death of father within one month after his return.

1947

Continued to write informal essays under the general title of "Yashe xiaopin" 雅舍小品 [A cottager's sketchbook] and contributed them to *Shijie pinglun* 世界評論 [The world review], a periodical published in Nanjing.

One-month lecture tour at Northeastern Chung Cheng University 東北中正大學 in Shenyang 瀋陽.

Appointed by Tianjin yishi bao 天津益世報 as editor of its Saturday literary supplement, *Xingqi xiaopin* 星期小品 [Weekly essays].

1948
Faced with the imminent danger of civil war, the family left Beijing and took separate routes to Guangzhou 廣州 in autumn.

1949
Arrived in Guangzhou from Hong Kong on New Year's Day and began teaching at Sun Yat-sen University 中山大學 during the spring semester.

Resettled with his wife and their youngest daughter in Taipei 台北 in June. Was appointed professor and chairman of English Department, Taiwan Teachers College 台灣師範學院 (expanded and renamed Taiwan Normal University 國立台灣師範大學 in 1955), where he continued to teach until his retirement in 1966.

Essay: *Yashe xiaopin chuji*《雅舍小品》初集 [A cottager's sketchbook, volume 1] was published in Taipei by Cheng Chung Book Company 正中書局 in November.

The Fine Art of Reviling (see above) was reissued in San Francisco by Wallace Kibbee and Son.

1951
Translation: *Su'er de qiangpo laogong* 蘇俄的強迫勞工 (*Forced Labor in Soviet Russia* by D. J. Dallin and B. I. Nicolaevsky) was published in July.

1953

Translation: *Faguo Gongchandang zhi pouxi* 法國共產黨之剖析 (*Communist Party in France* by A. Rossi) was published in February.

1954

Translation: *Shashibiya de xiju gushi* 莎士比亞的戲劇故事 (*Stories from Shakespeare* adapted by H.G. Wyatt et al.) was published in March.

Translation: *Xiandai xiju* 現代戲劇 (*Modern Drama* by Allardyce Nicoll), with Fu Yiqin 傅一勤, was published in December.

Essay: "*Meiguo shi zenyang de yige guojia*" 美國是怎樣的一個國家 [What kind of a country is the United States?], with Zhang Fangjie 張芳杰, was published in December.

1955

Was appointed Dean of the College of Arts, Taiwan Normal University in June, following the restructuring of Taiwan Teachers College.

English translation of *Jinxiu heshan huace* 《錦繡河山》畫冊, edited by Ding Xingwu 丁星伍, was published in Hong Kong by Xianggang guoji chubanshe 香港國際出版社.

1956

Established the Chinese Research Institute and the English Research Institute within the College of Arts of Taiwan Normal University and doubled as director of the latter institute.

Translation: *Baishou tu* 百獸圖 (*Animal Farm* by George Orwell) was published in November.

1957

Translation: *Hengli sishi shangpian* 《亨利四世》上篇 (The First Part of *Henry IV* by William Shakespeare) was published in Taipei.

1958

Continued to teach at the University but resigned from all the administrative positions.

Biography: *Tan Xu Zhimo* 談徐志摩 [An essay on Xu Zhimo] was published in Taipei by Far East Book Co. Ltd. 遠東圖書公司 in April.

Collected works: *Shih-chiu zixuan ji* 實秋自選集 [Selected writings of Liang Shih-chiu] was published in Taipei by Shengli shuju 勝利書局 in October.

1959

Tested positive for diabetes.

Translation: *Chensi lu* 沉思錄 (*Meditations* by Marcus Aurelius) was published in Taipei by Xiezhi chubanshe 協志出版社 in October.

1960

Member of the Chinese delegation to the Sino-American Conference on Academic Cooperation 中美學術合作會議 held in Seattle in July.

An English translation of *Yashe xiaopin*, vol. 1 《雅舍小品》初集 (under the title of *Sketches of a Cottager*) was published in Taipei by Far East Book Co. Ltd. 遠東圖書公司. The translator, Shih Chao-ying 時昭瀛, was a former classmate of the author at Tsing Hua College.

Translation: English translation of Baodao Taiwan *huaji* 《寶島台灣》畫集, edited by Ding Xingwu 丁星伍, was published in Hong Kong 香港 by Xianggang guoji chubanshe 香港國際出版社.

Editor: *Far East Practical English-Chinese Dictionary* 遠東實用英漢辭典 was published in December. Enlarged and renamed *Far East English-Chinese Dictionary* 遠東英漢大辭典 in 1975.

1962

Memoirs: *Tsing Hua banian* 清華八年 [My eight years at Tsing Hua College] was published in November.

1963

Appointed for a second time director of the English Research Institute, Taiwan Normal University.

Collected essays: *Qiushi zawen* 秋室雜文 [Miscellaneous writings of Liang Shih-chiu] was published in Taipei by Wenxing shudian 文星書店 in September.

1964

Collected essays: *Wenxue yinyuan* 文學因緣 [Essays on literature] was published in Taipei by Wenxing shudian 文星書店 in January.

Reprint: *Pianjian ji* 偏見集 [A collection of prejudices] was published in Taipei by Wenxing shudian 文星書店.

Translation: twenty plays by Shakespeare (mostly reprints) were published in May and July.

1966

Retired from Taiwan Normal University on August 1.

Edited *Shashibiya danchen sibai zhounian jinianji* 莎士比亞誕辰四百週年紀念集 [*A commemorative volume on the occasion of Shakespeare's 400th birthday*), to which he contributed three monographs.

1967-1968

Translation: *Shashibiya quanji* 莎士比亞全集 [The complete works of Shakespeare] was published in forty volumes in Taipei by Far East Book Co. Ltd. 遠東圖書公司.

Memoirs: *Qiushi zayi* 秋室雜憶 [Reminiscences] was published in Taipei by Zhuanji wenxueshe 傳記文學社 in October 1968.

1969

Co-editor (with Jiang Fucong 蔣復璁): *Xu Zhimo quanji* 徐志摩全集 [*The complete works of Xu Zhimo*], in six volumes, was published in Taipei by Zhuanji wenxueshe 傳記文學社.

1970

Took his wife to Seattle to visit their youngest daughter, son-in-law and grandchildren, then went on a tour of several major cities in the United States. This "belated honeymoon" lasted nearly four months. The couple returned to Taipei on August 19.

Essay: "Lüetan zhongxi wenhua" 略談中西文化 [A discourse on Chinese and Western cultures] was published in Taipei by Jinxue shuju 進學書局 in January.

Collected essays: *Shih-chiu zawen* 實秋雜文 [Miscellaneous writings of Liang Shih-chiu] was published in Taipei by Xianrenzhang chubanshe 仙人掌出版社 in October.

1971

Collected essays: *Shih-chiu wencun* 實秋文存 [Selected works of Liang Shih-chiu] was published in Taipei by Landeng chubanshe 藍燈出版社 in February.

Reprint: *Yashe xiaopin* 雅舍小品 [A cottager's sketchbook] was issued in Hong Kong by Wenyi shuwu 文藝書屋.

Edited: *A New Practical Chinese-English Dictionary* 遠東實用漢英辭典 in December. Enlarged and renamed *Far East Chinese-English Dictionary* 遠東漢英大辭典 in 1991.

1972

Essays: *Xiyatu zaji* 西雅圖雜記 [Random notes written in Seattle] was published in Taipei by Far East Book Co. Ltd. 遠東圖書公司 in January.

Arrived with his wife in Seattle for a second visit to their youngest daughter in May.

1973

Collected essays: *Yashe xiaopin* xuji《雅舍小品》續集 [A cottager's sketchbook, vol. 2] was published in Taipei by Cheng Chung Book Company in October.

Embarked on the monumental work of writing a history of English literature in Chinese.

1974

Accidental death of his wife on April 30. She was buried in the Acacia Memorial Park in Seattle.

Memoirs: *Kanyun ji* 看雲集 [The cloud watcher] was published in Taipei by Zhiwen chubanshe 志文出版社 in March.

Memoirs: *Huaiyuan mengyi* 槐園夢憶 [Reminiscences at the Acacia Memorial Park] was written in four months and published in Taipei by Far East Book Co. Ltd. 遠東圖書公司 in December.

Returned to Taipei in October; appointed Chairman of the Board of Directors, Tatung Institute of Technology 大同技術學院, Taipei, in December.

1975

Married his second wife Han Jingqing 韓菁清 on May 9.

Selected essays: *Liang Shih-chiu zixuan ji* 梁實秋自選集 [Selected writings of Liang Shih-chiu] was published in Taipei by Liming wenhua gongsi 黎明文化公司 in May.

1978

Collected essays: *Liang Shih-chiu lun wenxue* 梁實秋論文學 [Liang Shih-chiu on literature] and *Liang Shih-chiu zhaji* 梁實秋札記 [Reading notes] were published in Taipei by China Times Publishing Co. 時報文化出版公司 in September and October respectively.

1979

Completed his *Yingguo wenxue shi* 英國文學史 [A history of English literature] and *Yingguo wenxue xuan* 英國文學選 [Selected readings in English literature] in June.

1980

Collected essays: *Baimao wangzi ji qita* 白貓王子及其他 [The white cat prince and others] was published in Taipei by ChiuKo chubanshe 九歌出版社 in January.

Flew to Hong Kong for a reunion with his son after a separation of thirty-one years in June.

Edited: *Far East English-Chinese Dictionary of Idioms and Phrases* 遠東英漢成語大辭典.

1982

Received the Award of Distinguished Service from Taiwan Literary Writers Association on May 4.

Flew to Seattle for a reunion with his oldest daughter after a separation of thirty-four years in June.

Collected essays: *Yashe xiaopin* sanji《雅舍小品》三集 [A cottager's sketchbook, vol. 3] was published in Taipei by Cheng Chung Book Company正中書局 in March.

1983
Collected essays: *Yashe zawen* 雅舍雜文 [Miscellanies] was published in Taipei by Cheng Chung Book Company正中書局 in March.

Translation reprint: *Paoxiao shanzhuang* 咆哮山莊 (*Wuthering Heights* by Emily Brontë) was reissued in Taipei by Yuanjing chuban shiye gongxi 遠景出版事業公司 in May.

Essay: "Yongheng de juchang: Shashibiya" 永恆的劇場：莎士比亞 [The eternal playhouse: Shakespeare] was published by in Taipei by China Times Publishing Co. 時報文化出版公司 in August.

1984
Received the National Award for Contribution to Literature in May.

Collected essays: *Kanyun ji* 看雲集 [The cloud watcher] was published in Taipei by Crown Publishing Ltd. 皇冠出版社 in August. It differs in content from another collection with the same title published in 1974.

1985
Collected essays: *Yashe tan chi* 雅舍談吃 [On culinary art] was published in Taipei by ChiuKo chubanshe 九歌出版社 in Januray.

Translation: *Yashe yicong* 雅舍譯叢 [Selected translations by Liang

Shih-chiu] was published in Taipei by Crown Publishing Ltd. 皇冠出版社 in February.

Collected essays: *Yashe sanwen* diyi ji《雅舍散文》第一集 [Prose writings of a cottager, vol. 1] was published in Taipei by ChiuKo chubanshe 九歌出版社 in June.

Reunited with his son who had come to Taipei to stay in August.

His *Yingguo wenxue shi* 英國文學史 [A history of English literature] and *Yingguo wenxue xuan* 英國文學選 [Selected readings in English literature] were published in Taipei by Xiezhi gongye chubanshe 協志工業出版社 in August, each in three volumes.

1986
Collected essays: *Yashe xiaopin* siji《雅舍小品》四集 [A cottager's sketchbook, 4 vols.] was published in Taipei by Cheng Chung Book Company 正中書局 in May.

Received the Special Contribution Award from *The China Times (Taiwan)* 台灣中國時報.

1987
Reprints: *Abola yu Ailüyisi de qingshu* 阿伯拉與哀綠綺思的情書 (*The Love Letters of Abelard and Héloïse*) in January and *Pan Bide* 潘彼得 (*Peter Pan* by James M. Barrie) in May.

Collected essays: *Yashe sanwen* di'er ji《雅舍散文》第二集 [Prose writings of a cottager, vol. 2] was published in Taipei by ChiuKo chubanshe 九歌出版社 in July.

Died of heart failure on the morning of November 3.

1988
Memorial volume: *Chiu zhi song* 秋之頌 [Ode to Autumn], edited by

Yu Kuang-chung 余光中, published in Taipei by ChiuKo chubanshe 九歌出版社 in January. It contains articles by his friends and associates and a detailed chronology of his life and works (in Chinese).

Memoirs: *Chang xiangsi* 長相思 [Eternal memories], written by Liang Wenchiang, was published in Taipei by China Times Publishing Co. 時報文化出版公司. This book was written by his youngest daughter and contains firsthand accounts of his family life, down to the final moment of his long life.

1994
Reprint: *Maren de yishu* 罵人的藝術 [The art of reviling] was published in Taipei by Far East Book Co. Ltd. This volume contains all the articles in the original collection and four appendices, one of which is *The Fine Art of Reviling*, translated by William B. Pettus (see above).

1995
Yashe chidu 雅舍尺牘 [Letters of Liang Shih-chiu in his own handwriting], edited by Yu Kuang-chung 余光中 et al., was published in Taipei by ChiuKo chubanshe 九歌出版社 in June.

1996
Yashe xiaoshuo he she 雅舍小説和詩 [A selection of Liang Shih-chiu's early writings], edited by Chen Zishan 陳子善, was published in Taipei by ChiuKo chubanshe 九歌出版社 in May. It contains poems and short stories written from 1921 to 1925.

1999
Yashe xiaopin buyi 雅舍小品補遺, edited by Chen Zishan 陳子善, was published in Hong Kong by Cosmos Books 香港天地圖書有

限公司. It is a collection of short articles that appeared under various pseudonyms in a number of publications in China between 1928 and 1948.

2002

Yashe tan shu 雅舍談書 [Liang Shih-chiu on books] was in Taipei by ChiuKo chubanshe 九歌出版社 in December, with a preface by his son.

2003

Yashe de chunhua qiushi: Liang Shih-chiu xueshu yanjiu taolunhui lunwenji 雅舍的春華秋實：梁實秋學術研究討論會論文集, co-edited by Li Ruiteng 李瑞騰 and Cai Zongyang 蔡宗陽, was published in Taipei by ChiuKo chubanshe 九歌出版社. This collection of critical essays was published in commemoration of his 100th birthday.